Baroque Music T
Music As Spee

NIKOLAUS HARNONCOURT

Baroque Music Today: Music As Speech

Ways to a New Understanding of Music

Translated by
Mary O'Neill

Reinhard G. Pauly, Ph.D.
General Editor

AMADEUS PRESS
Portland, Oregon

© 1982 as *Musik als Klangrede* by
Residenz Verlag, Salzburg and Wien

Translation © 1988 by Amadeus Press (an imprint of Timber Press, Inc.)
All rights reserved

Paperback edition printed 1995

ISBN 0-931340-91-8

Printed in Singapore

Amadeus Press
The Haseltine Building
133 S.W. Second Avenue, Suite 450
Portland, Oregon 97204, U.S.A.
1-800-327-5680 (U.S.A. and Canada only)

Library of Congress Cataloging-in-Publication Data

Harnoncourt, Nikolaus.
   [Musik als Klangrede.   English]
   Baroque music today.

   Essays and lectures.
   Translation of: Musik als Klangrede.
   1. Music—Performance.   2. Music—17th century—History and criticism.   3. Music—18th century—History and criticism.   I. Pauly, Reinhard G.   II. Title.
ML457.H313   1988   780'.903'2   88-6207
ISBN 0-931340-91-8

Contents

Preface 7

I. BASIC PRINCIPLES OF MUSIC AND
   INTERPRETATION 9

   Music in Our Lives. The Interpretation of Historical Music. Musical Understanding and the Training of Musicians. Problems of Notation. Articulation. Tempo. Tone Systems and Intonation. Music and Sound. Old Instruments: Yes or No? The Reconstruction of Original Sound Conditions in the Studio. Priorities: The Relative Importance of the Various Factors.

II. INSTRUMENTARIUM AND MUSICAL
    DISCOURSE 99

   Viola da Brazzo and Viola da Gamba. The Violin: *The* Solo Instrument of the Baroque. The Baroque Orchestra. The Relationship Between "Words" and Tones in Baroque Instrumental Music. From Baroque to Classicism. Origin and Development of Music as Speech (*Klangrede*).

III. EUROPEAN BAROQUE MUSIC—MOZART 137
    Program Music—Vivaldi: Opus 8. The Italian and French Styles. Austrian Baroque Composers—Attempts at Reconciliation. Telemann—The "Mixed" [Eclectic] Style. Baroque Instrumental Music in England. Concerto Grosso and Trio Sonata in the Works of Handel. What an Autograph Can Tell Us. Dance Movements—The Suites of Bach. French Baroque Music—Excitingly New. French Opera: Lully-Rameau. Reflections of an Orchestra Member on a Letter by W. A. Mozart.

   Discography (with Addendum to the 1995 Edition) 200

   Index.. 208

Preface

During the many years in which I have been active as a musician and teacher, a large number of essays, talks and lectures have accumulated, from which I have selected the present texts. I have revised them slightly, though I have tried in some instances to retain the feeling of the spoken word. The essay "On the Interpretation of Historical Music," written in 1954, is my first written observation on this topic; it also represents the "credo" of the Concentus Musicus, which was founded at the same time. The opening chapter, "Music in Our Lives," is the acceptance speech which I gave on the occasion of being awarded the Erasmus Prize in 1980 in Amsterdam; it is the most recent piece in this book.

In making my selection, I gave preference to general themes. I excluded detailed studies of Monteverdi, Bach and Mozart, whose works have formed the focus of my own endeavors; these will be published together in another volume.

I would like to express my special appreciation to Dr. Johanna Fürstauer, who collected and organized the various texts; this book would not have been possible without her efforts.

Nikolaus Harnoncourt

I.
Basic Principles of Music and Interpretation

Music in Our Lives

From the Middle Ages to the French Revolution, music was one of the foundations of our culture, indeed, of our very lives. The understanding of music was part of a general education. Today, music has become simply an ornament used to embellish idle evenings with trips to the opera or to concerts, to evoke public festivity or even to banish or enliven the silence of domestic loneliness with sounds from the radio. A paradox has emerged: quantitatively, we have much more music today than ever before—almost uninterrupted music—, but it is no longer very relevant to our lives. It has become simply a pretty adornment.

We find importance in other things than did the people of earlier times. How much strength and suffering and love they squandered in constructing their temples and cathedrals, how little they expended for the machinery of comfort and convenience! For people today, an automobile or an airplane is more valuable than a violin, the circuitry of the computer's brain more important than a symphony. We pay all too dearly for what we regard as comfortable and essential, while we heedlessly discard the intensity of life in favor of the tinsel of creature comforts—and what we have once truly lost, we will never be able to regain.

This fundamental change in the significance of music has taken place with increasing rapidity over the past two centuries. At the same time, a change has occurred in our attitude toward contemporary music—as well as art in general: as long as music was an essential part of life, it could emanate only from the contemporary world. It was the living language for something which could not be said in words; it could be understood only by contemporary human beings. Music brought about changes in people, in listeners as well as in musicians. It had to be continually recreated, just as human beings had to keep on building new homes, in keeping with new patterns of living, new intellectual climates. Thus old music, the music of previous generations, could no longer be understood and used, although its great artistry was occasionally admired.

Since music is no longer found at the center of our lives, all this has changed: now that it is regarded as an ornament, it is felt that music should first and foremost be "beautiful." Under no circumstances should it be allowed to disturb or startle us. The music of the present cannot fulfill this requirement because at the very least, like all art, it reflects the spiritual and intellectual situation of its time, and this is true of our present time as well. Yet honestly coming to terms with our spiritual and intellectual situation cannot be merely beautiful: it has an impact on our very lives and is therefore disturbing to us. This has resulted in the paradoxical situation that people have turned away from contemporary art because it is disturbing, perhaps necessarily so. Rather than confrontation, we sought only beauty, to help us to overcome the banality of everyday life. Thus art in general, and music in particular, became simply ornamental and people turned to historical art and to old music, for here they could find the beauty and harmony that they sought.

As I see it, this interest in old music—by which I mean music not written by our generation—could only occur as the result of a series of glaring misunderstandings. Thus we are able to use only "beautiful" music, which the present is unable to offer us. There has never been a kind of music that was merely "beautiful." While "beauty" is a component of every type of music, we can make it into a determining factor only by disregarding all of music's other components. Only since we have ceased to understand music as a whole, and perhaps no longer want to be able to understand it, has it been possible for us to reduce music to its beautiful aspect alone, to iron out all of its wrinkles. And because music has in general terms become simply a pleasant garnish for our everyday lives, we can no longer fully comprehend old music— that is, what we actually call music—, because we have not been able to reduce it to a purely aesthetic dimension and to iron it smooth.

We find ourselves today in what amounts to a dilemma, therefore, if we continue to believe in the impact of music—in its power to change us, for the general spiritual condition of our times has shifted music from its central position to one on the periphery, from something with moving force to something that is simply pretty. We must not allow ourselves to be satisfied with this; indeed, if I were to believe that this is the ineluctable fate of our art, I would immediately stop making music.

I believe, therefore, with ever greater hope, that we will soon recognize that we cannot renounce music—and the unwitting reduction of which I spoke *is* renunciation—, that we can unhesitatingly submit to the power and message of the music of Monteverdi, Bach or Mozart. The more deeply and totally we try to understand this music, the more we shall see what this music still is, above and beyond mere beauty, how it opens us up and unsettles us with the diversity of its language. And finally, once we have understood the music of Monteverdi, Bach and Mozart, we will have to find our way back to the music of our own time, the music which speaks our language, embodies our culture and moves us forward. Does not the fact that art no longer strongly affects our lives underlie much of what makes our times so unharmonious and terrible? Are we not reducing ourselves with a shameful lack of imagination to the language of the "sayable"?

What would Einstein have thought, what would he have achieved, had he not played the violin? Only the imagination can produce the daring, creative hypotheses which then must be demonstrated by logical thought processes.

It is no coincidence that the reduction of music to the beautiful, and thereby to the generally comprehensible, occurred at the time of the French Revolution. There have been many periods throughout history during which attempts were made to simplify music and to confine it to the emotional sphere, so that it could be understood by anyone. Each of these attempts failed, resulting in new diversity and complexity. Music can be generally comprehensible only when it is reduced to a primitive level or when each individual person learns to understand the language of music.

The most far-reaching attempt to reduce music to a level which could be understood by all occurred as a result of the French Revolution. This was the first time that a great nation had ever attempted to employ music in the service of new political ideas: the ingenious pedagogical program of the Conservatoire was the first effort to reduce music to the common in the history of the art. Even today, musicians the world around continue to be trained in European music by the methods developed in revolutionary France, and listeners are taught—in keeping with the same principles—that it is not necessary to study music in order to comprehend it: all that is called for is simply to find it beautiful. Each individual therefore feels entitled and qualified to form his own judgment as to the value and the performance of music—an attitude which was perhaps valid for post-revolutionary music, but which in no way applies to the music of the preceding ages.

I am deeply convinced that it is of critical importance for the state of western European intellectual life that we live within our own culture. As far as music is concerned, this requires two new departures:

First, new methods—or methods similar to those used over two hundred years ago—must be used to train musicians. Rather than teaching music as language, our academies drill only techniques of performance. This focus is, however, merely the lifeless skeleton of technocracy.

Secondly, general training in music needs to be rethought and accorded the status it deserves. We will then be able to gaze with fresh vision upon the great works of the past, in all of their stirring, transforming diversity. And this will in turn prepare us for what is yet to come.

We all need music; without it we cannot live.

The Interpretation of Historical Music

Since historical music plays such a dominant role in the musical life of today, it is worthwhile to address the problems that stem from this fact. There are two fundamentally different approaches to historical music, each corresponding to quite different methods of rendition. One method transplants older music to the present, while the other attempts to view it in terms of the period in which it originated.

The first view is the natural one that has been customary during periods which possessed a truly vital contemporary music. It was also the only one possible throughout the history of Western music, from the beginning of polyphony to the second half of the 19th Century, and many great living musicians embrace this approach yet today. This attitude is based on the view that the language of music is always inextricably linked to a particular time. For example, compositions from the first decades of the 18th Century were regarded as hopelessly old-fashioned by mid-century, even though their intrinsic value was recognized. We are constantly amazed at the enthusiasm with which contemporary compositions were extolled as great pioneering achievements in earlier times. Old music was regarded as a preliminary stage, at best utilized as study material or arranged very infrequently for some special performance. For these rare performances of old music—for example in the 18th Century—, it was thought that updating was absolutely necessary. Today, however, composers who arrange historic compositions know very well that these compositions would be just as acceptable to an audience if they remained unrevised; such revisions arise not out of absolute necessity as in earlier centuries (when historical music, if played at all, was rendered only in a modernized fashion), but rather in the highly personal views of the arranger. Conductors like Furtwängler or Stokowski, whose ideal was grounded in the late Romantic period, presented all earlier music from this perspective. Bach's organ works, for example, were scored for Wagnerian orchestras and his Passions were performed in an overly romantic way, with a gigantic ensemble.

The second view, that of so-called faithfulness to the original, is much more recent than the first approach, dating only from about the beginning of the 20th Century. Since that time, there has been growing demand for the "authentic" rendition of historical music; leading interpreters describe this as the ideal towards which they are striving. An effort is made to do justice to old music as such and to render it in accordance with the period during which it was composed. This attitude toward historical music—the unwillingness to bring it into the present, but rather undertaking to return oneself to the past—is a symptom of the loss of a truly living contemporary music. Today's music satisfies neither the musician nor the public, both of whom reject a large portion of it. In order to fill the vacuum which this loss leaves, we fall back on historical music. In recent times we have quietly come to regard all music primarily as historic music: contemporary music is relegated to a realm of peripheral significance at best. This situation is thoroughly novel in the history of music. We might cite a small example to illustrate this: if we were to banish historical music from our concert halls and perform contemporary compositions exclusively, the halls would soon be deserted—yet the same thing would have happened in Mozart's time had the public been prevented from hearing contemporary music and been offered only older music (for example Baroque music). Today, historical music, particularly music of the 19th Century, forms the basis of musical life. Since the rise of polyphony, such a thing has never happened. By the same token, never before had audiences felt that historical music must be rendered faithfully, as is demanded today. This kind of historical perspective is totally alien to a culturally vital period. This can be seen in the other arts as well: for example, a Baroque sacristy could without hesitation be annexed to a Gothic church, magnificent Gothic altars were discarded so Baroque versions could be erected in their stead, while today, everything has to be painstakingly restored and preserved.

This attitude toward history has, however, a positive aspect: it enables us for the first time in the history of Christian/Western art to assume an independent position from which we can survey the entire creative achievements of the past. This is why historic music is included in concert programs with increasing frequency.

Late Romanticism was the last musically vital and creative period of Western music. The music of Bruckner, Brahms, Tchaikovsky, Richard Strauss and others was still a most vivid expression of the times. But after these men, musical life came to a standstill. Even today, the music of this period is the most beloved and most often listened to, and the training of musicians is still based on principles which evolved during that period. It almost seems as if we do not wish to be confronted by the fact that many decades have passed since then.

Our cultivation of historical music today does not resemble that of our predecessors. We have lost the "unselfconsciousness" necessary to use the present as the ultimate standard; the composer's intention has become for us the highest authority. We view old music by itself, in its own period, and therefore feel compelled to try to render it faithfully, not for curatorial reasons, but because this seems to us the only way to present older music in a vital and appropriate manner. However, a given rendition is only faithful if it approximates the views of the composer at the time of composition. It is obvious that this is possible to only a limited degree. The original conception of a work can only be intimated, especially in the case of music composed in the distant past. Some clues which may indicate the composer's intention include the expression marks on the score, the instrumentation, and the many traditional practices of performance, which have undergone constant modification, a knowledge of which composers could presume among their own contemporaries. But for us intensive study is required, an approach which can lead to serious error: a purely intellectual involvement with old music. The outcome is found in those familiar musical performances which are often historically impeccable, but which lack all vitality. Clearly, an interpretation that was historically uninformed but musically alive would be preferable. Musicology should never become an end in itself, but rather provide us with the means to make the best rendition, since a performance is only faithful to the original when a work is allowed to come most beautifully and most clearly to expression, something which happens only when knowledge and a sense of responsibility ally themselves with the deepest musical sensitivity.

Until recently, little attention has been paid to the continual transformation of musical practice; indeed, such change has even been considered unimportant. The reason for this is the notion of a "development" from primitive forms through more or less defective intermediate stages to a final "ideal" form. The latter is naturally thought to be superior in all aspects to the "preliminary stages." This notion is a holdover from the past, when art was a living reflection of its times; it remains widespread today. To people of earlier days, music, technique and instruments had developed "upward" to the highest level, i.e. whatever standard characterized a given period. However, today when we have been able to achieve an overview, this view of progress has been reversed; we can no longer make value judgments of the music of Brahms, Mozart, Bach, Josquin or Dufay—the theory of upward development can no longer be maintained. Yet to speak of the timelessness of all great works of art, as this concept is generally understood to imply, is just as erroneous as the theory of upward development. Like every art form, music is linked to a particular time; it is the living expression of its own period and can be completely understood only by its contemporaries. Our "understanding" of old music allows us only a glimpse of the spirit in which it is rooted. We see that music always reflects the spiritual and intellectual climate of its time. Its content can never surpass the human power of expression, and any gain on one side must be compensated by a corresponding loss on the other.

Because it is unclear just how and to what extent many specific changes in musical practice took place, let us briefly discuss this matter. By way of example let us look at notation, which underwent constant alterations into the 17th Century and whose "unambiguous" symbols were thereafter variously understood until the end of the 18th Century. The musician of today plays precisely what is indicated by the notes, little realizing that mathematically precise notation became customary only in the 19th Century. Furthermore, the enormous amount of improvisation, which until the end of the 18th Century was part and parcel of musical practice, is a source of great confusion.

Delineating the distinct phases of development during each particular historical period requires comprehensive technical knowledge, whose consistent application is reflected in formal and structural aspects of performance. However, it is the *sound itself* (tone color, character, loudness of the instruments, etc.) which allows this distinction to be clearly and immediately perceived. For just as the interpretation of notation or the practice of improvisation underwent constant modification in keeping with the *Zeitgeist*, changes were also taking place in concepts of sound and in what constituted an ideal sound, and thus also in the instruments themselves, the way in which they were played, and even in vocal techniques. Another aspect of sound is the space in which music is heard, i.e. the size and acoustical properties of a given room.

Nor is it possible to speak of "upward development" in connection with changes in the manner of playing, or technique: like the instruments themselves, technique has always been modified to the requirements of a given time. It could be said that technique has become more and more demanding; while this is certainly true, it applies only to certain aspects of technique, and simultaneously other aspects became less demanding. To be sure, no 17th-Century violinist could play the Brahms concerto, for example; but it is also true that no Brahms violinist could render a flawless performance of difficult works from the violin repertoire of the 17th Century. Completely different techniques are required for these two situations: they are equally difficult, though fundamentally different.

Similar changes can be observed in instrumentation as well as in the instruments themselves. Each period has precisely the instrumentarium best suited to its own music. In their imagination, composers hear the instruments of their own time and often write with certain instrumentalists in mind: idiomatic writing has always been expected; only poorly composed pieces were unplayable, and creators of such pieces only made themselves look foolish. Although many works of old masters are regarded today as virtually unplayable (wind parts in Baroque music, for example), this is due to the fact that musicians approach these works with present-day instruments and a modern style of playing in mind. Unfortunately it is almost impossible to expect a modern musician to be able to play on historic instruments, using historic techniques. Therefore, one should not blame early composers for writing unplayable parts, as often happens, nor should the musical practices of earlier times be regarded as technically inadequate. We must assume that leading musicians of all periods have been able to perform the most difficult works of the composers of their own times.

All of this only serves to indicate the monumental difficulties to be surmounted in any attempt to perform music fully faithful to the original. Compromises are unavoidable. How many questions are still unanswered, how many instruments can no longer be located or musicians found to play them? But whenever it is actually possible to achieve a high degree of true fidelity to the original, undreamed-of riches are the reward. The works appear in a completely new-old light, and many problems simply disappear. Given such a rendition, the works sound not only historically more correct, but also more vital, because they are performed with the means most appropriate to them, and we get an intimation of the spiritual forces which made the past so fertile. Involvement with old music in this way takes on a deep meaning, far surpassing that of purely aesthetic enjoyment.

Musical Understanding and the Training of Musicians

There are many indications that we are heading toward a general cultural collapse from which music of course would not be excluded, for music is but one aspect of our spiritual life and as such, can only reflect what is happening within it. If the situation is really as critical as it appears to me, then it is not right for us to simply stand by idly until everything is over.

The education of musicians plays a most significant role in this matter. By the term "musician," I mean all those who participate professionally in the life of music, including those who listen to music professionally, and the public as well. Against this background, let us first take a look at the relative importance of music throughout human history. It may be interesting to note that in many languages, "poetry" and "song" are expressed by the same word. In other words, at the moment when language reaches a profundity surpassing that of any concrete message, it is immediately linked to song, because with the help of song anything over and above pure information can be conveyed more clearly. This relationship is difficult for us to comprehend because it no longer is a part of our contemporary understanding of music. Thus the spoken word, the meaning of words, can be intensified by tones, melodies and harmonies, which make it possible to reach a kind of understanding that goes beyond the purely linguistic.

The role of music, however, did not remain limited to an intensification and deepening of linguistic expression; music soon found its own aesthetic (although its relationship to language always remained recognizable) and so a large number of special means of expression unique to it: rhythm, melody, harmony, etc. In this way, a vocabulary and syntax emerged which gave music an incredible power over the body and soul of man.

People listening to music can be seen to move; sitting motionless in the presence of music requires the utmost discipline. That motion can indeed be heightened to the point of ecstasy. Even in the simple progression from dissonance to resolution, tension and relaxation visibly occurs. Something similar happens in the realm of melody: every melodic progression follows a certain pattern so the listener, after hearing four or five notes, knows what the sixth and seventh notes will be and this sequence, this expectation, realized, brings about physical release and relaxation. If the composer wishes to evoke tension in the listener, he frustrates this expectation by melodically misleading him, only to evoke relaxation at a later point in the composition. This is an extraordinarily complicated procedure that has been utilized by composers for centuries in Western music. When we attend a concert and listen truly intensely—assuming, of course, that the music is played intensely and well—, we feel this tension and relaxation, we "apprehend the music physically" and changes demonstrably occur in our circulatory system. The same is also true in the musical representation of emotions, from those of a peaceful, cheerful or painful nature, to the excitation of the most intense joy, fury or rage; all are expressed in music in such a way that they indeed evoke strong emotions and physical responses in the listener. Among the changes that music can evoke in people are, of course, those of the spirit as well. So, music also has a moral role; for centuries it has profoundly influenced man and transformed him spiritually.

Music is grounded in time. It is an expression of specific periods, and, like all human cultural expressions, is a necessary element in the business of living. This relationship between life and music has existed for a millennium in Western music: music has been a basic component of life—and I mean here the music of a particular generation. When this unity could no longer be sustained, a new basis for understanding music had to be found. Present-day music is commonly divided into the categories of "folk music," "popular music," "serious music" (a concept which holds no meaning for me), etc. Within these categories, elements of the original unity still exist, but the unity of music and life and the view of the oneness of music has been lost.

We can still consider folk music as being one with the culture of a particular social group; but where only enclaves remain, this music is actually a component of folkloric tradition. (And it thereby represents cultural decline, since folklore is not something which is "cultivated," but is rather an intrinsic component of life. The moment we describe it as "folklore," it has already become a museum piece.) On the other hand, in popular music we still find a residuum of the old function of music. The physical impact on the listener is obvious. We should reflect carefully on the fact that current popular music plays an essential role in our cultural life, but no contemporary "serious music" plays a comparable role.

Popular music incorporates many of the elements of earlier music: the unity of poetry and song, which was so important in the origins of music; the unity of listener and performer; and the unity of music and time. Since popular music never endures more than five or ten years, it belongs to the present. Perhaps we can best understand what music once meant in people's lives by invoking the example of popular music, because, limited though its resonances and meaning may be, it remains an integral part of life.

Now we come to our pitiful stepchild, "serious music," which we may further divide into "modern" and "classical" music. Modern music, which is "cultivated" by musicians who are just as important and significant as they have been for a thousand years, is of significance only for a tiny circle of traveling devotees who are the same everywhere. I do not mean this ironically, but rather regard it as a symptom of a collapse that is neither easy to understand nor to explain. For if music disengages itself from its public, neither music nor the public is to blame. Nor can the reason be sought in art in general, or in music in particular, but rather in the spiritual condition of our time. It is in the present spiritual climate that changes would have to occur. Music is necessarily a mirror of the present; if we wish to change music, we must first change the contemporary world. There is no crisis in music; rather music is reflecting the crisis of an age. So endeavoring to change music would be just as absurd as a doctor treating a patient's symptoms rather than his illness. It is not possible to "cure" contemporary music by means of "cultural policies," by promoting certain "acceptable" directions, for example—anyone who believes in such a nostrum clearly fails to understand the function of music in human life. A true composer writes, whether intentionally or not, as the spiritual and cultural conditions of a period dictate; otherwise he would become a parodist, simply supplying imitations on request.

But what have we done? We have undertaken to "save" ourselves, we have attempted to flee into the past just when the unity of contemporary cultural creation and life no longer exists. The so-called "cultured" person therefore seeks to rescue for his time only that portion of the cultural and musical heritage of the last thousand years which he can now comprehend, because there is no longer a living present, by sifting out two or three components from the whole which have meaning for him, and which he thinks he understands. As a consequence, music is made and listened to today in this way: from all of the music of the past thousand years, we sift out and respond only to its aesthetic component. We simply opt for that which pleases our ear, which is "beautiful," completely overlooking the fact that we thoroughly degrade music by so doing. It is of no significance to us at all when we simply fail to hear essential components of classical music, because we are responding only to those beautiful elements which often play only a modest role in the totality of a work.

These reflections lead me to a further question: what role should music play in our own age? Is change possible, is it meaningful to attempt to alter anything? Is the place that music holds in our present life completely wrong?—In my opinion, we are in a difficult situation and one in which, if we do not succeed in combining our listening habits, our need for music, and our musical life—whether by re-establishing an equilibrium between supply and demand in contemporary music, or by fostering a new understanding of classical music—, the end is in sight. If we fail we will become nothing more than the curators of a museum, able to display artifacts of the past, which we have lovingly collected. I do not believe many musicians are interested in or moved by such a scenario.

Now to the role of the musician. During the Middle Ages, the roles of theoretician, practitioner and "total" musician were clearly delineated. The theoretician understood how music was constructed, but almost never performed it. He could neither play nor compose music, yet he understood its inner structure and its theoretical basis. He was highly regarded among his contemporaries because music theory was regarded as an independent science, for which musical performance had no real meaning. (This attitude is occasionally found among musicologists today.) The practical musician, on the other hand, could play music but had no knowledge at all of musical theory. Even though he could not explain things in a theoretical way, even though he understood little of its history, his musical understanding was instinctive and he was capable of supplying whatever music was required. This point can be illustrated using the example of language. The linguist possesses a body of knowledge about the composition and history of language, while his contemporary, the man in the street, has no grasp at all of such arcane matters, but can use the language fluently and trenchantly because it is the speech of his own time. The instrumentalist and the singer were for a thousand years of Western history in a precisely analogous situation; they did not *know,* they *were able,* and understood without knowing.

Lastly there was the "total" musician, a person who was both theoretician and practitioner. Those in this category knew and understood musical theory, but did not regard it as an isolated subject removed from practical application, sufficient unto itself; they were able to compose and play music because they were familiar with and understood all of its related elements. The total musician was held in higher regard than either the theoretician or the practitioner, because he had mastered all aspects of ability and knowledge.

What is the situation today? The contemporary composer is typically a musician in the latter sense. He possesses theoretical knowledge, is familiar with practical possibilities which exist, but lacks living contact with the listener, with those human beings who absolutely *need* his music. Apparently what is missing is a vital need for a completely new music created specifically to meet this need. The practitioner, the performing musician, is just as uninformed as he was centuries ago. He is interested above all in performance, technical perfection, immediate applause and acclaim. He does not create music, but only plays it. Because the unity between his time and the music which he plays has been dissolved, he lacks the knowledge of music which the musicians of earlier periods possessed as a matter of course. We must remember, however, that they played only the music of their contemporaries.

Our musical life is in a disastrous state. Opera houses, symphony orchestras, concert halls abound, offering a rich program of music. But the music we play in these places is music we do not understand at all, music which was intended for people of quite different times. The most remarkable aspect of this situation is that we are completely unaware of it. We believe that there is nothing to *understand,* since music addresses itself directly to our feelings. All musicians strive for beauty and emotion; this is natural for them and forms the basis of their power of expression. They are not at all interested in acquiring the knowledge that would be necessary precisely because the unity between music and its time has been lost; nor can such a pursuit interest them because they are unaware of any deficiencies in their knowledge. As a result, they portray only the purely aesthetic and emotional components of music, ignoring the rest of its content. This situation is shored up by the image of the artist that evolved during the 19th Century. The Romantic period in the 19th Century gradually transformed the artist into a kind of superman, who, with the help of intuition and creativity, develops insights far surpassing those of "normal" human beings. Thus he became a kind of "demi-god," even came to regard himself as such and allowed himself to be fittingly honored. This "demi-god" was quite a marvelous phenomenon in the Romantic period—one need only think of Berlioz, Liszt or Wagner, all of whom fit this development to a T. It was right that admirers kissed the hem of Wagner's dressing-gown, since such behavior was completely acceptable in that period. However, the portrait of the artist that emerged in this decadent late period has been preserved in stone, like so many other things from that time.

Now the question: what should the artist actually be? This question derives perforce from the way music must be understood today. If the musician really has the task of rendering our entire musical heritage—insofar as it is of any concern to us at all—and not just its aesthetic and technical aspects, then he must acquire the knowledge necessary to do so correctly. There is no other way. The music of the past has become a foreign language because of the progression of history, because of its remoteness from the present, and because it has been taken out of the context of its own period. Individual aspects of a piece of music may well be universally valid and timeless, but the message as such is linked to a particular time and can only be rediscovered when it is translated, as it were, into our contemporary idiom. This means that if the music of past epochs is in any way relevant to the present in a deeper and wider sense, if it is to be presented with its total message intact, or at least to a greater extent than is the case today, the understanding of this music has to be relearned from the principles that underlie its very essence. We have to know what music intends to express in order to understand what we want to say with it. Knowledge must therefore be added to the purely emotive and intuitive dimensions. Without such historical knowledge, neither historical music nor our own so-called "serious" music can be performed properly.

A few words regarding the training of musicians. In earlier times an individual musician instructed apprentices in keeping with the degree of his musical mastery; this means that for many centuries, the master/apprentice relationship was used in music, just as it was in craftsmen's trades. Students went to a particular master in order to learn "the trade" from him, his manner of making music. Attention was first focused on musical techniques, on composition and the playing of instruments; but rhetoric was also studied so that music could be made to speak. A constant theme in writings on music, especially in the age of Baroque music from about 1600 to the last decades of the 18th Century, is that music is a *language based on tones,* involving dialogue and dramatic confrontation. The master must teach the apprentice his art in all its aspects. He taught not merely how to play an instrument or to sing, but also how to present music. There were no problems in this natural relationship; changes in style took place gradually from generation to generation, so that learning was actually not relearning, but rather simply organic growth, organic metamorphosis.

As time progressed there were several interesting breaks which altered and brought into question this relationship between master and apprentice. One of these was the French Revolution. Out of the great upheavals it brought about, we see that not only musical training as a whole but musical life itself was given a fundamentally new orientation. The relationship between master and apprentice was replaced by a system, an institution: the Conservatoire. The system embraced by the Conservatoire can be described as politicized musical education. The French Revolution had almost all the musicians on its side, and it was clearly perceived that people could be influenced by art and particularly by music, which uses not words, but rather mysteriously effective "potions" to achieve its impact. The political utilization of art to indoctrinate citizens or subjects, either overtly or covertly, had been known since antiquity; but never before had music been used in such a systematic way.

The French method, which aimed at unifying musical style down to the last detail, attempted to integrate music into an overall political plan. The idea was that music had to be simple enough to be understood by anyone (although the term "understood" no longer really applies); it had to be able to move, arouse, soothe anyone, whether educated or not; it had to communicate in a "language" that everyone understood without first having to learn it.

These requirements were only necessary and possible because the music of the previous age had been presented primarily for "the well-bred," i.e. those who had mastered the language of music. Musical education had always formed one of the basic components of education in the Western world. When, therefore, traditional musical education was eliminated, the elite community of musicians and educated listeners disappeared. If everyone had to be reached and the listener need no longer understand anything about music, then everything that had to do with utterance,—which requires understanding—had to be eliminated; the composer must write music that speaks directly to the emotions in the simplest and most accessible fashion. (Philosophers rightfully point out that when art is merely pleasing, it pleases only the ignorant.)

In response to these dictates, Cherubini eliminated the old master-apprentice relationship in the Conservatoire. He had didactic works written by the greatest authorities of the period, which were supposed to embody the new ideal of *egalité* in music. With this in mind, Baillot wrote his violin method and Kreutzer his études. The most important music teachers of France had to formulate the new ideas of music in a specified system, which meant, in technical terms, replacing verbal with pictorial elements. This is how the *sostenuto,* the sweeping melodic line, the modern *legato* came about. The great melodic line had existed before, of course, but it had always been heard as a synthesis of smaller elements. This revolution in musical training was carried out so radically that within a few short decades, musicians all over Europe were being trained in accordance with the system of the Conservatoire. To my way of thinking, it is quite grotesque that this system remains *the* basis of modern musical education! After all, it wiped out everything that had formerly been considered important.

It is interesting to note that Richard Wagner was one of the greatest admirers of this new way of making music. Wagner conducted the orchestra of the Conservatoire and waxed enthusiastic at the smooth connection of upbow and downbow of the violins, at the breadth of the melodies; music could henceforth be used to paint a scene. After that experience, he repeatedly remarked that he could never achieve such legato with German orchestras. I am convinced that this approach is optimal for Wagner's music, but thoroughly disastrous for music prior to Mozart. Strictly speaking, today's musician is trained by a method that neither he nor his teacher understands. He learns the systems of Baillot and Kreutzer, which were devised for musicians of their day, and applies them to the music of completely different ages and styles. Without further thought we continue to train musicians in all those theoretical fundamentals which were quite meaningful 180 years ago, despite the fact that we no longer understand them.

When current music is historical music as is the case today (a fact of which we may or may not approve), the training of musicians should be radically different and based on quite different fundamental principles. In the long run, this training must not be limited to teaching where on the instrument the fingers must be positioned in order to play certain tones and to develop dexterity. This type of narrow, technical focus does not produce musicians, only hollow technicians. Brahms once said that in order to become a good musician, one should spend just as much time reading books as practicing the piano. This says it all, even for us today. Since we perform music from about four centuries, unlike the musicians of the past, we must study the optimal performance conditions for every historical type of music. A violinist possessed of the ultimate Kreutzer/Paganini technique should not delude himself into believing that he has thereby acquired the qualifications needed to play Bach or Mozart, for he has not undertaken to understand and to master the technical requirements and the meaning of the "verbal" music of the 18th Century.

Thus far we have dealt with only one side of the problem, for the listener, too, has to come to a much broader understanding. Without realizing it, he is still suffering from the emasculation resulting from the French Revolution. Beauty and emotion are for him, as for most musicians, the sole elements to which musical experience and understanding have been reduced. Of what does the education of the listener actually consist, if not the musical instruction that he receives in school and the concert life in which he participates? And even those who have had no education in music and never attended a concert have nonetheless received musical training, since in the Western world probably no one does not listen to the radio. The sounds that daily inundate the listener inform him musically by characterizing for him the value and the significance of music—whether this be positive or negative—, without his even realizing it.

One other consideration, from the point of view of the audience. Which concerts do we actually attend? Certainly only those at which familiar music is played. This is a fact that any concert organizer will confirm. Insofar as the program plays any role at all, the audience wants only to hear music that is already familiar. This has to do with our listening habits. If a musical work is designed so that the listener is totally involved in it, indeed literally overwhelmed by it, then this presupposes that he does *not* know the work, that he is hearing it for the first time. Thus instead of fulfilling our expectations, the composer can suddenly shock us by leading us to a normal cadence which he then transforms into a deceptive cadence; but a deceptive cadence that one already knows no longer deceives, no longer *is* a deceptive cadence. There are infinite possibilities of this kind, and our musical heritage is based on leading the listener by means of surprises and shocks to the understanding and experience that underlie the idea of the work. Today, however, there are neither surprises nor shocks: when we listen to a classical symphony which contains hundreds of such composed shocks, we lean forward with interest two bars in advance to hear "how will they perform it?" If we were to be exacting about this, such music should really not be performed at all, since it is already so familiar that we can be neither surprised nor shocked nor enchanted—other than perhaps by the "how" of the performance. Apparently a stimulus cannot be used too often, as we no longer want to be thrilled or surprised; we want only to enjoy and to know "how do they do that?" A familiar "beautiful" passage can appear to be even more beautiful, or a drawn-out passage can be extended a bit further, or perhaps be shortened a bit. Our listening exhausts itself in these comparisons of minor differences in interpretation, and thus our sense of music has been reduced to a ridiculously primitive stage. The essential difference between the listening habits of earlier times and those of today lies in the fact that we desire to listen often to a work that we love, whereas people of earlier times did not. People today are happy to listen again and again to works that are familiar, but would not care to listen *only* to those which are new. We are like children who want to hear the same story over and over again, because we remember beautiful parts we encountered the first time it was read to us.

If we are not able to interest ourselves in the unfamiliar—whether it be old or new—if we are not able to rediscover the reason for musical effect—an effect on our minds as well as our bodies—, then making music will have lost its meaning. Then the efforts of the great composers to fill their works with musical statements—statements which no longer affect us in any way, which we no longer comprehend—will have been in vain. If all they had wanted to incorporate in their works was simply that beauty which seems to be the only thing that still means anything to us, they could have saved themselves much time, effort and sacrifice.

It is not enough to simply master the technical aspects of music. I believe that only if we succeed in teaching musicians to understand the language of music again, or better yet, the many languages of the many different musical styles, and at the same time educate the listener to appreciate this language, will this apathetic and aestheticizing approach to music no longer be acceptable, nor the monotony of concert programs tolerated. (Are these few pieces which are played over and over again from Tokyo to Moscow to Paris really the quintessence of Western music?) And as a logical consequence of this, the separation between "popular" and "serious" music and ultimately also between music and time will disappear and cultural life will once again form a whole.

This should be the objective of musical education in our time. Since the necessary institutions already exist, it should be easy to infiltrate and change their objectives, thereby giving them a new content. What the French Revolution brought about by means of the program of the Conservatoire—which amounted to a radical transformation of musical life—, the present age should also be able to achieve, assuming that we are clear about the need for such a transformation.

Problems of Notation

Musicians are constantly confronted with the question of how a composer sets down his ideas and preferences so that they can be conveyed to his contemporaries as well as to posterity. Over and over again, we see the limitations of the efforts made by various composers to avoid ambiguity by supplying precise instructions. Thus each composer developed a kind of personal notation, which can be deciphered today only when studied in terms of its historical context. The prevailing misconception that notational symbols and indications of affect, tempo and dynamics have always meant what they do today is disastrous. This view has been fostered by the fact that for centuries, the same graphic marks have been used in the writing of music; not enough attention has been paid to the fact that notation is not simply a timeless, supra-national method of writing down sounds which has remained unchanged for centuries. On the contrary, the meanings of the various notation signs have undergone constant modification in keeping with stylistic shifts in music, the ideas of composers and the views of performing musicians. Their meaning at any given time can occasionally be discovered in writings of the time but must in many cases be derived from the musical and philological context of the period, which always involves the possibility of error. Notation is thus an extremely complicated system of encoding. Anyone who has tried to write down a musical thought or a rhythmic structure knows that this is a relatively simple task. But if a musician is asked to play what has been recorded, it will quickly be seen that he by no means plays just what was intended.

We believe we possess a system of notation which will inform us about both the individual tone as well as the course of the musical piece. However, every musician should know that this notation is very inexact, that it does not precisely say what it does say: it does not tell us the length of tone, the pitch, nor the tempo, because the technical criteria for this kind of information cannot be conveyed by notation. The duration of a note can only be precisely described by a time unit; the pitch of a tone can only be represented in terms of vibration frequency; a constant tempo might be indicated by a metronome—if there were such a thing as a constant tempo.

Is it not astonishing to believe that musical works which are completely different in essence and style, such as an opera by Monteverdi and a symphony by Gustav Mahler, can be written down using the same notational symbols? To those familiar with the extraordinary diversity of musical genres, it is quite astonishing that beginning in about 1500, this same symbol system has been used to set down the music of every age and every style, no matter how fundamentally they differ.

Further, despite the seeming certitude of this notational system, two quite different principles govern their use:
1. The *work,* the composition itself, is notated: but the details of its interpretation cannot be deduced from the notation.
2. The *performance* is notated: in this case, the notation includes directions for performance; it does not indicate, as in the former case, the form and structure of the composition (the interpretation of which must be deduced from other sources), but rather describes the interpretation as precisely as possible: this passage is to be played in this way. The work then, in theory, emerges automatically, as it were, during performance.

In general, music prior to about 1800 is notated according to the *work*-principle and thereafter as a direction for *performance.* Nonetheless, there are numerous deviations: for example, as early as the 16th and 17th centuries, the tablatures (finger notations) for certain instruments are strictly directions for *playing*—and therefore do not graphically represent the *work.* These tablatures indicate precisely where the player should place his fingers—when plucking the lute for example—so that the tonal reproduction is exactly as planned. We cannot imagine any tones from looking at a tablature; rather, we see only the finger positions. This is an extreme example of notation as direction for performance.

In the case of compositions written after 1800, using notation as the directions for performance (e.g. works by Berlioz, Richard Strauss and others), the primary consideration is to describe as precisely as possible how the written work is supposed to sound; only when these notes are precisely performed, only when all instructions are observed, does music emerge.

On the other hand, if we wish to play music which is scored using *work*-notation, i.e. music prior to the watershed of about 1800, we lack precise "instructions." We must resort to other sources for this information. This changing use of notation also poses a serious pedagogical problem, since normally the musician learns notation first and only later how to create music; notation is assumed to be valid for every style of music, so instructors do not tell students that music which was written prior to the notation watershed must be read differently from music written subsequently. We fail to draw our own attention as well as that of the student to the fact that in the one case we are dealing with complete instructions for playing, while in the other we are dealing with a composition written in a fundamentally different way. These two ways of interpreting one and the same notation—work notation and direction for performance—should be called to the attention of every music student from the very outset of instruction in theory, instruments or voice. Otherwise, the student will always play or sing "what is written down," a common demand by music teachers, although it is impossible to do justice to *work* notation without having first examined and understood it.

Perhaps this can be best explained by using the concept of orthography. There is a "right way to spell" in music, derived from musical teaching, musical theory and harmony. Special features of notation result from this musically proper spelling, for example suspensions, trills and appoggiaturas are often not written out. This can be quite annoying if one thinks he must play exactly what is written. In another example embellishments are not spelled out: if they were written down, no latitude would be left for the creative imagination of the performer; but this is precisely what was encouraged, particularly in the case of free embellishments. In the 17th and 18th Centuries, a good "adagio player" was a musician who freely improvised embellishments which suited and enhanced the expression of a particular work.

When I see a piece of music, I first try to assess the work and determine how it should be read, what these notes signified for musicians of the time. Notation depicting the work rather than the manner of playing requires, after all, the same reading knowledge on our part that it demanded of the musicians then.

Let us take an example which is surely obvious to present-day musicians: Viennese dance music of the 19th Century, a polka or waltz by Johann Strauss. The composer tried to write down whatever notes were necessary, in his opinion, for the musicians who sat before him in the orchestra. After all, they knew quite well what a waltz or a polka sounded like and how such dances should be played. If this music were given to an orchestra which lacked this knowledge, which was unfamiliar with these dances, and the musicians were to play exactly in accordance with the notes, the music would sound totally different. It is not possible to write down such dance music precisely as it should be played. Often a note must be played earlier or later, or shorter or longer than it is written, etc. Thus we could play this music as precisely as possible, even with metronomical precision—and yet the result would have nothing to do with the work as it was originally intended by the composer.

If the correct understanding of notes is this problematical for the music of Johann Strauss, despite its unbroken tradition—how much more problematical it must be in the case of music whose playing tradition has completely vanished, so that we no longer know how such music was actually played during the lifetime of the composer. Let us imagine that Strauss was not played for one hundred years, only to be once again "discovered" and performed anew as intriguing music. It is impossible to imagine how such a performance would sound! Something similar happens, I suppose, with the great composers of the 17th and 18th Centuries, with whose music we have no continuous connection because their works were not played for centuries. No one can say definitively how such music should be read, which specific conventions must be observed when this music is performed.

Of course, much information is available in the sources, yet it is also true that everyone reads into these instructions whatever he himself has in mind. If, for example, we find in the sources that each tone should be played shorter by half than its written value, we can take this literally: each tone is therefore held for only half its value. This instruction could be understood in a different way, however; there is also an old rule which holds that each tone should fade away into silence. The tone originates and fades away—rather like the tone of a bell; it ends "by dying away." The precise end cannot be heard because the listener's imagination extends the tone and this illusion cannot be separated from the actual experience of hearing. So the duration of a tone cannot be precisely determined. The tone can be regarded as a fully held note or as a drastically shortened note, according to whether or not illusion is also taken into consideration.

Furthermore, there are a few cases in which it is technically or musically impossible to hold a note according to the notation; such cases show at the very least that notation and practice often differ. This can be clearly seen in chord playing on stringed instruments, in which case not all notes can be sustained for technical reasons, or in the case of an instrument on which the notes cannot be fully sustained e.g. piano, harpsichord and other plucked instruments. We cannot hear a long, sustained note on a harpsichord or a lute; we hear only the onset of the tone, which then fades away. The imagination supplies the rest, while the actual tone disappears. This disappearance does not mean that the tone ceases, rather it continues to be heard by the "inner ear" and is cancelled only by the onset of the subsequent note. If this tone were to continue to sound at its full strength, it would disturb the transparency of the composition's texture and would cover up the entrance of the next tone; this outcome is often heard in the case of organ concerts as it is theoretically possible to hold any tone on the organ for as long as it is notated. The reality of a sustained sound is not better than the illusion of the sound; on the contrary, under certain circumstances the former can mask and interfere with our understanding of the latter. In those fugues contained in Bach's *Die Kunst der Fuge* in which there is an augmentation of the subject, this difference can be clearly recognized. For these fugues can be understood more readily on a harpsichord than an organ, which can sustain the notes as the harpsichord cannot. There is no four-part chord which can be sustained in all four parts on the violin for an entire measure, for just as the player reaches the E-string, nothing is left of the bass tone on the G-string and it is not possible to begin the four notes of the chord simultaneously, as written. This provides a clear example that we must regard the notation as an orthographic image of the composition and the execution as a musical representation intended to correspond to our technical resources and the receptiveness of our listeners. In other words, the chord has to be played successively and not simultaneously. This is not only true of the stringed instruments and the lute, but at times also of the harpsichord and the piano in those cases in which the chord does not lie within the span of the hand, as well as when the harpsichord player prefers not to play the notes simultaneously.

Clearly, mastering the historical texts will not suffice. To contend that each note must be played shorter or that each has its correct strength or weakness is to misapprehend the nature of notation. Even if we followed the rules they contain literally, much older music would end up sounding like a malicious caricature. It would probably sound even more distorted than if a musical person out of ignorance were to do everything "wrong." The rules of the old treatises become interesting for actual practice only if we understand them—or at least once they convey a meaning to us, whether or not we understand them in keeping with their original meaning.

I am very skeptical as to whether complete understanding remains possible today. One must always keep in mind that all these treatises were written for contemporaries, so an author could count on the existence of a large body of generally familiar knowledge; he did not need to discuss it at all. After all, his instructions were addressed to his contemporaries, not to us. All of this valuable information would therefore acquire its full import for us only if we, too, possessed the same accepted basic knowledge.—What was not written down, that which was self-evident, was probably more important than anything that was written!—For my part, I believe that misunderstandings resulting from study of the sources are not only common, but probable, and that the numerous collections of excerpts which have been published in recent years should never be introduced as evidence, for one could just as easily "prove" the opposite using other quotations similarly taken out of context. Therefore I must warn against overestimating our historical understanding of music. Only if we really comprehend the meaning behind the old prescriptions and theories will we be able to use them to interpret this music.

The information available to us comes from a series of 17th and 18th Century treatises. If we read just one of them, e.g. the flute method by Quantz, we feel that we have learned a great deal. And then we study a different text only to discover that it contains quite different, often contrary, information. If to compensate we read several authors, we find many contradictions, and only by comparing a large number of sources can we begin to see that these are not real contradictions. Only then do we begin to form an overall picture. If we codify the differing instructions, we can see exactly where each author stands. Music and musical practice, after all, were by no means uniform at the time. One author holds fast to what his forefathers wrote or said; his orientation is directed more towards the past. Another describes the musical customs in a particular location—or is a devotee of some new style or movement.

These differing approaches can be easily observed when we compare sources. Basically we find that a common practice, those normal, common aspects of musicianship, were never recorded in such texts. Rather, the tendency was to record something when it seemed it would soon be forgotten, or when a devotee of already outdated practices wished to preserve them, as is beautifully illustrated, for example, in Le Blanc's defense of the viola da gamba. Then, of course, there were authors who "mounted the barricades" to introduce something new. Muffat, for example, towards the end of the 17th Century sought to spread the current French style beyond the borders of France. He summarized the essential features of this style as a means to explain it to musicians totally unfamiliar with it. We must also consider where a source belongs stylistically. It does not make much sense to play a work dated 1720 according to playing directions from 1756. All of these considerations must be seen in context and repeatedly re-evaluated and reconsidered.

The example of Johann Strauss, which I referred to earlier, seems to me quite useful, because his music, as I understand it, is still played in Vienna in the original and natural way. In their youth, some of today's older musicians were still in touch with people who played under Strauss and his successors. They simply know—without much conscious reflection—how light and shadow are to be distributed in the dynamics, where notes should be shorter or longer, how the music realizes the right lilt for dancing and wherein the wit of the whole lies. Without any unbroken tradition, this kind of intuitive knowledge is lost to us. We can draw conclusions about the tempi and the unwritten fine points of musical performance only from descriptions. We know, at least from the point of view of physical sensation, far too little about the old dances, which is critical for determining tempo. If we know the rules of the dance steps, this knowledge can easily be applied to the music. We have therefore a certain concrete, movement-related possibility of interpreting the notation. Since the dances were at one time generally known and follow pre-determined rhythms and tempi, they are relatively easy to reconstruct, and are probably the most significant source of information about the manner of playing, timing and manners of accentuation.

In other music, the basic rhythm, tempo and accentuation must be deduced from the time signature and bar-lines. At the beginning of the 17th Century, these probably functioned only as an aid to basic orientation. They are put in "any old place" (in any case, I have yet to make any sense of them). Only in the course of the 17th Century was the bar-line "correctly" placed as we understand it today; and from then on, it provides very important information about the accentuation of the music. It allows the—already self-evident—hierarchy of accents which are derived from language to be rendered in a visible system. This hierarchy is—as I will later explain more extensively—perhaps the most elementary and most important aspect of the music of the 17th and 18th Centuries. It expresses something very natural, i.e. (to put it extremely simply) that following the principle of linguistic stress, a weak point follows a strong point, something light follows something heavy; which is also expressed in the manner of playing. Probably for this reason, musical instruments, and particularly string instruments, are designed in such a way that this change from strong to weak, from light to heavy, can be done very easily and naturally. The up-bow is always somewhat weaker than the down-bow, especially using a Baroque bow. Therefore the strong beat (in 4/4 time the one and the three) is usually played on the down-bow. There is a whole palette of tonguings for wind players with which a similar variability can be expressed. There are traditional fingerings for keyboard players which achieve the same effect.

Today's instrumentalists often believe it possible to achieve desired effects by other means as well; this is true in certain cases—an up-bow can certainly be accented—but it is more natural the other way around. I believe musicians today should first try this natural way and only when a particular effect cannot be thus realized should they try a different method of execution. This difference is clearly illustrated in comparing violin methods of Leopold Mozart and Geminiani: according to the former, *every* accent should come on the down-bow, while the latter claimed that accents could be made the other way, as well.

The music of earlier centuries was governed by written and unwritten rules, knowledge of which was taken for granted among contemporary musicians, knowledge which we today must arduously reacquire. One of these rules dictates that a dissonance must be stressed while its resolution should fade away. Many musicians—including those often dealing with older music—disregard this important and very natural rule of stress and so overlook charming accents which were introduced by the composer precisely by means of such dissonances, often against the usual rule of accentuation. Even the normally unaccented fourth beat is occasionally stressed, then resolving into silence as it reaches the otherwise stressed downbeat. Unfortunately, most musicians today ignore this extremely important variance.

By way of further example of how the meaning of notation has changed, let us look at how dotted notes are read and played today, as compared with the 18th Century. The modern rule says that a dot prolongs a note by exactly one-half of its value, and that the following short note has precisely the same rhythmical value as this prolonging dot. Our methods of notation cannot deal with the infinite number of ways of playing dotted rhythms—from almost equal note values to the severest over-dotting. Yet every dotted rhythm looks exactly the same on the music sheet, regardless of how it may have been intended. It is, however, evident from countless text books of earlier historical periods that there were an enormous number of ways in which dotted rhythms could be played, particularly those which exaggerated the dotting, i.e. those in which the short note after the dotted note had to be played later than the "correct" time, and often at the very last moment. The subdivision in a ratio of 3:1, which is the only one customary today, was employed only in very rare cases.

In most "modern" interpretations, note values are sustained in strict accordance with their supposedly correct duration, and the dotted rhythms are executed with downright ostentatious precision. The reason for this emphasis on rhythmical accuracy probably has to do with the fact that musicians, by their very nature and justifiably, prefer to play a less precise rhythm, so that the conductor must more or less wrest from them a rendition that is correct according to the notes.

Articulation signs such as dots and ties are also frequently misunderstood, because their various meanings in notation prior to and after the year 1800 are not sufficiently understood and so not taken into consideration. Our approach is largely based on the music of the 19th Century, in which the latitude of the interpreter was radically restricted by the "autobiographical" manner of composition. The details of interpretation were fixed as precisely as possible, each nuance, each slight *ritenuto,* each minute variance of the tempo, was prescribed. Since all notes were now regulated including dynamics, timing and phrasing, musicians became accustomed to slavishly transforming the score in keeping with all its instructions. This method of reading and playing, which is appropriate for the music of the 19th and 20th Centuries, is, however, completely wrong for the music of the Baroque and Classic periods. Despite this shortcoming such an approach is used for this music and for every type and style of music, largely out of ignorance. The result is therefore all the more inappropriate, since musicians of the Baroque period sang and played music using quite different assumptions than we do today. Music of the 18th Century carries virtually no indications as to dynamics, only a few tempo indications and modifiers, and almost no indications of phrasing and articulation. Editors of older music published in the 19th Century supplied the "missing" indications. In such editions, we frequently encounter the long "phrasing-slur," which greatly distorts these works in a "linguistic" sense; one might almost say they have been converted into 19th-Century compositions. To be sure, musicians knew that slurs could be supplied. But the real misunderstanding occurred in the first half of our own century, in connection with the vogue of so-called faithfulness to the work: older scores were "purified" of 19th-Century additions and performed in a dessicated form. Yet the principle of the 19th Century in which what the composer intended had to be found expressly in the notes was retained—and vice versa: anything not found in the notes was not intended and represented an arbitrary distortion of the work. The composers of the Baroque and Classic periods did not, however, observe such rules because they had not yet been formulated. Rather they were concerned with the principles of *articulation,* a topic which I will discuss later. These principles are closely interwoven with the problems of notation, because they presuppose playing methods which were only occasionally written into the score, and which therefore had to be furnished by the players, in accordance with their own insight and good taste. These principles were articulated quite clearly by Leopold Mozart, among others: "But it is not enough if one simply plays these figures according to the indicated bowing; one must also perform them in such a way that the change (in the stroke of the bow) can be heard immediately.... One must therefore not only observe the written and indicated slurs as precisely as possible: but when ... nothing is indicated, one must know how to introduce the slurs and accents *oneself,* tastefully and at the *appropriate places.*—It grieves me to hear experienced violinists ... play quite simple passages ... not at all in keeping with the intention of the composer." It was therefore a question of both adhering to the articulation which is precisely indicated by dots, lines and slurs on the one hand—for which methods of bowing or tonguing, but also dynamic playing were necessary—and, on the other hand, of finding the proper forms of articulation for those passages in which no articulation was prescribed by the composer.

Music has unfortunately been played, for some years and in many places, from "purified" editions; and from the point of view of "faithfulness to the work." As a consequence the liveliest and most imaginative interpretations of Baroque and Classic music are frequently labeled as "romantic" or stylistically wrong.

Fundamental problems also result from the notation of recitatives. Here I wish to point above all to the difference between the Italian and the French recitative. The same problem exists in both, i.e. rendering the melody and rhythm of language in music. The Italians do this in their easy-going fashion by *approximately* notating the rhythm of language; they always write in four-four time, for notational convenience. The accents are placed where the rhythm of speech calls for them, which may be on the second, fourth or first beat. The very simple basses are positioned below in long note values despite the fact that they may be *played* as short notes. This has been proved beyond question and so serves as a further example of the difference between modern scores and the sound that was intended. The vocalist is expected to follow only the rhythm of speech, not the notated rhythm. Strangely enough, this clear requirement is the basis of frequent argument and is regularly called into question in the preparation of operatic performances as well as in vocal instruction. All of the sources with which I am familiar speak in favor of a completely free recitative, which is notated in 4/4 time purely for orthographic reasons. For example, Türk (1787) says: "Beating time during purely narrative recitatives is an extremely nonsensical custom... (it) is quite contrary to expression and betrays great ignorance on the part of an orchestra leader." Hiller (1774): "It is left to the singer... whether he wants to declaim rapidly or slowly, and the content of the words alone... must serve as his guideline... It is well known that recitative is sung everywhere... without observing the beat." Carl Philipp Emanuel Bach writes: "The other recitatives are sung... without regard for the beat, even though they may be divided in written form into measures." And finally, the vocalist is constantly admonished to speak more than to sing recitatives. Niedt: "This style must be closer to speech than to song." G. F. Wolf (1789): "It should be a singing that is closer to speech than the actual song, i.e., musical declamation." Scheibe: ". . . one cannot say of the recitative, however, that it is singing... It is... singing speech." Rousseau notes in the *Encyclopédie*: ". . . the best recitative is that in which one sings the least." Examples of this type of recitative frequently appear in German music, as well. When the free recitative in speech rhythm is to cease, *a tempo* or something similar is indicated; this notation indicates that the preceding need not be performed in time, but rather in free rhythm; but after this point, the measure must be observed once again.

This sort of liberality is not consistent at all with the spirit of French rationality. Therefore, Lully—who was Italian himself—derived a sort of catalogue of speech rhythms from the lofty and impassioned speech of French actors, which he then attempted to express precisely in notation. This resulted, of course, in complicated times such as 7/4, 3/4, 5/4. Such time signatures were completely inconceivable in the music notation of that period; nothing other than two and four or two and three or four and three was possible, so composers wrote 4/4 or 2/2 or 3/4; the 2/2 being faster by exactly half.

Rameau, Castor et Pollux

Thus in French recitative, five different time signatures often appear in five successive measures. 7/4, 6/4, 5/4, 4/4 or 3/4 time are formed by the succession of 4/4, 3/4 and 2/2. This system thus contains all sorts of possibilities for the most complicated times; as long as it is remembered that the *alla breve* (2/2) is exactly twice as fast as the 4/4. This system of notation is very precise by contrast with the Italian system and thoroughly in keeping with the French love of order. As a consequence, the texts acquire a wonderfully scanning rhythm.

I should here also briefly discuss a form of "stenographic" notation. Strictly speaking, a thorough bass is nothing more than a shorthand score which shows the instrumentalist the harmonic flow of the piece. It does not spell out what he has to play, which depends solely on his knowledge and taste. The French operas of the 17th, and to some extent of the 18th, Century—i.e. to about the time of Rameau—as well as much Italian, particularly Venetian, opera, are also to a certain extent notated stenographically. They were written down in such a way that the performer often had only a skeleton, as it were, of the work before him, consisting usually of only an instrumental bass and a vocal part. In French opera, indications of the instruments to be used are occasionally found. This manner of writing opera down permits the performer to employ any one of a number of traditional ways of arranging the work in accordance with his abilities and taste, even to filling in the entire orchestral part. Several orchestral parts of contemporary performances arranged in this way have been preserved, offering illuminating comparisons of truly historical performances which differ greatly from each other. Thus we find the same opera scored on one occasion for an orchestra with horns and trumpets, another for a small string orchestra; completely different middle parts are typically recorded in each set of performance materials; and a work might be scored for three parts, at other times for five.

These radical differences derive from the fact that the composer wrote down only the outer parts; everything else was left to the performer. It is unfortunate that we cannot study the use of these practices as closely in the case of Italian opera, because almost no performance material has been preserved, whereas a great deal of French performance material remains from the 17th and 18th Centuries. The principle can clearly be observed in these cases. However, there are also Italian scores in which staves for the instrumental parts are left blank, so that the performer had the option of supplying an orchestral part in such places. It is clear that this discretion was usually regarded as the domain of the performer, not the composer. The work and its performance were thereby clearly differentiated. The creative latitude offered the interpreter, in which each performance became a unique and unrepeatable experience, is by and large unknown and alien to present-day musicians. In order to present adequate performances of early music today this huge treasure of once self-evident knowledge has to be resurrected and passed on to the ordinary musician—not just to the so-called "specialist" in old music. Even though the question of a stylistically correct performance will remain eternally unsolved (thank God!)—the notation is much too ambiguous to permit this—, nonetheless we must constantly search for and discover new facets of the great masterpieces.

Articulation

Articulation is the technical process in producing speech, the way in which different vowels and consonants are produced. The 1903 edition of *Meyers Lexikon* defines articulation: "to organize, express something point by point; to permit the individual parts of a whole, particularly the sounds and syllables of words, to appear clearly. In music, articulation signifies the linking and separation of tones, the *legato* and *staccato* and their mixture, sometimes misleadingly called 'phrasing.' " Problems of articulation are especially apparent in Baroque music, or more generally in music from about 1600 to 1800 since, as a rule, this music is basically related to speech. The parallels to speech were strongly emphasized by all theorists of the period. Music was often described as "speech in tones." To put this in simplified and somewhat approximate terms, I like to say that music prior to 1800 *speaks,* while subsequent music *paints.* The former must be *understood,* since anything that is spoken presupposes understanding. The latter affects us by means of moods which need not be understood, because they should be *felt.*

In the music of the 17th and 18th Centuries articulation was, on the one hand, something taken for granted by musicians, who had to observe only the generally accepted rules of accentuation and connections, i.e. the musical "pronunciation." On the other hand, there were and are for those passages which the composer wanted articulated in a particular way, certain signs and words (e.g. dots, horizontal and vertical strokes, wavy lines, slurs, words such as *staccato, legato, tenuto,* etc.) to indicate the intended performance style. Here we encounter the same problem as in the case of notation: these articulation signs have remained the same for centuries, although their meaning has often changed, and radically, after 1800. When a musician ignorant of the speaking, dialogue-like character of Baroque music reads the articulation signs as if they had been written during the 19th Century, his interpretation will *paint* rather than *speak.*

We all know how a foreign language is learned. By analogy, Baroque music is for us a foreign language, since we obviously do not live in the Baroque period. Therefore, as in the case of a foreign language, we must learn vocabulary, grammar and pronunciation—musical articulation, the theory of harmony, the theory of phrasing and accentuation. The simple application of these theories to the performance of music by no means implies that we are making music; this is simply spelling in tones. Even if the spelling is well and correctly done, we can only create music when we no longer need to think of grammar and vocabulary, when we no longer translate, but simply *speak,* in short, when it becomes our own natural speech. This is our goal. We must, therefore, learn the "grammar" of old music. Unfortunately, uninformed musicians often undertake this task, for we constantly hear musicians who have only mastered the grammar of music, but, like linguistics professors with dust in their veins, simply *translate* music. However, we cannot blame the rules for this unhappy outcome, since we cannot do without them.

As was true of all aspects of life during that period, Baroque music is hierarchically arranged. I do not want to get into the question of whether this is good or bad—much has already been said and written on this issue—, but only want to point out that this hierarchy exists. There are "noble" and "ignoble," good and bad notes. I find very interesting the fact that this hierarchy practically ceased to exist after the French Revolution, both in terms of music and the social order as well. According to the musical authors of the 17th and 18th Centuries, in ordinary 4/4 time we have good and bad tones, *nobiles* and *viles,* i.e. a noble one, a bad two, a not-quite-so noble three and a miserable four. The concept of "noble" and "ignoble" refers of course to the stress. This means therefore: ONE - two -*three* - (four).

nobiles = n, viles = v. It is no coincidence that these two signs, both in use at a very early stage, look very much like the signs for down-bow ⊓ and up-bow ∨.

The dynamic curve

This accent scheme as a kind of curve of changing weight is one of the basic tenets of Baroque music. It was also *expanded* to apply to groups of measures—a "good" group is answered by a "bad" group. We can apply the same curve to entire movements, even to entire works, which thus offers a clearly recognizable structure of tension and relaxation. This accentuation curve of the measure was also *reduced in scale* so that it applies to eighth as well as to sixteenth-note passages. Thus a complicated, interwoven pattern of hierarchies exists, but the same organizing principle governs each. This form of organization is ubiquitous in the Baroque period, since art and life were governed by the same concepts.

If all Baroque music were to be played in keeping with this strict accentuation system performances would be very tedious, indeed monotonous. Such performances would be almost as monotonous—a concept completely antithetical to the Baroque sense—as the performances with their machine-like regularity which are common today. Both approaches are incorrect and boring, because after ten measures we know precisely what is going to happen for the next half hour. Thank God there are other superior hierarchies which defeat the inevitable monotony of stresses, the most important of which is harmony. A dissonance must always be stressed, even if placed on a weak or bad beat. The resolution of the dissonance—and each dissonance in Baroque music has a resolution—must be unstressed, since otherwise there would be no "resolution." We physically experience a similar sequence with a physical pain that gradually subsides, then disappears, followed by a feeling of relief. To describe the way such resolutions should be conceived, Leopold Mozart in his violin method used a lovely phrase: "fading away." Thus we have a powerful counter-hierarchy, which immediately breathes rhythm and life into the main hierarchy. All of this is like a scaffolding, a skeleton, a system that has a definite order. This system is breached over and over again by stresses of dissonances.

There are two additional sub-hierarchies which modify the major accent hierarchy in an interesting way: rhythm and emphasis. If a longer note follows a short note, the former is normally stressed, even if it falls on an unstressed, "bad" position in the measure; this emphasizes syncopations and cross rhythms.

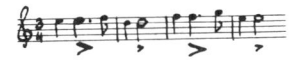

The emphatic stress falls on the top notes of a melody—thus singers are usually correct in emphasizing high notes, even holding them longer. It is clear that a large number of counter-hierarchies are superimposed on the basic framework of the hierarchy of measure. In this way, otherwise very dull order is constantly circumvented in interesting ways and enlivened at a number of levels.

The application of the rules of stress discussed above to eighth and sixteenth-note groups result in the actual articulation. Joining and separating individual tones and the smallest groups of tones or figures are the means of expression. We have several pronunciation signs for articulation: the slur, the vertical stroke and the dot. But these signs were seldom used. Why? Because their application was to a large extent self-evident to knowledgeable musicians. They knew what they had to do as instinctively as we speak in our mother tongue. As teacher and cantor at the St. Thomas School in Leipzig, Johann Sebastian Bach worked almost exclusively with young, inexperienced musicians, who evidently did not yet know how to articulate well, so that he wrote out the entire articulation of many works for them—much to the astonishment and annoyance of his contemporaries, who did not do so. He has happily thereby given us a series of models from which we can deduce how Baroque music was articulated, how, that is, it spoke through tones. Using these models, we can not only articulate the works of Bach appropriately, but the works of other composers of that period, which have come down to us with no or only a few articulation signs.

When we speak of articulation, we have to begin with the individual tone. Its execution is described very vividly by Leopold Mozart, who says: "Each tone, even the most strongly attacked tone, has a small, if barely perceptible weak point before it. Otherwise it would not be a tone, but merely an unpleasant, incomprehensible sound. This weakness can also be heard at the end of every tone." And elsewhere: "Such notes must be strongly attacked; be sustained without emphasis and gradually die away, as the ringing of a bell . . . gradually dies away." He also points out that one must be careful to sustain dotted notes well. At the same time, however, he holds that the dot should be "joined to the note in a dying-away manner." This apparent contradiction is typical of the way in which a source can be incorrectly interpreted because of a slight misunderstanding. Many use Mozart's instructions to hold the tones as "proof" that even at that time one had to sustain a given note value *sostenuto,* i.e. at a uniform strength. But at that time the "bell tone" was a generally accepted, self-evident concept, and "sustaining" was a warning not to play the following tone too early. Sustaining a note at full strength (as is customary today) had to be indicated specially by the prescription *tenuto* or *sostenuto.* In such cases we have to consider what was intended by a statement and also remember that the old authors wrote not for us, after all, but for their contemporaries. The most important aspect for us is often what they did *not* write, because that was what was generally known, what was regarded as self-evident. There is not one treatise that we could use today in order to say: Once I have studied this, I know everything. We must therefore be very cautious about using quotations and take the entire context into consideration as much as possible. "Contradictions" are in most cases misunderstandings.

The individual note is therefore articulated (pronounced) like an individual syllable. Organists often ask how a tone that is supposed to fade away can be played on the organ. I believe that space plays an important role in this regard. Each organ is meant for a certain space and a good organ builder takes this space into account when making the instrument. Until about 30 or 40 years ago, it was thought that the organ was the instrument of sustained sound. In recent decades, however, we have recognized that an articulated "speaking" way of playing is also possible. Furthermore, good, old organs have a transient phenomenon at the beginning of each tone called "chiff," which evokes the curve of the sound of a bell. On good instruments in appropriate spaces, the best organists are able to create the impression of a bell's tone fading away and therefore of a "speaking" type of playing, depending on when and how they end a tone. It is an illusion (similar to the "hard" or "gentle" touch of a pianist), but in music, only the illusion, the impression that the listener receives, counts; the technical reality that organ tones are incapable of *diminuendo,* that the striking of keys cannot be hard or gentle is absolutely secondary. We observe again and again that the great musicians are by experience also acoustical artists. In every space they know immediately how to proceed, how they have to play in that space; they constantly re-establish the relationship between space and sound.

The individual tone in music after about 1800 appears to me two-dimensional in its *sostenuto,* while an ideal tone in earlier music had a physical, or three-dimensional effect because of its inner dynamics. The instruments also correspond to these ideals of *flat* or *speaking,* as can easily be heard if, for example, the same phrase is played on a Baroque oboe and on a modern oboe. We then immediately comprehend the idea which underlies both of these sounds.

Now to the tone groups or figures. How should fast notes, for example the eighths in *alla breve* ¢ or the sixteenths in 4/4 C *allegro,* be played? According to most present-day music pedagogues, identical note values should be played or sung as regularly as possible, just like pearls on a string, all precisely the same! This style was perfected after World War II by a few chamber orchestras and established a certain way of playing sixteenth notes which evoked great enthusiasm throughout the world (this playing was given the most inappropriate name conceivable: "Bach-bowing"). This way of playing does not give the effect of speaking at all. Rather it smacks of something mechanical, but because our age has enslaved itself to machines, no one has noticed that this was wrong. But now we are looking for what is correct. What is supposed to happen with these sixteenth notes? Most composers, after all, do not write articulation signs in their music, except for Bach, who, as we have pointed out, left us many very precisely marked works. In the instrumental part of the bass aria of Cantata 47, for example, he articulates a group of four notes by dotting the first and slurring the other three. Yet in the same Cantata, the same figure occurs vocally, with the text: "Jesu, beuge doch mein Herze," and here, groups of two notes are joined together.

Violin and oboe

This example is very important to me because what Bach is saying by this is: there is not just *one* correct articulation for a musical figure, but several; here they even occur simultaneously! Of course, there are possible ways of articulating that are absolutely wrong, which we must identify in order to avoid them. In any case we see that in the same piece, the composer wanted two quite different articulations for the same passage. Just how precisely he wants these variants distinguished can be seen from the articulation dot in the above example.

This leads to a further consideration. In oil paintings using glazes, the paint is transparent; we can see through one layer to the next, so that we look through four or five layers to the drawing that lies beneath them. Something similar happens when we listen to a well-articulated piece of music. Our ears penetrate it in depth and we clearly hear the different levels, which nonetheless merge to form a whole. On the foundation level we hear the "design," the plan; on another level we find accented dissonances; in the next, a voice which is softly slurred in its diction, and another which is strongly articulated. All of this is at the same time, synchronized. The listener is not able to comprehend everything contained in the piece at once, but wanders through the various levels of the piece, always hearing something different. This multi-layered concept is extremely important for understanding this music. It is almost never satisfied with a mere two-dimensional approach.

Bach's vocal parts often contain an articulation different from that of the accompanying instruments, as seen in the example above. Unfortunately, this difference is today usually construed as an "error" by the composer and is "corrected." It is very difficult for us to understand and to accept the intricacy, the simultaneity of differing usages; we want order of the simplest kind. On the contrary, the 18th Century wanted richness, even excess: at whatever level one listens, one receives information, nothing is reduced to a common denominator. Things are looked at from all sides at the same time! There is no such thing as an articulatory synchronicity of the *Colla parte* instruments. The orchestra articulates in a different way than does the chorus. Even most "Baroque specialists" are not familiar with this; they always want to even things out, to have everything as much alike as possible and to hear beautiful straight columns of sound, but not diversity.

Various levels of articulation exist not only between vocal and instrumental parts, however, but also within the orchestra, and even within a particular section. There are numerous examples, for instance in the instrumental parts of the *Mass in B Minor* and the *St. Matthew Passion,* where the very same passage calls for different articulation in different parts. Improbable as this may seem from our ordered point of view, such diversity sounds in actual practice all the more beautiful, varied and "speaking."

What does the *slur* signify, then, for a string instrument player, a singer, wind instrument player, or keyboard player? It basically means that the first note under the slur is stressed and held the longest, while the following notes are played more softly. This is the Baroque principle. There is nothing here of the "even" notes called for today in formal music instruction. Of course there are exceptions, but this gradual diminution is the rule. After 1800, the slur was used in a completely different way. It was no longer a pronunciation mark, but rather a technical instruction. In this sense it is meaningless and of no use in Baroque music. If we do not know this distinction, then it makes no difference at all whether slurs are written or not, since every musician today will attempt to make the articulation inaudible, as if a great legato slur had been written over the melody.

In Baroque music, the basic meaning of the slur is that the first note is to be emphasized. As was previously noted, the fundamental hierarchy of stress within the measure is broken up by articulation and dissonance. And this breaking up is what is interesting; just as an irritant in an oyster makes a pearl, in music, irritation makes the listener keenly attentive. Again and again it is said that the listener is transformed by music. This can only happen if the music has a physical and spiritual effect. Let us imagine a dominant seventh chord. When we hear it, we also feel a physical tension: the dissonance demands a resolution; when it has occurred, we experience relaxation and relief. It is with this bodily reaction, tension and relief in the listener, with which the composer works. No one can avoid the compulsion to react with physical motion when listening to music; test yourself and observe audiences in any concert hall. This is part of the experience of music. The result is that the entire complex of articulation involves not only performing music, but also listening to it. Well-articulated music is heard in a completely different way than music which is played two-dimensionally. It affects us physically and forces our minds to listen actively, to engage in a dialogue.

The *dot* is a very important articulation sign. Normally we think that a dot shortens the note, because that is the customary rule today. Many musicologists call them "shortening dots" in their critical commentaries for scholarly editions of music. However, this concept did not exist during the Baroque period. In a large number of places in which Bach writes dots, we see that they always cancel whatever one would normally do at this point. In places where one would play broadly, a dot means a shortening; in places where one would otherwise play very short notes, it calls for emphasis. Very often these dots can be regarded as indicating emphasis, in which case they can even mean a lengthening of the note. In many instances they simply mean that slurring should be avoided here—or that notes which are otherwise played in an uneven rhythm (*inégale*) should be played evenly. In the hierarchical organization of Baroque music, we find not only the meaning "loud-soft, strong-weak," but also "somewhat longer-somewhat shorter," a distinction in terms of length. If dots are placed above notes, the differences are canceled. The dots then make everything the same.

Finally, dots also occur in those places where the composer wants to clearly indicate that the slur ends. We may have seen the handwriting of Bach and other Baroque composers; when they write a slur, it means: this should be played legato; the "how" was known by the performer. A dot, however, ends this slurring very precisely. We have to remember that a handwritten slur—usually written down hastily can never have the explicitness of one that is printed. The performer must therefore decide in every case what the composer might have intended by this or that slur. For performance there is a kind of correct spelling, of convention; but there is also an almost magical suggestion that emanates from every manuscript.

If a slur covers larger groups of notes, a frequent practice in the music of Bach and his contemporaries, this means that here the musician should articulate in the manner with which he is familiar; the player is called upon to perform appropriately. A long slur therefore can also mean—and we must be clear about this—a subdivision into many short slurs.

We noted earlier that a dissonance must always be linked to its resolution. This is a very strict rule, although unfortunately it is often violated today. There are, however, some pieces—the composer must, after all, have the latitude of achieving a certain effect by breaking a rule—where both the dissonance and the resolution have dots, so that both are stressed. This practice surely must have shocked a listener of that day because it was contrary to the language to accent the resolution as well. The result is the same as accentuating a word inappropriately in order to give it a certain emphasis.

The terms *spiccato* and *staccato* occur frequently in Bach and Vivaldi. Though we still use these terms, they have a different meaning today. In contemporary usage *spiccato* means bouncing the bow, so it is a term that has to do with bowing technique. Until the founding of the French Conservatoire, it only meant separated, articulated, as did *staccato*. It did not mean any particular kind of separation, but only that one should *not* play *legato,* nor *cantabile* in a great legato line; the notes were intended to be separated. We often find the term *"largo e spiccato"* to designate long note values. This designation is incomprehensible, even outright contradictory, for musicians of today, because *largo* (a slow tempo in long note values) and *spiccato* are mutually exclusive. The original understanding of this designation was simply that of a slow piece in which the notes were not to be slurred.

Slurred groupings in preludes and other free pieces frequently do not agree with metrical groupings, e.g. slurring in threes in metrical groups of four. This results in a further departure from hierarchical stressing, by adding a completely new rhythm to a piece. This kind of alteration of a passage possesses a baffling charm. Because of the superimposition of several "hierarchies," the orderly rhythmical structure seems to collapse temporarily. We understand why Hindemith could say that the rhythm of Bach's solo works is so extraordinarily rich.

Accentuation
Original phrasing

One and the same passage can be modified by various types of articulation until it can scarcely be recognized; articulation can make the melodic structure of a passage clear or completely unrecognizable. This means that simply by setting the articulation marks in a different way, the composer can superimpose a rhythmic model on a passage which makes the melodic sequence practically unrecognizable to the listener. For example, the rhythm of motivic imitation comes through stronger than the sequence of notes. Therefore we can make an imitation recognizable simply by rhythm. Accordingly, articulation is a device so powerful that it can destroy the melody. I want to make it clear here that articulation is absolutely the most important means of expression in Baroque music.

Now a few words regarding dynamics. The first thing a musician wants to know about in the matter of interpretation is the nuances, by which he means *forte, piano,* etc. What is loud? what is soft? is considered today the most essential principle of interpretation. In Baroque music, this type of dynamics is only secondary. Scarcely a work of this epoch is altered in its essence whether played loudly or softly. In many cases, the dynamics can simply be reversed, playing *forte* passages *piano* and *piano* passages *forte.* If they are played well and interestingly, either approach makes sense. In other words, dynamics were not composed. To be sure, dynamics played an ever increasing role in composition after 1750, but in the Baroque period, dynamics in the modern sense were not critical because the dynamics of the Baroque period were those of language. They operated on the small scale of individual syllables and words. They were of great importance, in the Baroque, but they were not called dynamics; they belonged instead to the complex of articulation, because they referred to single tones and the smallest groups of tones. A passage can of course be played *forte* and then *piano.* However, this is not an essential feature of the work or the structure, but rather an added piquancy, a type of ornamentation. What *is* essential is the small dynamics, which means *pronunciation,* since it makes the "tonal discourse" clear.

Dotted rhythm is particularly important in connection with articulation and musical "pronunciation." It is one of the primal human rhythms and is much more elemental than, say, a steady *staccato.* It is extremely difficult for a vocalist or an instrumentalist to perform a series of completely even tones. (For almost two hundred years the conservatories of Europe have attempted to "tame" the natural, rhythmical irregularities which occur in every type of folk music, and to change them into equal note values, nice and regular.) There are an infinite number of intermediate values between this regularity, which occurs only infrequently in Baroque music and which must be expressly indicated with dots or words, and very extreme dotting. The mildest, almost imperceptible form of dotted rhythm occurs when regular chains of eighth notes, for example, are played in pairs, with the first held a trace longer than the second, giving them a slightly lilting, "swinging" sound. In the next stage, we come close to a triplet rhythm and at some point or other, the composer will feel the need to notate this rhythm. He therefore writes a dot behind the long note and shortens the second by one-half. This by no means implies that the first note should be precisely three times as long as the second. It is simply one long and one short note—how long and how short is defined by the context. The notation therefore shows only one of the intermediate levels.

 Between the first and second pairs of notes, the only difference in dotting is one of degree.

Common sense tells us that dotted rhythms as such resist any precise classification. The length of the long and the brevity of the short notes are determined by the character of the piece and compositional consideration. There are, to be sure, some authors of the 17th and 18th Centuries who held that the short note in a dotted rhythm ought to be taken at the last moment; nonetheless, I believe this advice applies only to unusual cases and ignores the other and more common cases since they were taken to be self-evident. If we were to take every rule literally and apply it universally, without understanding its limits, we would soon end up in serious difficulties. In my view, fundamentalists are the worst enemies of religion: blind faith in the sources is dangerous.

Granted that the way dotted rhythms are played today, i.e. by holding the dotted note precisely three times as long as the following short note, is a precise interpretation of the written text, it remains in most cases simply wrong. It leads to a kind of regular sub-rhythm which destroys the dotting. Clearly a deficiency in notation exists. It is simply not customary to express the desired relation in numbers; one cannot write nine, for example, above the long note and two above the short note. Baroque composers often wrote a dotted quarter note and three thirty-seconds. The many professional pedants who have unfortunately gravitated to music do not approve of such ideas, so they calculate how many thirty-seconds are contained in one eighth note, i.e. four. This they write down and link the first of these with a tie to the long note.

In the 17th and 18th Centuries   Today

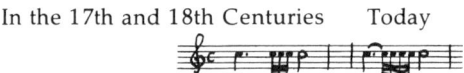

The composer could surely have done this, had he wished to. But he simply *wanted* a dotted long and three short notes. His intentions should not be changed in new editions, because a dotted rhythm is played more freely than one which is written down precisely.

Unfortunately, during the past 50 years, a dangerous trend toward "faithfulness" to the work has emerged, one of whose corollaries has been to banish all those good traditions which conveyed the correct *interpretation* of the score in favor of the authority of the *written* score alone. As late as 1910, the way a dotted rhythm should be played was still known and sensed, as old recordings show (e.g., a rehearsal with Bruno Walter). Only since Gustav Mahler insisted on a very precise way of playing exactly what was written has this knowledge been gradually lost. I find it regrettable that faithfulness to the notes has replaced faithfulness to the work—that we have forgotten many things which used to be living knowledge. This knowledge must now be rediscovered through arduous effort on our part. The same holds true for articulation. Many musicians today believe that when no articulation signs are given, they have to play such groups of notes in precisely the unarticulated way in which they are written—out of loyalty to the composer, i.e. out of "faithfulness" to the work, an approach which attempts to render the notes rather than the work. This oft-cited "faithfulness to the work" appears to me the worst enemy of an honest interpretation, because it attempts to make music out of what is written down—while ignoring the underlying meaning. Notation as such cannot convey a piece of music, but only serves as a point of reference. The only person who is faithful to the work, in the true meaning of the word, is the performer who recognizes what the composer intended to convey with the notes and plays them accordingly. If the composer writes a whole note, but means a sixteenth note, the "faithful" musician is one who plays the sixteenth note, not the one who plays the whole note.

One final word about articulation. By all means let us study the sources, try to learn everything we can about slurs and their execution. Let us try to feel exactly why the resolution of a dissonance must be played in a particular manner, why a dotted rhythm has to be played this way and not that. However, when we *make* music, then we must forget everything we have read. The listener should never be given the impression that we are playing something we have learned. It must have been assimilated into our very being, it must have become a part of our personality. We ourselves are no longer aware that we have learned something nor where we learned it. Perhaps we will again do something "wrong"—in literal terms. But a "mistake" which comes from conviction, from educated taste and feeling, is more convincing than any musical cogitation.

Tempo

Establishing the tempo in which a piece is to be played, the relation of the tempos to each other in a large work with several movements or in an opera, is one of the greatest problems in music. Tempo was conceived in a completely different way in ancient Greek music and in the monophony of the early Middle Ages. In those periods, the same piece of music might be played at different speeds. Speed depended only on one's personal temperament, just as some people speak faster or slower. Is it not true in speech that a sentence has no specific, inherent tempo? The forcefulness of the text is not influenced by tempo. We often find great differences in the tempo of plain chant without feeling that the music has been violated. In music of this kind, at least, tempo does not appear to have played a critical role.

Literary sources of the period indicate that in Greek music, rhythm and tempo were one. This sense is derived from the rhythm of verse, which was the basis for all music. Poetry and music were signified by a single word in the Greek language; singing and the reciting of poetry constituted the same act. From this one can conclude that singing was declaiming, declaiming singing. In Greece there were three different rhythms and basic tempos:

1. Rhythms using only short pulses, which are fast and used for sword dances and express passionate determination. Around 1600, they found their way into European music along with Renaissance ideas. They resemble tone repetitions which Monteverdi invented for the martial music of the *Combattimento* following the Greek model (Plato) and which he explained and justified in a very illuminating fashion.
2. The rhythms consisting of short and long pulses corresponding to the image of the round dance. This probably referred to jig-like rhythms.
3. The long rhythms which were slow and used in hymns.

Around 1600, when Greek music began to be incorporated into European music, these principles of emotional expression were recalled. The first and the third rhythm schemes in particular entered into the emotional repertoire of Western music. The first signified fiery, passionate and determined emotions while the latter referred to soft, indecisive, passive states.

By about 900 A.D. we find tempo letters in plain chant which are interpreted in different ways today. Over the neumes (signs schematically reproducing the hand motions of the choir director, thereby becoming the first Christian-European notation) were letters such as C: (*celeriter*), M: (*mediocriter*), T: (*tarditer*), i.e. fast, moderate, slow. The uses of different tempos were obvious in multi-part readings of the Passions. While the villains always spoke faster, the holier a character, the slower the rhythm, and the words of Christ were recited very slowly, in almost a hymn-like manner. Many of these ideas were in turn incorporated into the 17th-Century recitative.

The question of tempo only became problematic with the origin of polyphony. Now tempo and sometimes even rhythm had to agree, at least in certain passages. Since this was not possible using the old neumatic system of notation, a completely new notation, designed to indicate tempo and, to some extent, rhythm had to be invented. In its early stages, the euphony of the new style was considered so daring that only a "slow" pace could be considered. Several sources speak of *moroditas,* making the beauty of the music last. Beautiful polyphonic music was supposed to go on endlessly; music lovers could not get enough of it. Despite these very slow tempos, which were probably only used in the first phase of polyphony, precision and exactness were the rule, at least for the stressed "beats" (today one would say: on the first beat of each measure). The consonant octaves, fifths and fourths of all voices had to come together precisely on this beat. Between these consonances there was a certain rhythmic freedom, which today we would certainly regard as disorderly. This freedom led to the impression of the remarkable independence of the individual voice line, which operated within this spacious framework of consonances structured in a metrical way. This basic meter was set by the director beating time with a music scroll.

At that time tempo as such was still uncomplicated. Fast, slow and moderately fast were all relative terms. But with the advent of complex rhythms in the very early stages of polyphony, a more sophisticated notation was demanded. Music sung, for example, at the papal court in Avignon in the 14th Century—very likely only for a small circle of cognoscenti—was rhythmically so complex that it is still very difficult to decipher musical sounds from the scores of the time. More importantly, this music is impossible to render precisely using our current system of notation. It is therefore not possible in actual practice to render every imaginable kind of music in our notaton. Here, our belief in progress—that we have the optimal notation, the best engineering, the most efficient agriculture, etc.—proves wrong. The various notational systems of the past were not simply primitive stages of present day notation, but the appropriate form for the music of a given period. They suggested to contemporary musicians an adequate method of playing. Notation, as the graphic image of a musical event, provides an element of suggestion; it virtually forces the music to be played in a particular way. A given musical epoch has always found the symbols appropriate to it. So the notation used in the late Middle Ages and early Renaissance was able to express intermediate values and everything related to *rubato* and agogics.

The brevis (▭ twice as long as the present-day whole note ○) of former times was a short note; today it is very long. In the *tempus perfectum* it had three beats, in the *tempus imperfectum* only two. An extending dot was affixed only in ambiguous places: ▭· since a *brevis* in *tempus perfectum* was ordinarily considered to have three beats, even without a dot: ▭ . The subdivision of notes was indicated by the mensural notation sign at the beginning of the line (○ = *tempus perfectum;* C = *tempus imperfectum,* and many others). A note was first divided into three parts because division by three was regarded as perfect. Subdivision into four, on the other hand, was considered imperfect. This all had to do with the symbolism of numbers and the theory of proportions which were in vogue at the time.

The problem of tempo was resolved around 1300 by the complicated system of mensural notation signs. Since these signs expressed proportions relative to a given, unchanging basic measure (the *integer valor*), the beat, tempo and mensuration of music were fixed from about 1300 to the late 16th Century. Strange as it may seem, we can reconstruct the tempo of a piece from around 1500 much more precisely than we can in the case of Monteverdi, Bach or Mozart. In the 16th Century, the old system was increasingly diluted; although theorists still rigorously taught it, it received very little attention in actual practice. It was a marvelous construct in and of itself and did not need to be actualized in sound. The signs remained in use for a time, but without their strictly proportional meaning. Several signs remain in use today (C, ₵).

After 1600, differences in tempo were primarily expressed by various note values—even the individual note values were designated as "extremely slow..., natural..., neither fast nor slow..., moderately fast..., very fast." Because everything was expressed in the note values, the beat and tempo became a unity as tempo was determined by the note values. The earliest designations still confirmed the configuration of the notes: *tardo, lento, presto, allegro,* etc. were placed above those passages where long and short notes already indicated a slow or fast tempo. From old parts, manuscripts and prints we can see that such designations are frequently provided for only a single voice, and always in passages where there is a change of note value, though the absolute tempo remains the same. For example, *lento-presto* can alternate in one piece (these were the earliest designations for slow and fast), yet in those passages marked *lento,* there are long note values and in those passages marked *presto,* short ones. Moreover, these indications are often found only in the *continuo* part, which usually has long note values only, probably to advise the instrumentalist that the soloist in this passage plays fast notes, for example. In former times musicians did not play from scores, so the solo voice was only seldom written in the *continuo* part. Therefore *allegro* was written above the long notes of a continuo part, which meant only that the soloist had fast notes. But sometimes such a designation appears in the solo part too, where it can be seen quite clearly that an additional modification of the tempo in such a passage would be impossible, because the slow note values—when one plays the fast notes so fast that they are just barely performable—are already so slow that further retarding them would be meaningless. The tempo designation therefore only confirmed an already existing notational picture, without changing the absolute tempo. (This form of writing can still be found in some 18th-Century notation, for example in several of Bach's cantatas).

In the 17th Century, composers tried to describe the desired tempos in the prefaces to their works: the terminology used was only gradually moved into the pieces themselves as superscripts, where they then stood for specific forms.

Now I would like to illustrate briefly how our typical tempo indications originated from descriptions and instructions. Authors of the 16th Century tried to convey their wishes with phrases such as: "with a somewhat accelerated tempo," "the faster the better," "this passage must be played slowly," "must be performed very quickly, otherwise it does not sound right." By the beginning of the 17th Century (1615), we find the later tempo-affect terminology in the prefaces to printed music of Frescobaldi: "the beginnings should be played slowly (*adagio*) ... later, one should play more or less rapidly (*stretti*) ... one should play the partitas at the correct tempo (*tempo giusto*) ... one should not begin fast (*presto*) and then slow down ... Runs in the partitas should be played slowly (*tempo largo*)." These tempo terms, which derived entirely from the Italian vernacular, gradually became technical expressions written above the staves, as though they were part of the notation. They are of significance only in relationship to the music in question and therefore have no absolute effect on determining tempo; in many cases they should be regarded as terms to describe emotion rather than tempo. After all, the first thing that we have to determine about the tempo of a piece is its affect, its emotional import. It is either sad or merry—with all intermediate forms and ambiguities. Sad suggests slow; merry, fast. *Allegro* originally meant a joyful emotion (in the Italian vernacular, it still means gay), a fast tempo or simply fast note values in a neutral tempo. The most important 17th-Century terms are *lento, largo, tardo, grave, adagio, andante, allegro,* and *presto.* In 17th-Century music, therefore, these Italian tempo indicators, still in use today, determined the tempo and the musical expression, with the latter resulting, as it were, from the former. A *presto* passage is frequently found in the middle of an *adagio,* for example, but this is given only for the voice which plays the fast notes; again, the basic tempo remains the same.

The relationship of the tempos to each other is especially important. Renaissance music depended upon a basic tempo derived from the pace of walking or from the heartbeat, thus in some way from the nature of human beings. All other tempos were related to it. A system of complicated signs was devised, of which our *alla breve* sign ₵ and the sign C for 4/4 time are still carry-overs—to be sure, only as signs and without their original meaning. In the 17th Century, something of these tempo relationships was preserved for a time in the relation of 4/4 time to triple time, i.e. from an even to an uneven meter. This relationship was gradually weakened, however, as time and practice evolved. The strict relation of 2 to 3, which always causes one to feel the triple time as triplets in relationship to duple time, was no longer relevant as early as Monteverdi's time. This can be clearly seen when the same motif moves from triple to quadruple time; it frequently happens that the whole or half-notes of triple meter become eighths or sixteenths of 4/4 time. Then the basic movement simply continues. This practice is clearly illustrated by several passages from the later works of Monteverdi.

From the 17th Century on, therefore, tempo relations lose something of their former strictness. Thereafter it becomes more difficult to find the kind of regularity that was very clear in the previous period. Several writers have proposed that all unconducted Baroque music was played in a single tempo, which always results in whole number relationships, because the musicians would have kept time with their feet or beating with a large baton. For this reason, it is claimed, every *adagio*, for example, should be played exactly twice as slowly as an *allegro*, an approach which some consider valid right up to the Classic period. I am certain that in reality the relationships are much more subtle, and the fact that provincial musicians may have kept time by tapping their feet is no reason to use that as a criterion for determining tempos. Although there are several studies in this field, they should be viewed circumspectly because their authors are usually not practicing musicians and the theories they derive from their studies frequently turn out to be impracticable in actual performance. Nonetheless, a critical reading will yield some useful information.

Tempo transitions, *accelerandi* and ritards were, of course, originally improvised. From the end of the 16th Century, some composers evidently searched for ways of expressing them in the notation. We again refer to the prefaces of Frescobaldi in this matter. He writes trills in sixteenth notes and emphasizes in the text section that they should not be played in rhythm, i.e. "as written," but rather *veloce* (fast). This tells us that the notation in sixteenth notes represents only an approximate idea: the rhythmically free, improvisational execution is explained in the preface. This notation is later replaced by the symbol for the trill (tr). Similar methods of expressing free rhythms, at least by implication, were used by the English viol composers and teachers, such as Morley and Simpson. The latter frequently wrote fast passages which began with sixteenth notes and continued with thirty-second notes, a very appropriate method of notating an *accelerando*. Until such tempo terms came into use, composers tried somehow to approximate in the notes what they were looking for: an acceleration notated by degrees stood for an acceleration which was to be performed smoothly. A famous example of this is *Il trotto del cavallo* in Monteverdi's *Combattimento:* here Monteverdi portrays an accelerating horse trot in such a way that the same rhythm suddenly continues at twice the pace: ¾ ꜒o|꜒o|oɗoɗ| As in the previous example, this sudden acceleration actually means a gradual acceleration (the only way possible for a real horse), but in the notation of the period, this could simply not be expressed in any other way. Gradual ritards (*ritenuti*) were likewise expressed by simply doubling the note values. This way of writing down modifications in tempo is still found in Vivaldi and Handel; however, it is usually misunderstood and performed as a sudden change in tempo "as written."

In the 18th Century, certain figures (groups of notes) demanded a certain tempo. Musical "figures" are short sequences of tones, similar to musical building blocks or "tone-words," which require a certain coherent progression if they are to be articulated in a meaningful way which results in a certain tempo. Thus time signatures and tempo indications now belong to two completely different realms: the time signature is strictly rational, the tempo indication is irrational and must be related to something. The time signature does not clearly show the tempo even with a tempo word. Musicians said one had to guess from the piece whether it called for a slow or a rapid movement (Leopold Mozart). This could only have referred to the "figures"—they are thus the reference point for the time signature.

During Bach's time, the tempo of a piece could be derived from four facts without any further explanation: the musical emotion or affect (which a sensitive musician could guess); the time signature; the smallest-occurring note values and the number of accents per measure. The practical results obtained by using these criteria agree so exactly with other sources, such as instruction books, that they become an altogether credible body of information.

Obviously, rigid rules never did or should apply, since correct tempo also depends on various extra-musical factors, such as the size of the chorus and orchestra, acoustical properties of the room, etc. It was known and taught in earlier times as well that a large orchestra has to play slower than a small one, that one must play slower in reverberant rooms than in "dry" rooms, etc. And in reality, the same tempo sounds differently in different interpretations, with not only space and ensemble size, but also articulation being critical factors. A richly articulating ensemble has a faster and livelier effect than one which plays broadly and uniformly.

Generally speaking, we can tell from the sources that musicians of earlier times assumed much faster tempos than we assume today, especially in slow movements. But fast movements were also apparently played with *virtuosity* and briskly, judging from their orientation to the heartbeat (said to be 80 beats per minute after eating), and playing technique (the sixteenth-notes could still be played by the strings with single strokes and by wind players with double tonguing). Bach's son Philipp Emanuel (quoted in Forkel's Bach biography) writes of his father: "In the execution of his own pieces, he usually assumed a very lively tempo..."

Mozart uses richly differentiated tempo indications. For example, an *allegro* is very fast and spirited. In addition, he occasionally uses words of explanation (often added later) such as: *aperto, vivace, assai,* though the meaning of *allegro aperto* has not been completely explained. If I heard the term *allegro aperto,* without knowing the piece itself I would probably think that *aperto* speeds up the tempo. But if we compare the movements thus designated by Mozart, it seems as if they should be played somewhat slower, less tumultuously, perhaps even simply "more openly" (aperto = open). The *allegro vivace* demands liveliness in what is already a gay, fast movement. As in movements over which only *vivace* is written, this liveliness refers primarily to stresses of the small note values, so that the overall tempo is usually somewhat slower, but the impression of movement and liveliness is stronger than in the "normal" allegro. Such designations are often misunderstood, a fact which results in the movements appearing unarticulated and hectic. *Allegro assai* means a significant increase in tempo.

We can learn quite a lot from corrections (which unfortunately can be seen only in autographs, not in standard editions). An *allegretto* tells me much more if I know that the composer wrote it to replace the original *andante,* perhaps after working with an orchestra. Very instructive corrections like this are frequently found in Handel as well. A series of indications, such as *andante-più andante-più adagio* can lead to distortions if we do not understand the tempo words as they were used at the time. For example, in the fourth movement of Mozart's *Thamos* music, K. 345, there is a question of whether *più andante* is faster or slower than *andante.* Since *andante* at that time was regarded as a rather fast tempo, in the sense of "moving," the intensification (*più* or "more") is in the direction of acceleration. In this case, a melodrama, such a reading is clear from the dramatic situation; nonetheless, this passage is often performed exactly the other way around, with a retardation.

In conclusion, I would like to explain several other terms indicating tempo which are related to ornamentation. The first of these is *grave:* this designation of a slow tempo means "serious," which also means that, generally speaking, no embellishments should be introduced. In the case of Handel, for instance, every musician feels an urge to embellish particularly slow movements with improvisations, because of their melodic simplicity. This is appropriate in *largo* and *adagio,* but not in *grave*. Introductions to French overtures are almost always marked *grave:* they have a serious or festive processional character, are hardly cantabile, so should not be embellished.

The word *adagio,* on the other hand, usually means that in a slow movement the music can or should be embellished. Frequently the term *adagio* is indicated over individual notes or measures within a *grave* movement, though from the context a tempo change is impossible. Then it means approximately: here it is permissible to add embellishments. Quantz says that an *adagio* should not be *overloaded* with embellishments, yet the examples he cites as "sparing" embellishments appear to us very lush and overdone. We should probably not follow every recommendation in the old textbooks having to do with improvisation and embellishment, since improvisation is very closely linked to a particular style and a particular age. Rococo embellishments improvised by a rococo player in the 18th Century cannot be compared with rococo embellishments produced by us today. The uneasiness we feel when a Mozart aria is encrusted with too many embellishments is well founded. The entire aria is reduced to a kind of stylistic imitation. It is more important to portray a simple melody in an imaginative and interesting way than to divert attention from it using ornate and athletic embellishments. There is enough music from the 17th and 18th Centuries which is compatible with, and even demands, improvisional embellishment.

Improvisation and embellishment have always been regarded as an art requiring great ability, imagination and good taste; a performance employing improvisation becomes something unique. In descriptions of good musicians between 1700 and 1760, a "strong *adagio* player" meant a musician who could embellish a piece of music in a meaningful way. The simplest melody could inspire him to use embellishments, yet the emotional content of the piece was not allowed to be destroyed by them. Only if the basic emotion is preserved can an embellishment be considered genuine. Singers in particular, performing Baroque and Mozart operas, should use embellishments clearly in accord with the emotion embodied in the text. The singer had to bring out and enhance the emotion of the simple melody by means of correct and spontaneous embellishments. Embellishments which only demonstrate the technical skill of the vocalist or of the instrumental soloist are worthless, empty virtuosity. There had to be an inner musical need for the embellishments, and they were expected to enhance the expression contained in the work in a highly personal way.

Tone Systems and Intonation

A particularly important question for singers and instrumentalists alike is the absolute pitch standard. There are many old accounts suggesting that tuning was higher or lower in France than elsewhere; or tuning in the church was higher or lower than "in the chamber," i.e. in places where secular music was performed. But the only sure reference points are the human larynx, various old instruments, tuning forks and pitch pipes which have not been altered. We find after study that almost all the instruments dating from the age of Monteverdi in Italy, for example, were at modern pitch or even somewhat higher. The demands placed on the human voice extended to low C for the bass, which is very low indeed. But the old authors also claim that only a very well-trained bass can sing that low, while ordinary basses, as are found in the academies, can only sing to G. This is about the situation today for there are very few who can reach low C. (Thus tuning cannot have been lower in Italy at that time: "old tuning" varies therefore, and can be sometimes lower, sometimes higher.) In earlier times, singers tended to use the middle register and only very rarely the extremely high register. Things are different today when every singer—both male and female—wants to sing as much as possible in the highest register. A true soprano is unhappy if she cannot sing between D" and D'". Tenors, too, want to sing as high as possible; in the case of Monteverdi's tenor parts, the tenors complain that they should be sung by a baritone, that the music is too low for them. Yet we read in Praetorius (1619) that the human voice sounds sweeter and more graceful "when it is in the middle range and somewhat lower" than when it "has to screech high and loud." With regard to instruments, Praetorius notes that they also sound better in the lower ranges, though he observed that the general tuning is becoming increasingly higher. There is a tendency even today for the pitch of an orchestra to gradually rise. This can be confirmed by anyone who has observed the tuning of various orchestras over the last thirty years. This higher tuning is a significant problem for today's musician.

I believe that we should attempt to identify the origin of this unfortunate tendency to constantly raise the pitch. I played in an orchestra for 17 years and frequently observed that conductors told a musician he was playing too low, but never that he was playing too high. There is a reason for this, of course, for when intonation is impure, the ear automatically orients itself to the relatively highest sound. Anything lower is experienced as incorrect, even if it is objectively correct. So all of the supposedly too-low tones are pushed higher, until they are as high as the (too) high tones. What is the result? Every musician wishes to avoid having the conductor admonish him for playing "too low," so from the outset tunes his instrument too high. (This is especially true of the second player in a section of wind instruments, who is most frequently berated for playing too low. When musicians buy a new instrument, they immediately shorten it so that the pitch is higher.) The only way out of the dilemma of the evitably rising tuning pitch is to recognize the reason behind it and to orient oneself to a correct standard. The question of purity of intonation cannot be left to feeling, otherwise nothing will be in tune anymore, because no one wants to be the lowest. (There is a saying among musicians: "Better too high than wrong!") I think if musicians knew more about intonation and did not leave everything to feeling or to hearing, the pitch could easily be kept at one level.

The question of what constitutes pure intonation cannot be answered. There is no single, natural intonation system that is valid for all races. One is taught a tone system which can be either one of the five or six belonging to our own culture, or even a different one, in which the pitch is calculated from the length of grains of wheat or from stones—and anyone who is used to such a system hears and sings and plays in accordance with it. In many parts of Europe, folk music is played on natural wind instruments (such as horns), which can only play the natural tones. On these instruments, melodies can be played only on the fourth octave (from the eighth to the sixteenth partials), which makes the fourth degree of the scale sound very "impure," because the eleventh partial lies somewhere between F and F# and the fourth (C-F) is consequently much too wide.

Where such instruments are played, an identical interval is also *sung*, and people regard it as pure because they are used to it! We must understand that we cannot make *one* intonation system a standard for all; what sounds pure to us may sound wrong to others. Accordingly, whatever is right for a particular system is by definition pure. We in the modern West have trained our hearing mostly on the equal temperament of the piano. On this instrument, all twelve half-steps are tuned at precisely the same intervals, which results in actually only one single major key, transposable in half steps. Unfortunately, our ears are trained in and oriented to this system. With this system in our ears, when we listen to music that is intoned—no matter how perfectly—according to a different system, we have the impression that the music is being played out of tune. But the intonation system at the time of Monteverdi, i.e. the 17th Century, for example, was just such a different system! When we hear today music produced in perfect accordance with that system, we believe that everything is wrong, out of tune, excruciating to listen to. But if we were to turn this around and listen to today's intonation with that system in our ears, we would find it just as wrong. This shows that there is no such thing as objective and absolute truth as far as intonation is concerned. Thus purity of intonation can only be discussed within the context of a particular system. If I intone purely within *one* system, then my intonation is perfect, even if it sounds impure to ears that have been conditioned to another system.

Unfortunately, in our time, in which profound, genuine knowledge has been replaced, quite officially in many instances, by empty palaver, in which bluffing is carried out as a matter of course, it has become common to talk grandiloquently about things of which one has not the slightest knowledge. People do not try to inform themselves but take part in a conversation as if they understood the subject under discussion. Music is a subject that is insulted in this way with particular frequency. Almost everyone talks as if he knew something about it, whether in matters of purity of intonation ("What, you didn't hear how out of tune he played?"), or to keys ("In a mild E-flat major . . ."), and only fails to make a fool of himself because his conversation partner is equally uninformed. The subjects of intonation and the tonalities have given rise—even in the technical literature—to the worst kind of bluffing.

The music intonation of the 16th and 17th Centuries continued to be based in part on the "theory of proportion". This theory held that the ratios between vibration frequencies, i.e. the overtone series, served as the guideline to establishing pitch. The point of reference is the fundamental, the "one" of the series of partials, somewhat akin to the vanishing point in perspective; which symbolized *unitas,* unity, God. The simpler the numeric ratio, the nobler and more moral it is; the more complicated or further removed from the "one," the morally poorer, the more chaotic. Every interval can be expressed in proportions (for example the octave 1:2, the fifth 2:3 etc.) and its quality can be measured by its proximity to *unitas* ($c = 1,2,4,8$ etc.), as well as in terms of its simplicity. Modern concepts derived from the theory of harmony have no relevance in this case as the perfection of the sounds is revealed by numbers. And vice versa, all simple numeric ratios could be imagined as sounds. Kepler's harmony of the spheres, as well as harmonically "resounding" architecture, are based on this notion: if the visible proportions of a building could be expressed in simple numeric ratios, then these relationships could be seen and heard as "chords." In many ways, Palladio "composed" the ground plans for his structures as a kind of petrified music. According to theory, harmony in music rests on a principle similar to the golden section in architecture. Both impose order on the hearts and minds of men by virtue of their simple, natural relationships. The Baroque idea that music was a reflection or a likeness of the divine order was applied to all music, sacred as well as secular. The contrast between sacred and secular music did not play as important a role then as it does today. The unity between the individual genres of music had not yet been sundered; every form of music, was in some way regarded as sacred.

In the theory of proportion, harmonic intervals represent a God-given order: all consonances correspond to simple ratios (2:3 = the fifth; 3:4 = the fourth; 4:5 = the major third, etc.). Whatever comes closest to unity is perceived as more pleasing, more perfect than that which is remote, where disproportionality and even chaos reign. The relation 4:5:6 was regarded as perfect: it is based on the fundamental (c'), its numbers are in direct proximity to each other and result in three *different* consonantly harmonizing tones (C-E-G), a major triad; perfect harmony and the noblest euphony *(trias musica)*. It was the musical symbol for the Holy Trinity. So tuning followed the fourth, fifth and sixth overtones precisely! The proportion of the minor triad (10:12:15, E-G-B) is not as good: it is *not* based on the fundamental, its numbers are further removed from the one and are *not* consecutive since numbers (tones) 11, 13, and 14 intervene. So this chord was regarded as inferior, soft and, in the hierarchically negative sense, feminine (Zarlino calls the minor chord *affeto tristo,* a bad or malicious emotion.) Thus all harmonies were assigned a "moral" value, so it is understandable why every piece at that time had to end with a major chord, for it was not possible to conclude a work in chaos. (This rule could, however, be violated for special reasons.).

The role of the instruments used at the time was also governed by proportion theory. The trumpet, for example, on which only natural tones could be played, became the proportion theory "made sound". Hence it could only be used to symbolize God or the highest royal personages. C or D major with trumpets was reserved for the greatest lords; a situation from which trumpeters profited as they were accorded a status far superior to that of other musicians.

Numbers played an immense role in all Baroque music, even outside. of proportion theory. In the music of Bach, for example, numbers constantly occur which represent number or geometric games, biblical passages or biographical data. These numbers were encoded in many different ways; for example, the number of repetitions of tones, measures, of certain note values, of different pitches, etc. Knowledge of number symbolism and the numeric alphabet was so widespread at that time that a composer had no problem integrating such coded messages into his works, and certainly at least some of these codes would also have been understood by others when the music was heard or read.

Like numbers, a great variety of religious and astronomical symbols have been linked to music from antiquity onward. Column capitals in

Spanish cloisters represented certain melodies, as Marius Schneider describes in his book *Singende Steine*. When one walks through a cloister from a certain starting point, the sculptures on the capitals—symbolic figures from Greek literature and mythology which also represent specific tones—actually spell out the hymn to the patron saint of the monastery. Purely ornamental capitals interspersed among the others represent the rests.

In addition to the theory of proportions, the notion of *key characteristics* was another important factor in the portrayal of various emotions in Baroque music, a function they retain today. They probably have even more to do with intonation and its various systems than proportion theory. A short explanation may help clarify the importance of intonation as a means of expression.

From earliest times, portrayal of various emotional states by means of music has been resorted to. Musical means of distinguishing and identifying emotional status reach back as far as Greek music. First a system of symbols and characteristics depending upon *individual tones* was developed. An individual tone was linked to and embodied a symbol which stood for constellations, seasons, mythical animals, gods, all of which represented and evoked certain emotions. This led to a kind of key symbolism in which a scale based on a given individual tone assumed the characteristics of its ground tone. The use of this "key" evolved a corresponding association in the mind of the listener.

The Greek scales are made up of fifths unlike the natural tone series illustrated on page 60, which is based on natural tones of the third and fourth octave, i.e.

Pythagorean scale ⌒ Pythagorean third

The Pythagorean scale, constructed in this way, in turn became the required intonation system used in all Medieval music. The major third (Pythagorean third) which derived from this scale is a much larger interval than the natural third explained above (4:5), and is not consonant, like the latter, but *dissonant*. The Pythagorean scale sounds very beautiful and convincing when used for monophonic music, just as the Pythagorean third sounds very beautiful in a melodic context. The Greek scales were derived by beginning on different tones of this basic scale. These Greek scales finally led to the church scales of the Middle Ages, the modes. These scales bore the old Greek names (Dorian, Phrygian, Lydian, Mixolydian), each of which was associated with certain expressive characteristics. As long as music was monophonic, or polyphonic but based on fifths, fourths and octaves, the Pythagorean intonation system could be retained; indeed, it remains optimal for this form of music. But only when the sensuously pleasing euphonious *natural third* (a consonance) was introduced into practice, was polyphony able to develop to the fullest extent. The major chord (the *trias musica*) gradually became the central harmony which determined key and tonality. Finally, by the end of the 17th Century, the major scale was all that remained of the church keys. This outcome would have resulted in a great impoverishment of expression had it not been possible to give each transposition of this one scale its own character: i.e. such that B major, for example, evoked a different effect than C major, although in principle, both utilize the same scale. If the difference in the church modes lay in the interval sequence, the various major scales could be distinguished only by a different *intonation.* The need for different key characters is the basis of the well-tempered tuning systems.

From "Mean-Tone" to "Well-Tempered" Tuning

Once the basis of our tonal system had been discovered to lie in the pleasing natural third and thus the major triad, a variety of questions arose about how the problems of intonation which emerged in this process could be solved on various instruments. Only the natural wind instruments, horns and trumpets, were perfectly suited to this new system. In the case of keyboard instruments, organ, clavichord and harpsichord, a tuning system had to be developed which would make it possible to play the pure thirds of the new intonation, and if possible with twelve tones per octave. This system was found in "mean-tone tuning." It is based on the fact that the major thirds must be *absolutely pure,* at the expense of all other intervals. (It should be clearly understood that there can be no "pure" tuning system on a keyboard instrument, that each system favors certain intervals at the expense of others.) In mean-tone tuning there is no enharmonic equivalence, because each tone is unequivocal: an F-Sharp, for example, cannot be interpreted as a G-Flat. In order to realize pure-third tuning, all fifths must be considerably narrowed. This is the price that has to be paid for pure thirds.

Mean-tone tuning

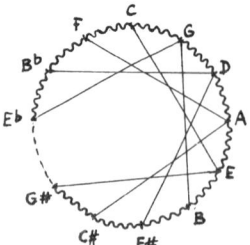

∿∿∿∿ narrowed intervals
- - - - - widened intervals
——— pure intervals

All of the fifths from E-flat to G-sharp are narrowed by 1/4-comma. The much too wide and musically useless "wolf" (out of tune fifth; G-sharp-E-flat), really a diminished sixth, is left. All indicated thirds are pure. All the other thirds are much too wide, useless. The circle of fifths cannot be closed.

Strangely enough, in a triad with a pure third, the fifth can barely be heard, because it is subdivided by the third. This tuning is called mean-tone because the large third (e.g. C-E) is divided exactly *in the middle* (by the D) and not, as in the overtone series, in the ratio 8:9:10, where there is a large whole-step C-D and a small step D-E. This pure third tuning sounds very soft and relaxed harmonically, although all *playable* tonalities sound exactly the same. Chromatic scales and transitions have an extremely interesting sound on instruments tuned in the mean-tone system. When individual half-steps are played consecutively, the effect is extraordinarily colorful and varied, since the half-steps vary in size. The term "chromatic" is truly appropriate here, for once. F-sharp is a different color from F. And the chromatic half-step F-F-sharp acts like a mere color change, while the much larger half-step F-sharp-G, which is not chromatic, is a genuine, solid interval.

Musicians today have a very hard time at first playing or singing pure thirds, because, accustomed as they are to the tempered thirds of the piano, pure natural thirds sound out of tune and too narrow.

Now to the "well-tempered" tunings. To temper means to balance; several intervals are thus consciously tuned incorrectly mathematically, but only to an acceptable extent, so that one can play all keys. The most primitive well-tempered tuning is "equal-tempered tuning." Here the octaves are divided into twelve identical half-steps; all intervals except the octave are somewhat impure. In this tuning, which is the norm today, there are no key characteristics; all keys sound alike, only at different pitches. If, however, by *well*-tempered we mean well and usefully tempered, as in the 18th Century, then this modern tuning is one of the worst. (It was known in the 18th Century, although it was not technically feasible. This became possible with the invention of electronic tuning devices.)

A "well-tempered" tuning (by Werkmeister)

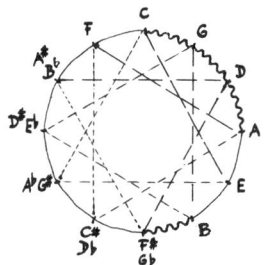

4 fifths are narrowed by 1/4 comma (C-G, G-D, D-A, B-F-sharp), all others are pure. The circle of fifths is closed.
The thirds vary in purity. Because of this variation, different keys have different characteristics. The best thirds are F-A, C-E; almost as good are G-B, D-F-sharp, B-flat-D; clearly worse are E-flat-G, A-C-sharp, E-G-sharp, B-D-sharp. All other thirds are Pythagorean thirds and as such are audibly too wide.

In "good" well-tempered tunings, not all major thirds are tuned alike: for example, F-A, C-E, G-B, D-F-sharp are tuned purer, or narrower, than the other thirds, and therefore the fifths also have to be tuned differently. It is still possible to play in all keys, although they sound differently: F major sounds much softer and more relaxed than E major. The various intervals are different in each key; some are somewhat purer, others somewhat less so, which results in different key characteristics. This outcome results from various strong tensions, created by intonation, which increase with distance from the C major center and which are also felt as a kind of longing for the beautiful, relaxed keys (F major, C major, G major).

In any case, we should never say prematurely that a musician is playing in or out of tune. After all, very different systems exist, and if someone plays in tune within a system to which our ears are not accustomed, we do him an injustice if we assert that he is playing out of tune. I am so accustomed to the unequally-tempered tunings that an ordinary piano sounds terribly out of tune, even though it is tuned extremely well. The primary consideration is that a musician play purely, within the context of the particular system used.

However, as actual practice shows, the music of the 16th and 17th Centuries can only be adequately performed with pure-third tuning. If we are working *only* with vocalists or string players, we need not use all of the features of mean-tone tuning, which is, after all, intended for keyboard instruments. We will not attempt to make the 8th and 9th overtones equally large nor to narrow the fifths; we will try, however, to intone the thirds absolutely purely. (In the case of the fifths, every musician attempts to do so in any case.) Absolute purity in all intervals is certainly not desirable, because every artistic effect is based on the longing for perfection. Actually achieving perfection would be inhuman and very likely excruciatingly boring. An important part of musical sensitivity and appreciation is based on the tension between the longing for perfect purity and the degree of purity which is actually attained. There are keys with a very high degree of purity, where this tension is minimal, and others that contain very little purity and consequently a high degree of tension. Intonation is thus a very important means of expression in interpretation. Nonetheless, there is no single intonation system that is suitable for all Western music.

Music and Sound

If, as a musician, one is very involved with sounds and believes that they have an important place in the framework of interpretation, it is inevitable that questions arise with regard to historical standards. We have a general idea of the vocal and instrumental scoring for music played in the 14th Century at the papal court in Avignon and for the various Italian, Burgundian and German court orchestras in the age of Maximilian (around 1500). We have a fairly precise idea of Lasso's vocal and instrumental resources at the Bavarian court (around 1560). The orchestral and vocal sound at the time of Monteverdi (after 1600) has been fairly well documented by Monteverdi himself, as well as by Michael Praetorius (1619). By doing the necessary research, we can get a fairly good picture of 17th-Century opera. Bach's orchestral and choral sound can be easily reconstructed today. We know something about the timbre of Mozart's music and we are familiar with the sound of the Wagnerian orchestra. At the end of this development is the symphony orchestra as we know it today.

Until recently, specialists in the fields of musical aesthetics and the history of instruments were of the opinion that this process involved a development from primitive stages through constant improvements to an optimal stage, which is always located in the present, a notion long abandoned in the field of art history. This viewpoint is supported neither by aesthetic principles nor by technical and historical considerations. We are only just starting to realize what has long been accepted in the visual arts: that we are dealing with shifts in emphasis, not in value, which always parallel—must parallel—shifts in intellectual and social history. It is high time that we realized that the instrumentarium, the "orchestra," of a given period is perfectly suited to the music of the period and vice versa—which is true with regard both to the entire instrumentarium of the age as well as to each individual instrument. I both see and hear that each instrument, by the time it is used in art music, has already reached an optimal stage where *overall* improvements are no longer possible. Any improvement in one area must therefore be paid for by a worsening in a different area. This is an hypothesis which I have found consistently confirmed in innumerable experiments and in constant dealing with this material, so that it has begun to assume for me the character of a demonstrated fact.

The question which arises with regard to each of these changes in the instruments, which were formerly regarded only as improvements, is: Am I prepared to pay the price that is inherent in a given "achievement?" To relinquish the possibility of subtle nuances and colors, as well as of technical facility, in exchange for an increase in volume (piano) or to achieve the completely dynamic and intonation-oriented equality of all playable half-steps at the cost of losing the tonality-related tuning and individual tone color of almost every individual tone (flutes and others)? Examples of this sort could be found for almost every instrument. However, in our fascination with each new "improvement," we failed to notice that something was being sacrificed, and we certainly did not notice what that something was. Today, having gained the necessary historical perspective, we must regard almost all "improvements" simply as changes within the history of music.

The obvious conclusion is that every kind of music should be played on the instrumentarium appropriate to it. This involves a variety of complex issues. Does not a different sound medium connote a basically different means of expression for the musician? Can the listener jump back and forth between different historical sounds, or does he finally decide, consciously or unconsciously, in favor of one tonal image, one tonal aesthetic? Do these questions not also apply to other secondary aspects of music: the acoustical properties of halls, which, after all, play a crucial role in shaping sound; the system of intonation, i.e., that which is felt to be pure and impure with regard to pitch, and whether and to what extent genuine expressive functions belong to this complex? And finally the question of whether music as such represents a language which can be understood across the ages (Ionesco: Do we truly understand Mozart?), a question which cannot be answered affirmatively as easily as one might believe. It is quite possible that the total realignment of our cultural life which has occurred over the last hundred years has altered the ways in which we make and listen to music to such an extent that we no longer perceive and understand just what Mozart, for example, was saying through his music and what it was that his appreciative contemporaries understood by it. We are totally unable to comprehend the extent to which music, just one hundred years ago and of course even much more so in earlier times, was an integral component of public and private life—there was hardly a joyous or mournful, festive, religious or official occasion where music was not performed, and not simply as a social adornment, as it is today. I believe that today we see and comprehend only a very small part of music—primarily its aesthetic elements—and that many possibly important facets remain inaccessible to us because we have lost the ability to perceive them. Moreover, this minimal portion which appeals to us is evidently so rich that we accept it gladly, without demanding more. It could thus be said that although we have lost the present, we have gained the entire past—but are able to perceive only a small segment of it with greatly limited understanding.

The question is: are we really in possession of the entire history of Western music (and of cultural history in general), are we able as performers and listeners to adequately come to terms with the stylistic diversity of musical idioms? If the answer were yes, then the differences in various bodies of sound, in the sounds of each musical epoch, would present no problems to the listener, but would help him grasp the much greater variety in the music itself. The alternative, and the one which is resorted to in our musical life today, is obviously unhealthy, in terms both of the repertoire and the sound. Our traditional, globally uniform repertoire is by no means the much touted "Selection of History"! A large part of this repertoire has never been submitted to the allegedly unerring judgment of the centuries. This oracle began its pronouncements only in the 19th Century and was thoroughly shaped by then prevalent tastes. And as far as sound is concerned, this very paltry selection, which was chosen by our great-grandparents at a time when they still had a very vital contemporary repertory, has been and is still being presented to us with the uniform sound of the 19th Century: Bach like Mozart like Brahms like Bartok—and the latter we foolishly call "modern," as the sound which characterizes our own age.

We no longer have the luxury of rooting around in the treasures of the past as did our forefathers in the last century; we must be able to discern a purpose in what we do, in order not to become completely pessimistic. We believe absolutely that a deeper understanding is certainly possible and that every useful approach is worth pursuing. The understanding and the conceptualization of a piece of music are largely independent of its realization in sound. The first and most important steps in meaningful musical interpretation are thus invisible and not at all spectacular; they are at most sensational, in the literal meaning of the word. What is visible is, as the final step, the work with its original instrumentarium. It is the most spectacular, the most conspicuous feature of an interpretation, although it is often applied in a meaningless way, without the corresponding technical preparation of the performers, and very often without any compelling reason. Faithfulness to the original sound can thus be a fundamental help in approaching many works, but for others, precisely because of its spectacular nature, it can degenerate into meaningless sound fetishism.

Old Instruments: Yes or No?

Naturally, the answer to the question old instruments, yes or no? is: it all depends! Playing music on old instruments, i.e. on instruments which for some reason or other have fallen into disuse, unfortunately has such a disreputable history that it is almost impossible to discuss it calmly and without misplaced passion. Although I myself am counted among the proponents of using old instruments—and with some justification—, I would prefer to be regarded as an exception on this issue. I believe that I am able to take part in the discussion in a thoroughly objective way and with *genuine* passion, something which I hope can also be said of my imaginary discussion partners.

As soon as one picks up an old instrument one is called a "purist," "historian," "stylistic ascetic," or someone who must constantly reflect before each note, thanks to a lack of intuition. Innocent concepts like faithfulness to the work often have negative connotations, and people who use them are often said to lack commitment and skilled musicianship. Why should this be the case? No matter how specious the argument, there is nothing negative in the concept of faithfulness to the work. The fact that this concept is often *wrongly* interpreted to mean faithfulness to the notation—and thus unfaithfulness to the work—can certainly not be blamed on this innocent phrase, but only on the incorrect usage to which it is put.

The connotation associated with the word "purist" today makes it possible to express something that is actually true with a very unattractive and defamatory wink of the eye—and it goes without saying that this is gladly done. As previously indicated, I believe that the remnants of the "pioneer days" of Old Music in the 20's and 30's are still with us, whether we approve or disapprove of old instruments. Old music then was not thought to be a part of official musical life, but was viewed as an ideologically-based anti-music which was discovered and cultivated by elite circles of enthusiastic dilettantes. The professional musical world took no notice of this, which did not bother the champions of old music in the least; they wanted to keep to themselves. They thought that Early Music was "Purity" and "Authenticity" itself—goals of the "youth movement" which sprang up after World War I as a broad protest against the hypocritical morality of contemporary society.

The established music of symphony concerts and opera houses was felt to be pompous and hypocritical; everything connected with the business of music was thought to be fraudulent. "Romantic" became a negative catchword, while "objective" was felt to be positive. Technical brilliance and perfection belonged to the world of professional music and was sufficient reason to make these concepts suspect. The music of the Renaissance and Baroque periods, which had been completely disregarded up to that time, seemed to mesh with the new ideals: sung or played slowly, the music posed only slight technical difficulties, and because it lacked tempo and dynamic marks, it appeared excellently suited for "objective" music-making.

Musicians were soon freeing themselves from conventional instruments; it was during this period that the recorder, gamba and harpsichord were rediscovered. The sounds evoked, which were somewhat meager due to the lack of good models and of an unbroken performance tradition, were considered to be austere, authentic and, therefore beautiful. Of course, there were many people who sensed the possibilities of timbre and technique that went beyond the results that were achieved so far, and who discovered in this music merits beyond those of pure *Weltanschauung*. It was not long before a few professional musicians began to take up this music and use the newly discovered instruments, but they were not taken seriously by their professional colleagues. Their activities were thought to be simply a hobby, something which was not at all welcome, since it was feared that this distraction would lead to a loss of quality in playing "normal" instruments and the "right" music.

Some highly undesirable developments which took place during this early period are still felt today. The primary example is that of the modern harpsichord. Instrument makers were not long in discovering the new market and were soon providing the growing number of devotees with recorders and gambas, and later with crumhorns, cornetts, baroque trombones and many other "old" instruments as well. The piano found in most homes could no longer be used as an accompanying instrument: it was *de rigueur* to have a harpsichord. The new harpsichord manufacturing business—there was soon an enormous demand— did not pattern its products after those older instruments which had been preserved, since it was thought wiser to apply the experience gained in modern methods of piano manufacturing. Thus keyboard instruments in all sizes and price ranges were built; they were constructed like pianos and their strings were plucked with plectra made of hard leather, or later of various plastics.

Although these instruments were called "harpsichords," their sound was as remote from that of a harpsichord as a child's tinny violin is from a Stradivarius. The mistake went undetected because those who were playing the music did not know what a harpsichord was supposed to sound like; industry took the path of least resistance and focused its efforts on expanding the market and keeping up with demand. Since these instruments quickly become available in large numbers, they were soon used for "fashionable" performances of the works of Bach in "large-scale concerts," while audiences became accustomed to interpreting their chirping and tinkling as "original sounds." Intellectually independent musicians such as Furtwängler rejected the "harpsichord," claiming that it was impossible to play music on such an instrument. However, it was almost impossible to hear a real harpsichord played, since surrogate instruments were flooding the market.

It was decades before this major misunderstanding was cleared up, and it will still take some time until all musicians and music lovers have modified their understanding of the harpsichord's sound to one that is good and correct and until all of the ill-begotten harpsichords have disappeared from concert halls. But, after all, a pioneering period must be allowed to make mistakes, just as long as subsequent generations recognize and correct them.

I have portrayed the origins of the old music movement and its influence on instrument building, because all this is very unusual and quite fascinating in terms of cultural history, and because the attitudes of professional musicians and critics as well as of the concert-going public were affected by this situation for decades. Thirty years ago, if a musician with a modern orientation had shown interest in the authentic interpretation of 17th and 18th-Century music because he was convinced that this music possessed the highest artistic merit, he would have been regarded almost as a deserter to the camp of the sectarian dilettantes. And to add insult to injury, if he had opted for old instruments for whatever reasons, virtually no one would have continued to regard him as a serious professional. It should be noted, however, that this was true in the traditional environment of symphonic music; the sworn believers in old music naturally welcomed the influx from the professional camp, even though they suspected that these professionals, because of their natural drive for perfection, were not in it for quite the same ideological reasons.

By now it has become clear that music can be produced just as well on old instruments as on others, so the key question is simply *why* a musician favors one type of sound over another.

Over the course of the next few years, the original prejudices will certainly be eliminated to such an extent that non-musical reasons, such as the enterpreneurial instinct or fear of discrimination, will no longer influence this decision. It is natural for every good musician to want to use the best possible instrument. Historical or curatorial reasons are able to hold our interest for a time, certainly: how was this formerly played, how might it have sounded? However, there is hardly a *musician* who would focus his professional interest in the long run on such pursuits; I tend to regard such a person more as an historian than as a musician. In the final analysis, a musician will always look for the instrument which appears best suited to *him*. In the following discussion, therefore, I refer only to musicians who base their preference for one or the other of these instruments purely on musical considerations; those who do it merely out of interest in old phenomena or conditions are not musicians, to my way of thinking: at best they are scientists, not performers.

Never before has the available repertoire been as large as it is today: works written 800 years ago are being performed once again. Given sufficient knowledge of the background of a given music (recalling my example of the harpsichord, the history of which typifies the development of many other instruments as well), a wide range of useful instruments from different historical periods is available to us. After all, the musician should have the right to play any work on the instrument he believes is best suited to it, or to select the combination of sounds that seems ideal to him.

In this decision, only one thing matters: what sounds better on this instrument, what on that? Every musician knows there is no such thing as an instrument that is perfect for every occasion; every one, whether historic or modern, has certain drawbacks. If the advantages and disadvantages of master instruments from various historical periods are compared it is clear that we do not simply have a case of on-going improvement in quality as in the case of the airplane or camera. Rather, each instrument at each stage of its development had both advantages and disadvantages, a fact which was well known to musicians and instrument makers alike. Thus it is only natural that there is a close relationship, indeed, a reciprocal interaction, between the ideas of instrument makers and those of musicians—both instrumentalists and composers. For example, several of the highly-touted "inventions" of instrument makers (such as the Heckelphone or the Arpeggione) were not accepted by musicians, despite initial successes, while others, such as the pianoforte, underwent very interesting metamorphoses as a result of collaboration between instrument makers and musicians.

It appears that this development ended some time ago: our instrumentarium has remained virtually unchanged for over 100 years, which is particularly striking if we consider that in previous centuries, almost all instruments were significantly modified every few years, or at least once in each generation.

With all this in mind, the question posed at the beginning of this section can be answered in two ways: Yes—because all instruments under discussion here are actually old instruments; and No—because the instruments have not needed any modification for the past hundred years because they had already achieved a state of perfection.

Only the first of these answers leads us anywhere, though. The development of the instrumentarium certainly did not come to a standstill because it had attained any degree of perfection—an appallingly inhuman thought—, but because at that time, the whole fabric of Western music, and of Western culture in general, was profoundly shaken. Only because contemporary artistic creativity has not been able to meet our cultural needs, only since we no longer look down on the music of the past from a superior position—something that was normal for every culturally healthy period—, are we able to judge this music fairly. This judgment, however, both in the field of music and in the visual arts, is no longer a *value judgment* in the sense of regarding the music of one particular period as inherently better than the music of another.

Since a musical instrument was always a "tool," a kind of technical device, faith in progress was retained in this area for a longer time. But the musical instrument is also a *work of art*. The names of the great instrument makers have always been as famous as those of the great painters. Antonio Stradivari, Johann Christoph Denner, Johann Wilhelm Haas, Andreas Ruckers, Andreas Stein, Theobald Böhm and others created musical instruments which were, as works of art, perfect and so admitted of no improvement. Any "improvement" would have reduced their value.

If we take by way of example a violin built by Stradivari around 1700, as *he* built it, outfit it with the gut strings, bridge, tailpiece and sound post which were used then, and play it with a master bow from the same period, it would sound much softer than one built by the same master, but reconstructed in the 19th or 20th Century and played with modern strings and a modern bow. However, it would also have a large number of subtle tonal qualities (overtones, kind of response, way in which the tones are joined, balance between high and low strings) that the modern violin does not possess.

Perhaps I should briefly mention that even the old string instruments, which have been used for centuries, have been subject to constantly changing requirements. They were frequently modified, sometimes quite radically, and hence have survived all the shifts of style and taste up to the present. Thus an old violin sounds completely differently today than it did two or three hundred years ago, and a violin virtuoso of our own time would be just as surprised to hear his "Stradivari" in its original condition, as would Stradivari, if he could hear and see what has been done to his instruments since their creation. There is practically no master instrument in existence today that has not been rebuilt many times. These alterations were directed mainly at increased volume, but also at greater evenness and smoothness.

Since the best of the old string instruments were supremely well-balanced, each improvement resulted in a loss of quality in other areas, especially in their sound quality. It comes down to a question of priorities. Comparing a silver flute by Böhm with a one-keyed flute by Hotteterre, we find that all the half-steps sound alike on the Böhm flute, while almost every tone on the Hotteterre flute has a different timbre, due to the differing sizes of the holes as well as to the necessary cross fingerings. Moreover, the Böhm flute sounds a great deal louder, but also smoother, more uniform and less varied in tonal quality. All of this could be put differently, depending, of course, on one's point of view and personal taste. Some may claim, for example, that the Hotteterre flute is a poor instrument, because the various tones do not sound alike on it—judged by the standard of the Böhm flute. Others might hold that the Böhm flute is an inferior instrument because all the tones sound alike on it—judging from the standard of the one-keyed flute.

These viewpoints, and many others as well, appear in contemporary reports from so many different periods, that we begin to realize how difficult it is to define *good* and *bad*. Rather, the composer, the instrumentalist and the instrument maker have to come to some agreement about what it is they want. If a musician, for whatever reason, prefers the uneven sound of the old flute to the even sound of the Böhm flute—and this is a perfectly legitimate decision, in historical terms—, then we should not criticize the unevenness in his interpretation as a *defect,* just as a critic with a different orientation should not describe the evenness of interpretation on a Böhm flute as a defect in performance.

Historic evaluations of innovations in instrument-building were only interesting as long as this involved the innovations themselves; but today all that matters is whether a given interpretation is meaningful in and of itself and whether it is convincing—assuming the listener is receptive. What these comparative experiments mean for many musicians, myself included, is that the advantages and disadvantages at any given stage in an instrument's development go hand in hand with the music the instrument was designed to play. The varying colors and dark tone of the Hotteterre flute are exactly right for French music prior to 1700, but are not at all suitable for German music around 1900, while the reverse is true for the even and metallic sound of the Böhm flute. Such comparisons could be made for any instrument, although an objective evaluation is more difficult in some cases because of the overriding question of whether a given instrument can be adequately played at all today.

Intrinsic quality is a vitally important criterion in the selection of any instrument. In addition to the question of whether a "modern" or an old instrument should be used, there is the question of what actually constitutes a *good* instrument. And if the purely tonal aspect of an interpretation is really so important that for artistic reasons one *must* decide in favor of instruments from a particular epoch, then this factor must also play a central role in any evaluation of these instruments.

It would therefore be absurd to select an inferior Baroque flute over a good Böhm flute, simply because the former happened to be a Baroque instrument. An inferior instrument is still inferior, even though it might be temporarily lionized as the result of a widespread lack of critical acuity on the part of musicians and music-lovers, due to swings in taste (remember the pseudo-harpsichord). We should guard against false prophets who, like wolves in sheep's clothing, persuade us that false is genuine, bad is good. A boom in old instruments must not be allowed to lead to a situation in which countless more or less nicely turned wooden pipes, equipped with six or eight holes and ballyhooed as "original instruments," are used as such, no matter how inadequate their sound. In making such choices, we must use our ears and good taste to settle only for the very best.

A responsible musician, aware of his responsibilities, will avail himself of every opportunity to play or listen to genuine instruments by the leading makers and then judge any copies, or much more frequently, *so-called* copies, against these originals. Once our ear has been attuned to subtle sounds and true quality, we shall be able to distinguish between the toy-like sound of fake "original instruments" and the rich sound of authentic instruments as well as good reproductions. Nor will the public allow itself to be talked into accepting cheap, inferior sounds as precious "Original Baroque" sounds. The term "original instrument" should never cloud our good judgment out of sheer enthusiasm for allegedly rediscovered authentic old sounds. The historical errors made in reconstructing the harpsichord should not be repeated with other instruments as well. It therefore behooves us to categorically reject anything inferior, something most musicians have always done as a matter of course.

The more musicians familiarize themselves with the specific style characteristics of various historical periods and various nationalities in Western music, the better they will recognize the profound interrelationships between a given type of music and its interpretation, both then and now. Conservative musicians, who have not progressed beyond the music of the turn of the century, are usually those who also prefer the instruments of that period—i.e. those instruments which are still viewed as *modern,* which is ridiculous—even though they play early music.

On the other hand, those musicians who are also open to contemporary music often turn to original instruments, if they play early music at all, because they understand that this significantly expands their range of expression. It is easy to see, therefore, that the differentiation frequently made by professional critics between a *modern* interpretation with standard instruments and an *historic* interpretation with old instruments completely misses the point. The modernity of an interpretation is hardly affected by the choice of instruments, least of all in the juxtaposition described here. An interpretation with old—but also with standard—instruments can be historical, but this depends not on the instruments, but on how the musician approaches the work. The only thing that matters is: which advantages outweigh which disadvantages in the eyes of the performer.

In addition to sound and technique, the problem of intonation confronts every musician who is seriously involved with pre-classical music. When all is said and done, we must acknowledge, here too, that every type of music demands its own system of intonation and that the various pure-third and unequal temperaments of the 16th, 17th and 18th Centuries are at least as important for the rendition of old music as the by no means *well*-tempered equal temperament. Here, too, old instruments can be of some help since, contrary to generally-held opinion, they can be played in tune or out of tune, just as can "modern" instruments, although original instruments adapt themselves more easily to the various temperament systems.

By way of a final argument, I would like to bring up the question of balance in an orchestra or chamber ensemble. Each age has a group of instruments that are perfectly adapted to each other; a composer writes with a particular type of orchestra and a certain combination of sounds in mind. If instruments are used which simply bear the same or similar names as their original counterparts, any relationship between the resulting sound and the ideal the composer had in mind will be purely accidental.

It is not my intention to argue on behalf of "historical" performances: the wheel of history cannot be turned back. But despite all our progressiveness, we still seem to need the art, the music, of bygone ages; the sound itself is and will remain a secondary consideration. Original sound interests me only to the extent that it is the best-suited of all available means for rendering a given piece of music *today*. I do not feel that the Praetorius orchestra is suited to play Richard Strauss, nor is the Richard Strauss orchestra suited for playing Monteverdi.

The Reconstruction of Original Sound Conditions in the Studio

Every noun in the above title evokes an emotional response in me, makes me want to offer excuses, explanations, antitheses. Even the words "Reconstruction of original sound conditions" raise numerous questions. What were the original sound conditions? Were they good, bad, indifferent? Why should they be reconstructed? Why not simply create new ones? And then "in the studio". This phrase borders on the absurd; if one thinks at all about the reconstruction of sounds, then surely it is in the context of Gothic or Baroque churches, where music is played on so-called original instruments, perhaps even the singing is performed with original voices, and where, regrettably, the authentic organ of the 17th Century can no longer be blown with the original air of the period (a justifiable point of view for strictly technical reasons, as well as environmental), despite the fact that this air must have possessed completely different sound-producing qualities.

It is not possible for me to deal with this topic objectively, since each of these challenging questions forces me to take a personal stand. Generally speaking, I take original sound conditions to mean those which the composer might have expected in an optimal performance in his own time. This idea intrigues me, since it is obvious that most composers conceived their works not simply as abstractions, but rather largely in terms of real sounds. The involvement of possible components is different for each composer, of course, and is determined to a great extent by the prevailing taste of the period. It is very important for a musician who performs not his own works but those of other composers to understand their ideas. Musical substance thus does not depend to the same extent on its actualization in sound at all times, for all composers and in all pieces.

Flemish compositions of the 16th Century leave the question of the ultimate sound completely open; it was not even important whether a composition be played or sung. Does this allow the performer total freedom (assuming he wishes to render the composition with integrity), or do all the infinite number of "right" ways have something in common which differentiates them from other ways which are "wrong"? We are treading here on the shaky ground of evaluation research in which, as in almost all areas of research, including the natural sciences, it is clear that the findings almost invariably support the expectations of the person doing the research. Largely based on my feeling for music, I do believe that the right ways have something in common—assuming, of course, that the work is to be performed as it stands, without transforming or re-composing it.

What they have in common are (1) tone color and the blending of sounds; but even more importantly perhaps, (2) the way sounds are created: whether a tone, for instance, is sounded and then dies out like a bell sound or whether it is steadily sustained; (3) the system of intonation, i.e. to reproduce intervals that are pure, or too large, or too small; and (4) acoustic conditions. Comformity to or deviation from these qualities are easily noted so their importance in interpretation is easily evaluated and used.

To put it briefly, there are, in my opinion, almost invariably many possible correct solutions, but—and this should be kept in mind—several that are totally wrong. To the extent that composers intend certain sounds for their works, they write idiomatically, i.e. in a manner geared to an instrument, the voice or a particular orchestra. Thus, while there are many different "original" ways of performing music from the age of Maximilian I, there is only *one* adequate sound image for the symphonic works of Richard Strauss. In the four centuries separating these two periods, a gradual shift took place which steadily reduced the number of "correct" possibilities.

Thus by original sound conditions, I mean all the legitimate possibilities a particular composer might have imagined. For the sake of clarity, I exclude all transpositions into a different period style; such changes I regard as similar to translations into a foreign language, which always alters the nature of a work of art. What matters here is the intent of the composer, and consequently I must endeavor to master *his* language.

Original sound conditions are thus of great interest to a musician for they make an essential contribution to the understanding of a work, above and beyond purely aesthetic considerations. The historical question of how a particular piece originally sounded is only of informational value to a musician, since the central issue for him revolves around how a piece ought to be conceived. When we talk about how music sounded in various periods, we usually focus on the sounds of the instruments. So the phrase "old instruments" begins to function as a value judgment, with all its related drawbacks and advantages. Only five years ago one might have heard, "It is amazing how lovely that sounds, even on those old instruments," but one is now more likely to hear: "This is very lovely, despite the fact that old instruments were not used." Standards have changed this markedly in such a few years. It is not at all clear if instruments really are the critical factor in the discussion of sound conditions. I am of the opinion that musical diction and articulation and the whole question of intonation in music of the 17th and 18th Centuries are far more important to sound than are the instruments, because they affect musical substance much more directly.

Intonation: here I do not mean adjustment of tones on the piano, organ and harpsichord, but rather the questions involving precise pitch.

Intonation is usually absolutized today as good or bad, in tune or out of tune. This is a wholly untenable assumption. There is no such thing as a *pure* intonation which holds true for all situations. An artist using consistent intonation, i.e. always the same, entones purely within his accepted tonal system. By nature, the human ear is like a blank sheet of paper, ready for the intonation marks of the piano tuner, the radio, the music teacher. Thus the ear must first be programmed, as it were, and thereafter perceives any deviation from this program as wrong. Consequently, perception is entirely subjective. But if each epoch uses its own intonation system, which differs from all others, we must ask ourselves whether it is possible to meaningfully render the music of every epoch employing a single system, for example the system which we use today. A string quartet may play a Mozart quartet perfectly, but if it uses the intonation system which has been taught for the past sixty years (to achieve melodic tension, players deviate especially on leading tones and major thirds by sharpening these notes), it strikes me as completely wrong. Mozart's quartet was written with a completely different form of intonation in mind. I have grown so accustomed to differentiated intonation systems, I have so reprogrammed my ear, as it were, that my mind balks at such a performance. But is equally obvious to me that the musicians intone very well, as they are playing perfectly consistently within the context of their learned system. Nonetheless, it is almost impossible for me to follow and understand the harmonic event. For me, this intonation is bad, even disastrous. Others undoubtedly regard as false an intonation which seems pure to me. It is therefore obvious that, prior to making any judgment, we must agree on the system to be used.

This is simply one example of the significance of a problem that has received very little attention. Its importance is compounded, logically enough, by the question of the meaning of the various major and minor keys. In a system of equal temperament, they are, after all, distinguished solely by pitch. I have long wondered how today, when scientific precision is so important, people still and without any concrete reason can believe that different keys have different emotional content, especially since there are no longer any keys, with the exception of transposed C major and A minor. The so-called equal-tempered system, a term which many people mistakenly use interchangeably with "well-tempered," did not come into general use until very late, not until the 19th Century. But even in this case, deviations in the tradition of the guild of piano tuners have been retained to the present time, which really make it possible to achieve a different quality in the various keys and thus genuine key characteristics on keyboard instruments as well. The instrumentarium prior to about 1840 naturally offers even more variations, since the different keys sounded very differently on the natural brass instruments and woodwinds of that time, because different fingerings altered the tone colors. Moreover, enharmonic tones often required different fingerings; the old Baroque and pre-Baroque intonation systems had a lasting impact, while later instruments strove for a chromatically even scale. It is evident that the very different intonation systems had a major influence not only on the key characteristics, but also on the blend in orchestras and ensembles. Some instruments, especially those of the 17th and 18th Centuries, have a rich spectrum of tones with clearly audible overtones, so it obviously makes sense that an orchestra which plays a triad in C major, must sound totally different when the high instruments intone the thirds, i.e. the E, the 5th partial of the bass, differently than the audible overtone of the bass sounds. This difference is heard as beats, which occasionally take on the character of a trill. Thus it is by no means simply a question of being in or out of tune but rather one of true aesthetic differences. I am convinced that each type of music absolutely demands both the intonation system and an historical instrumentarium appropriate to it. And further these two characteristics of every epoch are closely related.

The acoustical properties of the room in which a performance took place are another very important aspect of the original sound. This issue used to be more clearly defined, since the professional competence and knowledge demanded of composers went far beyond composition theory and counterpoint. Since they basically wrote for special occasions and specific halls, the instrumentation, the skill of the performers, the acoustics and the nature of the audience were all elements which entered into the composition. The composer was rightly blamed for an imbalance of sounds, serious errors in performance, incomprehensibility or over-simplicity of the work, since this meant that he had failed to give proper attention to all these various components. Ideally, music which was written for small chambers and a small circle of listeners should probably still be played in a smaller format, regardless of whether modern or old instruments are used. I do not believe that instruments were made to play louder only because performance rooms became larger, but rather that dynamics required constant extension. As they became an essential part of a composition, once one begins to play loudly, one must play louder and louder to achieve the same impact, until the threshold of pain is reached. Obviously in such a case the hall may also be rather large. The final outcome of such a trend results in a symphony orchestra of 120–130 musicians playing loud instruments. But in my view, the problem lies neither in the size of the concert hall nor in allegedly larger audiences. When we consider that the so-called "simple folk" took part in the life of music to an extent that is inconceivable to us today (at that time many concerts took place in the churches and great cathedrals of northern Italy, for example, for which a vast amount of new music was played Sunday after Sunday before thousands of people), we can surely conclude that this musical life possessed an intensity and immediateness far surpassing present-day concert life.

Every performer at some time finds himself in the unfortunate position of having to play in halls that are anything but ideal for a particular kind of music—for I am firmly convinced that the hall is one aspect of the total sound of music. But to be rigid about this would be fatal for musical activity, since it would mean that from the moment the ideal hall is found all concerts would be performed only in it, so the public would have to come there. Compromises along these lines are probably unavoidable. But there is also the danger of going too far with such compromises, so that one ends up playing in halls where most of the audience is forced to conclude that the sound is too thin resulting from soft-sounding instruments or the small size of the ensemble, often dictated by a particular composition (such as the third and sixth Brandenburg Concertos), which cannot be enlarged without altering the structure of the music.

There are very large halls with optimal acoustics, even for old instruments, and small halls with very poor acoustics. (The quality of a room depends not only on its size, since there are small halls with such poor acoustical properties that no music should ever be played in them). Yet I do not consider this an insoluble problem. As we are coming to better realize, certain kinds of music can be performed much better with certain acoustics, so halls which are quite unsuitable for more recent music because they have too much resonance, can be used very well for music of the 17th and 18th Centuries. But even in less suitable halls, correct playing techniques can make it clear to the audience that music is not a matter of allowing oneself to be lulled by pleasant sounds, but rather of active listening. Even if the sound is thin as a result of too little resonance, each individual line nonetheless comes through the way it should, if properly executed. The listener who can overlook the absence of brilliance and polish—which are often only fool's gold—discovers that he still has something to gain, something which he could not recognize or even notice in run-of-the-mill performances, in which musical sense was lost in the volume of sound and which was oriented to two-dimensional sounds, although the music was not at all composed two-dimensionally.

The degree of reverberation in a room is of particular importance in this matter. A room is "over-acoustical" (i.e. it resonates too greatly and the resonance lasts too long) when harmonic change cannot be heard clearly, when one harmony muddles the sound of the next. In this case a musician is forced by the qualities of the room to play slowly so the harmonies of the music can be understood. In other words, it is not a question of the tempo of the fast notes, but rather the tempo of harmonic changes which determine performance qualities. One of the important criteria for selecting a correct tempo is that a piece must be played slowly enough so that the echo of the preceding harmony does not obscure a subsequent harmony. We know that good composers built into their works, as it were, the acoustics of a room, the echo, the blending of certain sounds. Many Baroque scores, and certainly Medieval and Renaissance works, are completely misunderstood if acoustics are not taken into consideration. The greatest examples of the mastery of acoustics are found in the works of Bach.

We are familiar with the acoustics of the St. Thomas Church in Leipzig, for which most of Bach's works were written; we know that during his lifetime, the church had wooden paneling and that its echo time was similar to that of the hall of the *Musikverein* in Vienna, i.e. it had the reverberation time of a very good concert hall, in which it is possible to play very rapid tempos without blurring the integrity of the sounds. With this in mind it is easy to understand why Bach could employ the fast changes of harmony resulting from the very fast tempos which, according to his sons, he preferred. Other composers, such as Vivaldi, who use extremely fast tempos—typically played very fast by Italian ensembles today—performed in reverberating churches. The harmonic changes in works which were intended to be played in such spaces are placed so far apart that they remain clear while the fast notes are evidently not intended to be heard as single notes, but as a blurred effect. The intent was to achieve in this way a shimmering overall sound effect.

If, for example, a composer has written a fast sixteenth *arpeggio* so that in such a hall it will blend into a shimmering chord, and the performer of today plays the fast notes precisely and clearly, then he misconstrues the meaning of these notes and alters the composition—not out of arrogance, but rather out of ignorance! There is a danger—and this holds for some critical listeners as well—that the performer wants to hear the *score* rather than the music. He discovers that everything sounds blurred, and he does not like it. But this is because he wants to hear the *score*. On the other hand, if he listens to the *music*, he will discover that these fast notes, in reverberating, create an indefinite trembling and a vague color. This is an impressionistic manner of composition, chosen with the reverberation of a room in mind. In this context I also strongly recommend rethinking the way Mozart is interpreted today, in relation to the acoustical properties of rooms. I am firmly convinced that much of what we today want to hear so finely engraved, as if drawn in a blueprint, should have a more reverberant space, with a broadly blending edge. In any case, the primary concern with regard to the acoustics of rooms is not the size of the room, but rather its resonance and compactness of sound.

The great importance of the polychoral aspect of the Baroque concerto gives us an indication of the importance of space in Baroque music. The placement of musicians in various groupings in a room is of enormous importance for this music. Much of the music of the period was played not on a raised podium, as it is today, but throughout the room, which became an integral factor in the music. This polychoral technique was frequently used even for monochoral works. Simple four-part music was sometimes played polychorally by distributing several groups (each of which might play the complete movement) throughout the room, having them play alternately or together. (There are accounts of such performances of Willaert's four-part ricercars). This practice of separating parts of both chorus and orchestra was used in the Salzburg Cathedral until the second half of the 18th Century. Masses by Leopold Mozart, which were written in the monochoral style of the period, were performed polychorally in the Cathedral, making use of several additional wooden galleries constructed for this purpose.

The spatial setting had more to do with the performance than with the work itself. The concept of a room alive with sound was basically related to a religious outlook. Music was not simply a performance to which one listened, but rather a manifestation in sound of the sacred place. The church itself was an architectural hymn of praise to the deity. Believers entered this domain—and when it began to resonate with sound, the sound came not from any specific source, but rather from everywhere, coalesced with the architecture. The awareness of such a sacred space could have an overwhelmingly powerful effect. This inclusion of space in the conception of the composition was enhanced by the concept of the total unity of art, an idea which has unfortunately been long lost. Although we no longer regard art as a totality, we should at least be aware that this unity of space and sound was essential to Baroque music and intended to encompass and to transform the entire human being.

The use of sacred space in a musical composition is very clear in Monteverdi's Marian Vespers. In this work a polychoral quality is inherent in the idea of the composition, even though it is not expressly required. One choir consists of the soloists, while the *cantus firmus*—the other choir—is scored for a chorus. The soloists are answered by the entire chorus. The significance of separating the soloists is especially evident in the "concerto" *Duo Seraphim*. Here the suggestion that the seraphim are calling to each other across the heavens creates the need for a kind of music that embraces space. In *Audi caelo*, echo is used to portray nature's response to the song of the angels. These echo effects were so important to Monteverdi that in one passage in his opera *Orfeo* he calls for an additional *organo di legno* (an organ with wooden pipes) for just a few words sung by "Echo." Echo passages also constitute an important part of concertante dialogue, as for example in the fourth Brandenburg Concerto. This echo effect was so important to Bach that he called the two flutes which play the echo interpolations *flauti d'echo*. Only when these two instruments are separated and allowed to answer each other from a distance are Bach's intentions realized.

In light of the crucial role played by space in the music and performance of the 17th and 18th Centuries, we realize how critical the positioning of the orchestra, the placement of the instruments, is for Baroque music—even for many of Mozart's and Haydn's works as well. Not much can be achieved with the way in which symphony orchestras are seated today because the groups which are intended to be clearly differentiated from each other in a dialogue often merge together in an incomprehensible way. In keeping with the Baroque concept, the different groups should be positioned as far apart as possible, so that their dialogue is audible and comprehensible. This dialogue takes place between soloists and *tutti,* between larger and smaller groups in the orchestra, or even between individual instruments. It can be realized, for example, with a chamber orchestra and a solo trio, each spatially separated. A concerto by Corelli has been preserved which was performed in the palace of Cardinal Barberini with a hundred string players, groups of which were dispersed at various places throughout the entire building. It was customary everywhere to separate the concertino (the soloist group of a concerto) and the orchestra, so that the dialogue or echo effect could be more clearly expressed. But concertos for several harpsichords or pianos present a special problem. Today the instruments are usually placed so closely together that the dialogue which the composer intended is lost. Such positioning of the instruments tends to produce the effect of one single amplified harpsichord or piano, rather than that of several instruments which are communicating with each other. In order to create an ideal situation, one must experiment with positioning the instruments as far away from each other as possible so the best sound separation is achieved, without endangering the necessary ensemble precision.

Having discussed the importance of hall acoustics and of space in connection with polychoral music and the location of the musicians, I would like to turn briefly to the question of the studio used—for radio performances and recordings. My group, the Vienna Concentus Musicus, has been recording since 1958, in the early years for a number of different companies, all using different recording procedures. Conflicts for the musicians were unavoidable, since the room plays so critical role in the production of sound, particularly in the kind of music we play. As musicians, we feel comfortable only when we play in a room which is ideal for the music in question. The consequence is that original sound conditions can only be created "in the studio," from the musician's point of view, if the studio is not a studio, but rather a room with ideal musical properties.

A few examples may show that from the recording technician's point of view things may appear quite differently. The two extremes we were confronted with in those days were a recording session in an almost completely dead room and sessions in musically ideal Baroque halls. In the first case, musical conditions were so poor that we hoped never to repeat the experience. The players could hardly hear each other, one's own sound appeared dull and drab, and the sounds did not coalesce. In such a room, the instruments speak very badly, which makes truly inspired playing impossible. Everything might sound quite different in the control booth, much better and more real, since reverberating is artificially mixed in, but this is of no help to those actually playing the music. Even if the end result were a perfect sound, the method remains nonetheless inhuman. It is only by accident that such a recording turns out to be first-rate.

We also experimented with, or were forced to try, other combinations. On one occasion, each instrument was recorded separately on a different track and the final mixing, the stereophonic division and the sound of the room were added later, without any input from us. After we had gone through all of these troubles, growing out of differing attitudes toward the studio, at long last creating the finished album, we came back to the position from which we had set out years before: the best room for a particular type of music stimulates the best playing of this music, and only a performance of this sort is worth preserving; interestingly the results appear best in technical terms as well. So, to go back to the question of conditions best for recording, the conclusion must be that they occur only when the studio is not a studio.

But to return to the starting point of this chapter, the title of which moved me to reject it. I have attempted to explain original sound conditions as a complex matter involving much more than simply so-called old instruments. But now comes the decisive point, one which makes musicians furious: "re"-construction. I immediately feel myself carried away to an archeological site in Assyria where an ancient temple is being reconstructed. Can you imagine that a good conductor, while attempting to be as faithful to the work as possible, has the sense that he is "reconstructing" a Beethoven symphony while performing it? We are nothing but musicians playing the works of Bach or Monteverdi: why should we need to reconstruct something? Just as others long before us realized that it is musically better to perform works as much as possible in keeping with the ideas of the composers and insisted on extreme faithfulness to the notation, so we, too, have somehow gotten the notion that most music is better performed, *musically* better, using original, rather than modern instruments.

While this might be termed reconstruction, it is actually nothing more than a somewhat prolonged study of music. Just as one gradually masters the instruments which are generally used today, so too one can master the older instruments. However, since there is no direct tradition guiding the interpretation of the notation, and because criteria for performance practice no longer exist, one must necessarily search, compare, study old textbooks, but only as the means to an end, i.e. the best possible performance. We know that we cannot recreate 18th-Century performances today, nor would we wish to. We simply present the music with the best means at our disposal, which is the legitimate right and duty of all musicians.

The key question is actually: why do we play old music at all, since we now have new music? But the answer to this question is not my task at present. Having committed ourselves to the original, basic anachronism, that of finding the artistic expressions of by-gone days (which were written for people of other times) interesting and important, then it is no longer anachronistic to use period instruments, so long as they are, as is undoubtedly the case, much better suited than other instruments for performing this music today. I view our situation thus: today, for the first time in the history of Western civilization, the musical achievements of many centuries are available to us; we are familiar with the various tone systems and performance factors, and we know the sounds of the instruments of each period. Today's musician can therefore freely choose the most suitable means—provided he is aware of them.

We usually speak of a "historical" or "modern" instrumentarium, although the latter term is used quite absurdly and carelessly. After all, there is no such thing as a "modern" instrumentarium, with the exception of a few seldom-used instruments. The so-called modern instrumentarium is, like the music for which it was created, 120–140 years old. It seems silly to speak of a performance with the usual orchestra of, say, a Beethoven symphony as a performance "with modern instruments," and a performance using instruments of Beethoven's time as "with historic instruments." Both of these rely on historical sound images! In one case, the instrumentarium of 1850 is used, in the other case, that of 1820; there is no basic difference between the two. In the former case we savor the sounds of the second half of the 19th Century, in the latter those of the first half. This by no means indicates which is better suited for the work and its understanding today.

I would like to use a few examples to demonstrate the close relationship that exists between music of a period and a suitable instrumentarium. In the Baroque period, musical symbols, tone symbolism and the theory of affections played an important role in understanding the language of music. Trumpets, for example, were always assigned to divine or worldly rulers. Bach frequently used them in this way, employing the impure natural tones (the 7th, 11th and 13th partials, or B-Flat, F'' and A'') to represent terror, the dreadful, the devil. Though these tones seem rough and off-key, they sounded normal to the listeners at the time, since their ears were accustomed to the natural overtone series in trumpet and horn music. It is thus clear that both intonation and tonal beauty—a very questionable concept—were used to convey certain ideas. In some contexts, only the "ugly" sound intended by the composer can render the truth of a musical statement. These differences in tone cannot be expressed on a valve trumpet capable only of playing to the 8th overtone, while omitting the 7th. It plays everything as "beautifully" as possible, thereby eliminating any contrasts. Or: B minor is a wonderfully light and brilliant key on the Baroque transverse flute, while C minor sounds dull and is extremely difficult to play. The listener was familiar with these facts, and mastery of difficult keys was considered one aspect of virtuosity. Moreover, the difficulty of remote keys, which could be heard in the tone color (due to cross fingerings)—was part of the music's affective content. On the modern Böhm flute, C minor sounds just as good as B minor. The flute figures in the soprano aria "Zerfliesse mein Herze in Fluten der Zähren" from the *St. John Passion* are extraordinarily difficult and multicolored, since in F minor cross-fingering is needed for almost every combination of tones. This corresponds perfectly to the desperate emotion of the aria. On a Böhm flute, the figures sparkle as if they had been written in the easiest and brightest key; here too, the idea behind the instrumentation cannot be realized. I could cite many other such examples.

Such problems raise the question, whether the ugliness of the false natural tones and the dullness resulting from cross-fingering, which are used to achieve musical expression, are still desirable today. It used to be taken for granted that beauty is inextricably linked to ugliness, and that neither is possible without the other. Music appreciation formerly accorded an important position to the ugly and the coarse, but this can hardly be said of our understanding of music today. We no longer desire to comprehend works of art as a whole, in all of their multi-layered facets; only *one* component counts for us today: the element of unadulterated, aesthetic beauty or "artistic enjoyment." We no longer want to be transformed by music, but only to luxuriate in beautiful sounds.

I believe it should be possible to cast off these listening habits which are based on misunderstandings and to experience once again the diversity of Western music as a whole. And this brings me to my final point: the richness and diversity of Western music. For about the last 70 years, our concert programs have been made up almost exclusively of older music, rather than contemporary music—the music of Monteverdi, Bach, Mozart, Beethoven, Schönberg, and Stravinsky. By a very curious selection process, an imaginary community of music lovers and musicians has distilled a repertory of a very few works from the vast fund of our musical heritage, a repertory which people want to hear and to play again and again. Obviously, this music is generally familiar, and therefore the purpose of a piece of music designed to surprise the listener is lost. This preference for the familiar gradually leads to the complete rejection of the unknown, of anything new. Pieces which are seldom played are ultimately discarded, and in the end, probably very soon, we will forget how music should be listened to and understood. The musical record album is, or was, our last great chance: people have the opportunity of listening at home to a work in which they are interested as often as necessary to really understand it. But this opportunity is only rarely used, probably because constantly surrounding ourselves with the familiar prevents us from looking farther afield and stifles our desire for new encounters.

We often speak of the judgment of an age. But this judgment can only speak when it is asked to do so. Of course, each age produced countless inferior compositions, and for the past 40 years, publishing houses and artists have not been particularly successful in the selection of the most interesting and best works of the Baroque repertoire. Today's attitude toward old music is similar to what occurred in so-called classical music: unless it was written by Bach or Monteverdi we don't want to hear it. We therefore have to place our hopes in a new listening public, one which may be open to new music as well as to old music, and which will also accept a new aesthetic of music.

Priorities: The Relative Importance of the Various Factors

It is a weakness of educated Europeans to focus on only a few of the many important aspects of a problem, and then consider these few as the only important issues. This is a familiar error; all manner of sectarianism is based on this type of thinking and a lot of confusion in this world stems from it. But how does this apply to music? Of all the factors which inform an interpretation, we arbitrarily seize upon one—perhaps because we have just "discovered" it—and declare it to be the overriding consideration; in order to be taken seriously as a musician, one must do such and such a thing in such and such a way. The importance of "the joy of discovery" should not be underestimated; if someone really believes that he has discovered something special, he usually overestimates its importance and thinks that all other aspects of the problem pale in comparison. Thus while there are many important facets of interpretation, it is all too easy to select just one of them, perhaps even a minor one, and inflate it into a major concern. I have often been told by fanatics, who seem to abound in the field of early music, that every factor is equally important and that there are no priorities: an interpretation is only worthy of discussion if *all* its aspects have been taken into consideration. Yet we know that no one can achieve *everything* that is expected of him—as creatures we are much too imperfect. We must be satisfied with fulfilling only some part of our expectations; there is no such thing as everything or nothing, because there can never be such a thing as everything.

What remains then is to bring a certain order to the various aspects that we expect in a good interpretation. We may argue that *everything* is important, but in the final analysis there are some things which are more important than others. From this we can draw up a kind of list of priorities, ranked in order of importance.

I would like to mention an interesting example of what I mean by our obsession with making one *single* point the major one. There is a famous Baroque violinist who from the many, many rules and instructions for performance has focused only on the *one* point: every tone must be short. He is an excellent violinist, a virtuoso who has played many years with a symphony orchestra, but since he has been playing Baroque music, his playing is almost unbearable because he gives this one aspect precedence over all others. If we were to say to him: Fine, there is a rule that every tone should be shortened, but there is also a rule that says that song must be imitated—how are you going to resolve these two rules? This would do no good, for if someone is totally obsessed with one point, which he considers the most important of all, then say what you will, he will continue to regard *his* particular sense as primary. A responsible and artistic approach must therefore be found for these problems, any other leads only to eccentricity. We must always be willing to recognize something new and to acknowledge our mistakes.

Now to the various aspects which are at the heart of our interpretation of music: these are technical mastery, sound quality, probably also the instrumentarium, tempo, the historical setting, understanding of notation (to what extent the notation itself embodies the work or whether it requires further interpretation); there is also the social significance of the piece in question, for its time as well as for ours (to the extent that this has any influence on interpretation); there is music as language in tones, the articulation of small note values, analogous to the pronunciation of words, the *projection of levels of sound planes,* which rules out an articulation of words, the so-called *sweeping line,* and finally the size of the ensemble. No doubt there are other aspects I have failed to mention. When we look at this list of various ingredients, we see that almost any one could be regarded as the key aspect.

There are those who contend that a certain kind of music can only be played with a small, or alternatively, with a large orchestra. However, such assertions are difficult to address without first asking what role the group's size plays in the first place? What will happen if, instead of ten violins, I have only two or three? It makes no sense to say that *this* composer used only three first violins, so we will play his pieces with a small orchestra, and that another had ten, so we will play his music with a larger one. No, the size of the orchestra must be determined by the acoustics of the hall, the musical form and the sound of the instruments. There is thus a whole series of secondary aspects which influence the size of the optimal orchestra. Mozart performed his early symphonic works in Salzburg with a very small orchestra; therefore, many people today think that such "Mozart orchestration" is right for these works; indeed, performances with large orchestras are dismissed as lacking in good taste. Yet Mozart performed works from the same period in Milan, for example, with a very sizable orchestra, because the hall was quite spacious and the orchestra was good as well as large. Later, when he performed his early Salzburg compositions in Vienna, the string section was occasionally larger than what is used today in performances of late Romantic works. Something similar could be said about Haydn's performances. We know the size of the halls that were available to him in London, Eisenstadt and Esterhàz. The size of his orchestras varied from the smallest chamber group to very large ensembles.

Let us take a look at another secondary factor. The "sweeping line" is often singled out as being critical to a good performance. But whenever we focus on *one* particular point we have to ignore several others. If in early music we want to create a broad surface of sounds, as required by Romantic music after 1800, then we have no choice but to dispense with any kind of "speaking" articulation and the transparency of the music will suffer. In this case, aspects of one style are transferred to another, something which happens frequently because few musicians are aware that the performance style in which they feel at home—generally the style of late Romanticism—cannot be indiscriminately employed for the music of other periods.

Another secondary aspect is the instrumentarium. There are many musicians who have recently come to believe that when the music of a particular period is played with the instruments of that period, they have automatically met almost all the requirements for a "correct" performance. The relative importance of this problem has varied greatly throughout the history of Western music. Let us consider, for example, what importance the instrumentarium or the dimension of sound had in the music of the 16th Century, music which was not *"orchestrated"* by the composer. There was almost no difference in composition between vocal and instrumental music; the instrumentalists took the same music the vocalists sang and adapted it for their instruments. This was true for players of the flute, harpsichord, lute and other stringed instruments—the same piece could be played in very different ways that were stylistically correct. Therefore a very specific sound cannot have been essential for *this* kind of music.

It is therefore very important to determine the relative value of every single musical decision we make and to understand that this value can differ greatly among various works and periods. It may happen that due to an erroneous interpretation, the music fails to make any statement at all, or that despite serious errors in interpretation, which can hardly be avoided, a considerable portion of the work, of its musical intentions, is nonetheless preserved and communicated to the listener. We have to look to the persuasive power of the rendition, not to elements which are "correct" or "wrong"; in the long run this will make us much more tolerant of opinions which differ from our own, since the same spirit underlies both. That the most convincing rendition usually is also the "most correct" is another matter entirely.

We must find some way of categorizing these various decisions naturally and in order of their approximate importance. Understanding the work must be accorded first place, with everything else subordinate to it. Thus we must ask: how does the work communicate itself to the listener and what part do its stylistic features play in this communication? Is it a question of the style of a particular period, something which all compositions of that period have in common, or is it the personal style of the composer, i.e. that which distinguishes his personal style from that of the period? A musician should be able to recognize and sort these things out because otherwise, the requirements of the various periods could be so confused in a performance that the listener would not be able to understand anything (except perhaps "how beautiful it sounds"). We must first come to know and understand the style of a period,—then that which is stylistically unusual in a work will stand out. Essential stylistic differences exist, for instance, between: a) the German late Baroque of Bach, Handel and Telemann, b) *Empfindsamkeit, galanterie,* as well as the *Sturm und Drang* of Bach's sons and their contemporaries; or from the articulated music of the Viennese classical age of Haydn and Mozart to c) the middle and late Beethoven, Weber and Mendelssohn. From the standpoint of performance styles this means, very simply put: a) a "speaking" playing, articulation of the "words" in small, tone groups, dynamics primarily applied to the individual tone and as a means of articulation; b) overall dynamics specified by the composer (e.g. "Mannheim crescendo"), new kinds of instrumentation, "romantic" play of tone colors (idiomatic wind writing, pedal chords), vigorous contrast of dynamics; c) detailed articulation replaced by large *legato* surfaces and lines; tone-painting. (The suggestive effect is now derived much less from the relationship of details than from the overall impression). The musical language of the 18th Century also knows these moods, but there they are always linked to language. People talk differently depending on whether they have something sad or something happy to say: mood affects diction. In 19th-Century music, however, general moods were painted and could be extended to great lengths. Impressions were created; the listener is transported, but nothing is *said* to him.

Thus it is very important to understand the style of the period in which the composer thinks and with which he is well familiar. Is this music which is articulated, which "speaks", or is it general sound, intended to convey specific moods?

It is quite clear that the musicians of every age are so at home in the musical idiom of their own time that they believe they must render and understand the music of other times in this same idiom. Thus in the 19th Century, Bach's works (which have to be understood primarily from the point of view of language), were played in the style of a work of that period: i.e. broadly, as late-Romantic emotional music. This led to many pieces being newly orchestrated and so to the transformation of articulation into "phrasing." Articulation is completely lost; the articulation sign becomes a bowing mark that indicates a place—as inaudible as possible—for the change of bow. A greater contrast to genuine articulation can hardly be imagined. However, by subordinating every other factor to that of understanding the work, it turns out that articulation deserves a particularly high priority. Since it directly affects the understanding of the work, and in fact a work can be decisively altered by correct or faulty articulation, it ranks close to the top of my "list of priorities."

Every musician tries hard to express with his instrument or voice whatever the music demands. In this context, it is interesting to note that the development of musical instruments always goes hand in hand with the requirements of composers and the style of a particular period. It was long thought that technical development went its own way and always led from poorer to better technology. The bow invented by Tourte (around 1760) therefore had to be better than the bows used prior to his time; the flute invented by Böhm (around 1850) had to be superior to earlier flutes, and so on for all instruments.

This naive faith in progress remains very widespread, even among people who ought to have some understanding of the history of interpretation. This lack of comprehension probably has to do with their reluctance to recognize the full significance of the price that must be paid for each improvement. Viewed in historical terms, the defects to be eliminated were, after all, only *apparent* defects. The composer inevitably thinks in the sounds of his own age, not in terms of some future utopia. It is clear that the historical instrumentarium has a key position in interpretation. The advantages and disadvantages, special features with regard to sound, sound blend, dynamics and, last but not least, intonation must be studied. But before we opt for a completely "historical" kind of performance, we must ask whether our choice is based on characteristics other than the instrument's original advantages and defects: characteristics which it possesses only at a different time, namely the present: for example, it does not sound like what we are used to, but has a strange, rather "exotic" tone color. Since there is no unbroken tradition of playing, we have no idea how the instrument was really played. It is rare that a musician today can completely identify with the sound of these instruments. Sometimes he can render the tonal and technical potential even better with his modern instrument than with an authentic old instrument with which he has not "bonded" musically. In this very complex matter, we must decide each case separately by asking whether the advantages outweigh the disadvantages.

Take another example: the violin bow. The bow created by Tourte at the end of the 18th Century produced an *equally strong* tone along its entire length. Further, an almost inaudible bow change can be executed almost completely masking the difference between upbow and downbow. In addition, the violinist can play extremely loudly with this bow, while the bouncing bow technique sounds hard and drum-like. These qualities, which make it ideal for rendering the "broad sound surfaces" of music after 1800, must be paid for by the loss of many other qualities. With such a bow it is very difficult to create an elastic, bell-shaped tone, to shorten a tone so that it does not sound chopped off, or to give a different sound quality to the up and the downbow, something required in early music and easy to execute with the baroque bow. Of course a violinist may say that this is precisely what is wrong, that one *should* make up and downbows as similar as possible; that the modern (Tourte) bow is better than the old Baroque bow because it alone can produce an even sound. But when we proceed from the premise that music can be best performed when it is properly interpreted, we discover that all the apparent disadvantages of the Baroque bow are actually advantages. The tones that are usually paired sound different on the upbow and downbow; the individual tone has a bell-like dynamic, innumerable intermediate levels from *legato* to *spiccato* play themselves, as it were. We see that the Baroque bow is ideal for Baroque music—so there are good reasons for using it. This does not mean that it is the perfect bow bar none; we will not play Richard Strauss with it. But strangely enough, this is precisely what was done, only the other way around, with the Tourte bow.

The modern bow, which was designed for the *legato,* for less articulated playing, can also be used for Baroque music, if no other bow is available. However, professional musicians today are forced to play music from many different periods using the same tools. As any orchestra member knows, he will play contemporary music today, for example, and a symphony by Mozart or a work by Bach or Gustav Mahler tomorrow. They cannot use different instruments every day. This means that they must know the various musical idioms so well that they can play in completely different ways on the same instrument. This is only rarely successful, however. Although we do play the music of five centuries, we usually use only *one* language, *one* performance style. If we were only to recognize the essential differences in styles and rid ourselves of the unfortunate concept of "music as a world language," which is identical in all nations, cultures and centuries, a list of priorities would easily emerge. We would view a work as the artistic expression of an age and of one human being, placing special demands on listener and performer. We would literally be forced to investigate and to fulfill these demands concerning articulation, tempo, tonal balance, etc. Finally, we would probably no longer be satisfied with our instruments and would select instruments of the period, but only if and when they are right for the work and best-suited for performance. It is in this way that a musician in search of the best interpretation should arrive at the use of "original" instruments, very naturally and based only on the requirements of the work.

The other approach, often taken today, leads us astray, in my opinion. There are many musicians who believe that early music must be played on *authentic* instruments—but they do not have a precise notion of what these old instruments can and cannot do. They acquire an old instrument without understanding its meaning, only because they have been hired to play on old instruments and the "gig" pays well, or because they themselves find it interesting. The decisive element in their decision, the benchmark, as it were, is the old instrument, the "original" instrument—not what this old instrument can do. Such a musician, however, learned to play music on a completely different instrument so his notion of sound and his concept of music are based on a different instrument. Now he takes the Baroque instrument and tries instinctively to produce with it the sounds to which he is accustomed. Such a thing can be heard again and again, and the result is the pitiful sound of ensembles which perform, if one may call it that, on old instruments, for one can hear the outright longing of the musicians for the sounds to which they have been accustomed. But this simply does not work: it is impossible to play a beautiful *sostenuto* with a Baroque bow, although this does not prevent some musicians from trying; it is impossible to achieve a certain luxuriant sound, but it is nonetheless attempted. The result is pitiful, and of course the listener says: so this is the sound of the old instruments; the composers in those days were certainly limited, for they had nothing better to work with. And the musician who comes to an early instrument this way can never believe that what he is doing is meaningful, so at the first opportunity, will put it aside. In short, the musician must first *know* why he chooses an early instrument, which should be for musical reasons alone. If these musical reasons are not perfectly clear to him, then he should desist and work with the instruments which sound authentic and natural to him.

The question of priorities is of particular importance in the case of the instrumentarium, because serious mistakes have been made in this area. If historical instruments had been selected purely for musical reasons, and not just to appear "authentic" and "historical," or to seem interesting, then hundreds of thousands of so-called "early" instruments, which are not really musical instruments at all, would never have been sold. Entire shiploads of such recorders and harpsichords, crumhorns, cornetts and trombones have been sold—and we owe it solely to the admirable talent of a few musicians who manage to make these abominations sound tolerable. A David Oistrach can make music even on a miserable student violin. Therefore I believe that musicians and particularly those of us who play a great deal of "early" music should never give the instrument, the tool, precedence over the music, although unfortunately this often happens.

Perhaps those instruments which are more independent of the player in the creation of sound should be excepted from this principle. I do believe that it is much more important that organ music be played on an adequate instrument than, say, violin music. The relative importance of the instrument is different in the case of the organ and the violin. It is simply impossible to make good organ music on a completely unsuitable instrument; in this case the organ itself is the primary factor in determining musical expression, while this is not to the same extent true of the winds and strings.

Even without original instruments, I believe that Classical and pre-Classical music can be played much better than it is today. Such improvements will not be accomplished by simply pressing Baroque instruments into the hands of the musicians. They would play so miserably on them that after two rehearsals they would be convinced themselves that this was not going to work. I believe—and this is what I wish to articulate above all in calling for an ordering of priorities—, that a musician must first understand the musical means of expression of a particular period using the instrument upon which he is best able to express himself.

If we place *music* in the foreground, the question of musical instruments falls a good bit lower on the list of priorities. We must first endeavor to realize as much as possible the diction and articulation of this music using the instruments available. In time the point will inevitably come at which every perceptive musician feels he needs a different instrument, one that is better suited to this music. And when an entire group of musicians "discovers" early instruments in this way, they will use them with greater conviction and find their idiom better than those who are only following a fashionable trend.

To conclude my review of the priorities of various musical factors: immediately following the work itself, which must always be given first place, comes the interest and imagination of the performing artist. I regard any musician completely unsuited for proper interpretation who, while doing everything perfectly in a technical sense, observing all aspects of articulation, paying close attention to the sources, using the correct instrument, intoning in mean-tone, choosing the correct tempo, lacks one thing: musicality, or to put it more poetically, the kiss of the Muse. It is a terrible truth in this profession, but if a person has not been kissed by the Muse, he can never be a musician. In listing the priorities I have, to clarify my meaning, taken my arguments ad absurdum, and I do so here again. A true artist can do many things wrong, demonstrably wrong, and yet succeed in getting under the skin of the listener with his music, and really move him. This can only happen by way of the "kiss of the Muse." No matter how interesting the interpretation of an "unkissed" musician may be—he will not succeed in unlocking the essence of the music, in making a musical statement that speaks directly to, moves and transforms us.

II.
Instrumentarium and Musical Discourse

Viola da Brazzo and Viola da Gamba
A Chapter in the History of String Instruments

If we examine the instrumentarium of our own time by tracing the history of individual instruments, we quickly discover that there is no such thing as a purely modern instrument. Almost all of them have a history going back many hundreds of years. The study of the history of individual instruments, exploring the relationships between each technical detail and the historical conditions, is a fascinating undertaking as well as a critically important one for anyone seriously involved with historical music.

Of all of the musical instruments in use today, only the strings still retain the external form of their predecessors 400 years ago. *All other instruments were recast and replaced again and again by new designs* which were immediately recognizable, both outwardly and in the sound produced. These changes were made whenever musical taste or technical requirements called for decisive modifications. But why was this not also true of string instruments? Were no modifications necessary? Is the tone of the contemporary violin identical to the sound of the 16th Century violin? This question is justified, not only because present-day instruments look like those from the past, but because old instruments are still clearly preferred by musicians. All the great soloists play on instruments which are more than 200 years old.

The violin, which assumed its present form in the 16th Century, incorporates the structural features of several earlier instruments: the shape of its body comes from the fiddle and the *lyra da braccio,* the way in which the strings are fastened, comes from the rebec. The violin, which in Italy was called the *viola da brazzo* or arm viol, in contrast to the *viola da gamba,* had four strings from its beginnings and was tuned in fifths as it is today. Various models were rapidly developed, especially in northern Italy; some of these aimed at producing a more incisive sound, one richer in overtones, while others produced fuller and rounder sounds. Some are highly arched and made of thin wood, while others are flat with thicker sides, depending upon the sound desired or the traditions of a particular school. After the middle of the 17th Century, violin makers in southern Germany and the Tyrol became increasingly prominent. The models created here, especially by Stainer, represented the unchallenged sound ideal of string music north of the Alps for more than 100 years. Despite this multiplicity of models and tonal ideas, which at times differed considerably, the violin remained largely unaffected by any drastic changes in sound until the end of the 18th Century. The basic form was retained, modified in only minor ways to meet the needs of each period. Instead of the fuzzy and somewhat dull-sounding gut G-string, a metal-wound string was introduced; longer bows were developed and balanced for a more refined bowing technique. But otherwise, for over 200 years, the violin remained the stable element in the instrumentarium.

The sweeping historical changes which influenced and transformed every aspect of life in Europe at the end of the 18th Century also placed their mark on art. And just as composers like Beethoven introduced into the art of music a completely new spirit, which shocked and repelled many contemporaries, so, in keeping with this spirit, the sound spectrum of instruments in Western music was fundamentally transformed. Notably, the dynamic range of the instruments was extended to the greatest possible extent.

The dynamic scale of the violin no longer met the requirements of composers and listeners. But ingenious violin makers found ways to rescue the instrument from this crisis, a crisis to which the gamba and many other instruments fell victim—the structure of the latter could not bear the tension of the strings required to extend their dynamic range. The thickness of the strings is directly proportional to their tension which results in the pressure being transmitted via the bridge to the belly of the instrument: the thicker the strings, the greater the tension and pressure, and the more powerfully the bow can and must be drawn to make them vibrate. Since earlier violins were not designed for and could not withstand this increased pressure, the old bass bar was reinforced, i.e. it was replaced by a new form which could produce volume of sound three to five times that of the original. Thus reinforced, the belly of the instrument could withstand the greater pressure required. Furthermore, the old neck including the scroll, which had been cut from one piece of wood and which was fastened parallel or almost parallel to the instrument, was removed. A new neck to which a separate scroll was attached was glued on at an angle. As a result, the angle of the strings across the bridge became more acute and again greatly increased the pressure on the belly. Around the same time, Tourte designed his modern violin bow, which was critical to the success of this reinforcement. This bow is heavier than the old ones, which had been designed for lightness and were quite concave, which means that the tension on the hairs is heightened when pressure on the bow is increased. The new bow has twice as many hairs as its predecessor, and in contrast to the round, loosely fastened bundle of the old bow, the hairs are held flat by a metal ferrule.

Almost all of the old violins underwent this operation between 1790 and the present. All the old Italian violins which soloists use today have been modernized so their sound is *totally* different. These rebuilt violins, when played with Tourte's new bow, were completely different instruments. But, the great advantage of being able to play at three times the volume was acquired by an enormous loss in high overtones. Over the years, a virtue was made of this necessity, and the smooth, round violin tone came to be regarded as the ideal. This sound was smoothed even more as uncovered gut strings were gradually discarded in favor of wound gut strings and steel strings. The loss of high overtones is a necessary concomitant to any increase in weight. This reduction in high overtones was due not only to the stronger bass bar and tighter strings, but also to other adjustments: the solid ebony fingerboard, the tailpiece, etc. Not all instruments benefited from this operation; some, especially the thin, highly arched instruments of the Stainer school, lost much of their timbre; their tone often became shrill, while remaining thin. Uncounted numbers of valuable old instruments were literally destroyed in the process when their backs broke, unable to withstand the extreme pressure of the sound post. I have dealt extensively with the history of this remodeling because it contains the key to understanding the sound quality of the old string instruments.

If we compare the tone of the Baroque violin with that of the modern concert instrument, we see that the tone of the former is soft, but has an intense, sweet clarity. Variety is achieved primarily by a richly differentiated articulation rather than by means of dynamics. In contrast, the modern instrument has a round, smooth tone with a very broad dynamic range, so dynamics are now the dominant shaping factor. On the whole, the sound palette has been impoverished, since all instruments in the modern orchestra strive for a round sound, lacking in overtones, while in the Baroque orchestra the differentiation of the instrument groups was much more varied and therefore richer.

Using the example of the violin, we have followed the history of the remodelling of instruments in relationship to musical sound. Let us now turn to the other string instruments, in particular the viola da gamba (leg viol, because it is held with the legs), and its family. This instrument seems to have descended more directly from the Medieval fiddle than the violin has. But one thing is certain: both families, the violins and the gambas, originated around the same time, in the 16th Century. From their beginning they were sharply differentiated from each other. This can be seen in the fact that in Italian instrumental works of the 17th Century, the cello, which is held between the legs, or "da gamba," is described as *viola da brazzo,* i.e. as a member of the violin family, whereas the small French *pardessus de viole* are discant *gambas,* although they are usually held on the arm, or "da brazzo."

Gambas differ structurally from violins in their proportions: they have a shorter sound box in proportion to the length of the strings, a flat back and wider ribs or sides. Gambas are generally thinner and lighter. The contours of the gamba's sound box are quite different from those of the violin, but are much less standardized, and seem to have little influence on the sound of the instrument. On the other hand, the tuning in fourths and a third, as well as the frets, both of which were borrowed from the lute, are essential. Gambas were made in consorts as early as the beginning of the 16th Century. This means that instruments of different sizes were built in soprano, alto, tenor and bass ranges. These groups were mostly used to play vocal works which had been adapted for instrumental interpretation by means of appropriate embellishments. Early treatises by Ortiz of Spain and Ganassi of Italy describe the various forms of embellishment. At that time, the violin was used mainly for improvised dance music and was not yet considered fit for proper society.

Towards the end of the 16th Century, when the violin, so much in keeping with the extroverted Italian character, slowly began to take hold in Italy, the *viol consort* was establishing its first legitimate home in England. The viola da gamba must have appealed to the English in a very special way, because in a period of about a hundred years, a rich variety of exceptionally beautiful and profound music for two to seven gambas was written. In its timbre and its musical and historical significance, it can only be compared with the music written for the string quartet, which was created in the 18th and 19th Centuries. Every musical family in England possessed a "chest of viols," including instruments of all sizes. Fantasies, stylized dances and variations were written expressly for these instruments while the art of instrumentation on the continent had not gotten much farther than "for use with all kinds of instruments." Because of its structure and frets, the gamba had a much finer and more direct tone than the instruments of the violin family. The music was always protected from a dynamically exaggerated rendition, which would coarsen and destroy its effect, given the special nature of the gamba, whose range of expression lies above all in the finest nuances.

English musicians also employed the gamba very early on as a solo instrument. For this purpose they designed instruments somewhat smaller than the normal bass gamba in D, calling them division viols; an even smaller solo gamba was called the lyra viol. The tuning of these instruments was varied according to the piece played. Its music was written in tablature (finger notation). Due to the complexity of the tuning and the unfamiliar notation this very beautiful and technically interesting solo music is hardly ever played today.

The gamba was used in England as a solo instrument above all for free improvisation. Some wonderful examples of this art can be found in Christopher Simpson's *Division Viol,* an introduction to solo improvisation on a bass instrument. This form of playing was regarded at the time as the height of gamba playing since the musical and technical mastery as well as the fantasy of the players could be richly displayed. Throughout the entire 17th Century, English gamba players were in demand everywhere on the continent. When Stainer built a gamba in 1670 for a church in Bolzano, he relied on a description by an English gamba player as the highest authority.

But it was in France, at the end of the 17th Century, that the solo capabilities of the gamba were most fully realized. The range of the French gamba of this period was enriched by the addition of a low A string. Championed by the most distinguished patrons of music, the rich work of Marin Marais and the impressive, bold compositions of the two Forquerays, who had many imitators, were created at the court of Louis XIV within the space of a single generation. The technical demands imposed by these compositions are often so unbelievably extreme that we are curious about the predecessors of these virtuosos. Previously, at the time of Louis XIII, the lute had been the fashionable and virtuoso instrument par excellence. Its special fingering technique can be clearly recognized in the fingering indicated in almost all French gamba compositions. These composers also refined the gamba's range of expression and introduced a system of symbols for countless complicated and clever embellishments, *glissandi* and other special effects, which were always explained in a preface. At this point the gamba reached the pinnacle of its solo and technical possibilities and, if one might put it this way, of its place in society. In their leisure hours, most noble personages played the gamba. The intimacy of the gamba's sound, which is mentioned over and over again and which makes it the perfect solo instrument for use in smaller rooms, as well as its ability to render the most subtle, whispering sounds, brought about the demise of the instrument just as it had reached its peak. Initially scorned, the more powerful violin, which can be easily heard even in large rooms, gained in popularity, until it ultimately supplanted the delicate gamba in the second half of the 18th Century. The history of this struggle is vividly portrayed in a polemic work berating the violin and cello, written by the gamba enthusiast Abbé Le Blanc. In any case, the essence of the gamba's sound, its breathy delicacy and subtlety, was so well understood that no attempt was ever made to save the instrument from its fate by increasing its volume.

The gamba never played the same role in other European countries as it did in England and France. In Italy it had, with the rise of the violin, fallen out of fashion by the 17th Century. There is a whole series of compositions for gamba in Germany which have a curious intermediate position; they are oriented either to French models, such as several chamber music works by Telemann, or else the gamba is viewed simply in terms of its technical or tonal qualities, as in the case of Buxtehude, Bach and others. Their works do not exploit the essence of the instrument, for they could, without any serious loss of musical substance, be played on other instruments as well.

In the 18th Century, when the period of the gamba was at an end, a few special members of the gamba family came briefly into fashion, e.g. the viola d'amore and the English violet, which could be used only as solo instruments. An attempt was made to achieve a kind of artificial resonance with these instruments by adding seven to twelve metal strings just above the belly of the instrument. These strings were conducted through the hollowed-out neck to the peg box and depending on their number, were tuned either in a diatonic scale or chromatically. They could not be played directly, but were only meant to vibrate "sympathetically" when the instrument was played. This created a kind of thin veil of sound, which constantly wafted over the instrument's delicate and sweet tones. In the 18th Century, the viola d'amore was very much in fashion, and even after the disappearance of the gamba in the 19th Century, it still managed to retain a strange shadowy existence.

In the 18th Century, bass gambas were occasionally built with sympathetic strings. The baryton is probably one of the strangest instruments of this genre. As large as a bass gamba and with strings tuned like those of the gamba, the baryton's metal sympathetic strings not only affect tonal color, but can be plucked with the thumb of the left hand. The effect is rather curious: since the strong, harpsichord-like plucked tones cannot be dampened; they continue to sound for a rather long time, often simultaneously. The baryton would probably have been long since forgotten, were it not for the fact that Haydn wrote a large number of beautiful compositions for this instrument which reveal its particular charm to great advantage. Other than Haydn's works, there are very few compositions for the baryton. Since a relatively large number of these instruments has been preserved, some from the 17th Century, it can probably be assumed that it was mostly an improvisational instrument, which allowed a player to accompany himself, as it were, by using the plucked strings.

Unfortunately, when the gamba was rediscovered some 50 years ago, its special sound was no longer appreciated. Something that had never even been considered in the 18th century was now attempted: many beautiful old gambas were reinforced and often even shortened to the size of a cello.

Now that two generations of musicians have had a chance to experiment and gain experience with Baroque instruments and so-called Baroque instruments, we have a different perspective. We no longer want to "improve" older instruments, but are trying to understand their unique sound. This has led to a basic principle that is almost a law: the instrumentarium of each age is a finely coordinated whole, with instruments in proper balance. It is not possible to use early instruments together with modern instruments. An original, correctly adjusted gamba, for instance, sounds much too thin in a modern string orchestra, a problem that confronts many gamba players during the annual performances of the Bach passions. (In my view, no compromise should be made here: the solo should be played either on a cello or on a reinforced cello-gamba).

Once a musician has undertaken the journey to the interpretation of early music and discovered its characteristic sound, that is, original instruments as the ideal medium, as ideal aids to interpretation and a source of artistic stimulus, he will not rest until he has reached the last link in the chain. It is no small task to properly coordinate an entire instrumentarium, but once done, our reward is a convincing sound that is a wonderful medium for early music.

The Violin:
The Solo Instrument of the Baroque

The Baroque period was an age in which artistic, solo performance reached unprecedented heights, an age which gave rise to the virtuoso because people wanted to admire and celebrate not only anonymous works of art, but above all artists who accomplished the seemingly impossible. For the sake of the soloist, the Baroque period broke the barriers imposed on each instrument by nature. Like no other musical instrument, the violin embodies the spirit of the Baroque age. Its emergence during the course of the 16th Century was like the gradual embodiment of an idea. Out of the multitude of stringed instruments of the Renaissance, the fiddles, rebecs, lyres and their countless variants, the violin crystallized, made possible by the ingenious instrument makers of Cremona and Brescia.

This process went hand in hand with the development of music itself: the music of the preceding centuries depended for its power upon the artistic fabric of polyphony; the individual instrument, the individual musician was an anonymous part of the whole. Each instrument had to outline a melody as clearly as possible while at the same time adding a special color nuance to the musical picture. Then around 1600, new forces came into play. The musical-declamatory interpretation of works of poetry led to monody, accompanied solo singing. The *recitar cantando,* or singing speech, and the *stile concitato* were musical forms which joined words and sound in one compelling entity. Purely instrumental music was also borne along on this wave. The soloist moved out of the anonymity of the ensemble and adopted the new monodic manner of speaking in tones, without words, and henceforth "spoke" exclusively in this way. Since this solo music was literally thought to be a kind of speech, the theory of musical rhetoric evolved. Music took on the character of a dialogue, and all music instructors of the Baroque age demanded, above all, a "speaking" manner of playing.

Since Claudio Monteverdi, most Italian composers have played the violin. The new musical language of the Baroque led in an incredibly short time to a virtuoso literature which long remained unsurpassed. Monteverdi wrote the first genuine violin solos in his *Orfeo* (1607) and *Vespers* (1610). But it was above all his students and followers, Fontana, Marini, Uccellini and others, who within 30 years brought the solo violin to its greatest flowering with their bold, often bizarre works.

During the following decades, things quieted down somewhat. The violin had passed through its *Sturm und Drang* phase, and its playing technique had so matured that further development occurred very slowly. Just as the Baroque style conquered all of Europe with national variations, so too did the showpiece of its musical instrumentarium, the violin. Germany embraced it most quickly; even in the first half of the 17th Century, Italian virtuosos were playing at the courts of German nobility. Soon a unique and typically German style of solo violin performance developed there, in which chord playing, or playing polyphonically, became especially highly developed.

Many violin players and music lovers today assess the state of violin playing in the 17th and 18th Centuries incorrectly. They believe that the great difference between the technique of soloists today and that of musicians 100 years ago implies similar differences (i.e., less developed technique) before that. This view ignores the fact that the social restructuring of the musical profession in the 19th Century was accompanied by a general decline. Henry Marteau correctly pointed out around 1910: "If we could hear Corelli, Tartini, Viotti, Rode and Kreutzer today, our best violinists would probably be astounded and convinced of the decadence of present-day violin technique."

Many techniques of violin playing which we now take for granted, such as vibrato, spiccato, flying staccato and others, are regarded as achievements of Paganini and, with the exception of the vibrato, absent from Baroque music. Instead, so-called "Bach-bowing" was invented, which really only admits uniformity in place of the endless variety of Baroque articulation. Both the music itself and the old treatises make clear the technical devices that were available at any given time and place.

Vibrato, which is intended to imitate singing, is as old as string instruments themselves, being specifically documented as early as the 16th Century by Agricola. Later, Mersenne (1636), North (1695), and Leopold Mozart (1756) describe it repeatedly as something generally known. However, it was always regarded as a pure embellishment to be used only for certain passages and by no means universally applied. Leopold Mozart writes: "There are some players who tremble at every note, as if they had a chronic fever. One should use the tremolo (vibrato) only in those places where Nature herself would produce it."

Spiccato, or bouncing bowing, is a very old type of stroke. In the 17th and 18th Centuries, however, the designation *spiccato* did not mean bouncing bowing, but simply notes that were clearly separated. Most unslurred arpeggio figures and rapid repetitions of notes were played using this bowing practice. J. Walther (1676), Vivaldi and others called for it specifically by using the term *con arcate sciolte* or simply *sciolto.* But many kinds of forced bouncing bows, even long chains of flying staccato, are found in the solo literature of the 17th Century, especially in Schmelzer, Biber and Walther. Even the most varied and extreme kinds of pizzicati (with a plectrum and rebounding from the fingerboard in Biber, in chords in Farina, 1626) and *col legno* (striking with the bow stick) were widely employed in the 17th Century in the works of Farina,

Biber and others.

Capriccio stravagante, written by Carlo Farina, a student of Monteverdi, was published in 1626 and contains an amazing catalogue of special violin effects. Most of these were thought to have been invented only at a much later date, some not until the 20th Century! This work, with its precise bilingual (Italian/German) instructions for performance, is therefore important evidence for early violin technique. It describes playing in higher positions on the lower strings to create a special sound: at that time, higher positions were normally used only on the E string. "One moves the hand toward the bridge and begins . . . with the third finger on the prescribed note or tone." *Col legno* is described thus: 'These (notes) are produced by striking with the wood of the bow as if on a dulcimer, though one does not hold the bow still for long, but rather continues to move it'—the bow stick is probably supposed to bounce back as though from a drum. *Sul ponticello* (close to the bridge) is used by Farina to imitate wind instruments such as the fife and flute: "The flutes are imitated by slurring very sweetly, close to the bridge, about a finger's breadth away from it, like a lyre. The soldier's fife [effect] is similar, only that it is done somewhat stronger and closer to the bridge." A particularly common effect used in Baroque string playing, the bow vibrato, is used to imitate the organ's tremulant (organ register with a rhythmical vibrato): "The tremolo is played by pulsating the hand in which the bow is held, imitating the manner of the tremulant in organs."

The fingering technique was different from that of today in that high positions on low strings were avoided—the exceptions were bariolage passages, in which the change of tone color between the high positions on the low string and the open high string resulted in the desired sound effect. The use of open strings was by no means discouraged and in fact was often expressly called for; however, the open gut strings had a less penetrating sound than that of today's steel strings.

The Baroque Orchestra

In its tone colors and color mixtures, the orchestra in the first half of the 18th Century was like an exquisitely tuned "instrument." The individual voice groups were carefully related to each other in very specific proportions of strength. Like the registration of a Baroque organ, the specific tone colors of these groups played a decisive role in instrumentation: in the *tutti*, the basic texture was one of four or five voices, *varied* as to color by the addition or subtraction of instruments; the wind instruments and string instruments, therefore, played the same music. Obviously the special blend of sound is extremely important in this kind of instrumentation. For example, the mixed sound of oboes and violins is the backbone of the Baroque orchestra. This *colla parte* manner of writing was enlivened by concertante instrumental solos, with the various instrument groups (trumpets, flutes, oboes, strings) emerging singly from the blended sound of the *tutti* blocks—a practice which Bach used with great imagination.

The special features of late Baroque instrumentation cannot be replicated with a modern orchestra. Over the centuries, the individual instruments have changed greatly; most of them have become louder, and in all cases their timbre has been modified. If we were to hear a present-day orchestra using the same number of players found in a Baroque orchestra, a quite unbaroque sound would result. Modern instruments have simply not been designed for this register-like blended sound, but rather for the role which they assumed in the classical symphony orchestra, and especially during the Romantic period. But this was completely different: the composers of the 19th Century consistently wrote *obbligato* wind parts which float above a greatly increased string orchestra sound. The only relic of the old *colla parte* technique was the combination of contrabass-violoncello, which began to break up at the end of the 19th Century. The symphonic Bach sound of today's orchestra also influences the style of interpretation and makes it more difficult to comprehend the works themselves.

Paul Hindemith had a deep insight into the compositional methods of his great predecessors. In a speech given at the Hamburg Bach festival on September 12, 1950, he spoke about performance practices during Bach's lifetime and the way this practice is viewed today:

> "We still like to consider the small size of the orchestra as well as the sound and playing characteristics of the instruments which were customary at that time, as factors imposing intolerable restrictions on the composer... We have no evidence for such a notion... We need only study his [Bach's]

strictly orchestral scores, the suites and the Brandenburg concertos, to see how he relished the minutiae of distributing tonal weight among these small instrumental groups—an equilibrium that is often upset by doubling a few instruments, just as if the soprano lines of Pamina's aria [in Mozart's *Magic Flute*—ed.] were to be sung by a female chorus. We can rest assured that Bach felt quite at home with the vocal and instrumental stylistic means available to him. If it is important to us to present his music as he himself presented it, then we must reproduce the same performance conditions. This means that it is not enough to use a harpsichord as a continuo instrument. We must string our string instruments in a different way, and use wind instruments with the dimensions customary at the time..."

Hindemith's demands go far beyond that which is usually understood today as faithful rendition. Coming from the practical side, I have reached the same conclusions as Hindemith. Many concerts and years of experimentation with original instruments have demonstrated the very special sound conditions and balancing these instruments require.

Furthermore, these instruments were heard in halls with acoustical properties unlike those of modern concert halls. In the 17th and 18th Centuries, the resonance of music halls was much greater than we are accustomed to today, due to the stone floors, the height of the rooms and their marble paneling. These architectural characteristics lead to blending sounds together in a much more pronounced way. In such a hall, broken chords in fast notes, as found in almost all allegros of the time, sound like dramatically vibrating chords, rather than finely chiseled, as in modern concert halls.

The objection could be raised that tempos at that time were slower, which would counteract the "echoing" acoustics. Fortunately, we possess sources which establish the tempos of Baroque music with almost metronomical precision. One example is Quantz's flute method, in which tempo is related to the pulse beat; another is the tone technique of Père Engramelle, which expresses the duration of tones as units of length which can be easily converted. Thus, on the contrary, by studying these tempos, we come to the surprising conclusion that music was usually played much more briskly at the beginning of the 18th Century than we intuitively assume. The tempos today regarded as standard for the works of Bach or Handel are generally much too slow. This is probably due to our romantic monumentalization of this music, as well as the completely unjustified distrust of the technical abilities of musicians of that period.

Thus our grasp of "performance conditions of that time" leads to a new grasp of this music in general. The demands on the listener are just as great as those placed on the musician, since both must radically modify their musical views. We miss the modern scale of sounds, the colors and dynamics to which we have been accustomed since childhood. We must patiently train our ear to appreciate the unfamiliar, much softer sounds of early instruments, until we feel at home with them as well. Then a new (the old) world of characteristic and fine sound nuances will reveal itself: the true sound of Baroque music will become reality.

But what is the basic difference between the instrumentarium of the Baroque age and that of our own time? The *string instruments,* the nucleus of every ensemble, look almost exactly as they did 250 years ago, indeed, instruments from that period are still frequently played. In the 19th Century, however, they underwent far-reaching structural modifications to adapt them to new requirements, especially with regard to sound volume and tone color. Even though many master violins still in use today were built during the Baroque period, they really no longer are "Baroque violins." When the musical sound ideal radically changed around 1800, all string instruments then in use were rebuilt, mainly for the purpose of enhancing their volume. The result was the loud modern violin. The real "Baroque violin" is much softer, its sound clearer and richer in overtones. The instruments of Jacobus Stainer and his school corresponded very closely to the sound ideal of the German composers of the Baroque period. The Kapelle of Köthen, for which Bach wrote his violin concertos, had, for example, very expensive Tyrolean instruments, probably made by Stainer. These instruments were played with the short, light bows of the 18th Century. What we have said about the violin largely applies to the tonal character of the Baroque viola and violoncello as well.

Various wind instruments frequently joined this string group. As already observed, they almost never had their own part in a Baroque *tutti:* unlike the Classic or Romantic orchestra, the oboes played the same notes as the violins, and the bassoon followed the cello. Thus the addition of wind instruments was important to the Baroque orchestra only for the color they added to the piece, but hardly for the harmonic completeness of the composition.

Baroque *woodwinds* differ externally from modern instruments mainly in the smaller number of keys and in the fact that they are usually constructed of light brown boxwood. The taper of their internal bore is also different. These differences result in a completely different playing technique. Of the seven or eight holes, six are closed with the fingers, the others with keys. In theory, only a diatonic scale can be played on such an instrument, the basic scale of the instrument in question, which is at the same time its best key. One can also play in most other keys, but only by resorting to complicated "cross fingerings" with which all tones other than the basic scale have to be fingered. These tones sound quite different from those played with "open" fingering; they have a more veiled, indirect sound. Thus, in every key and every interval there is a constant interplay between covered and open sounds. This not only gives each of the different keys a characteristic quality, but also lends an iridescent brightness to the sound as a whole. This kind of tonal irregularity was not considered undesirable at that time. Not until the 19th Century was a conscious effort made to achieve a completely regular "chromatic" scale, or more precisely, a scale of twelve half-steps. The early wind instruments also require a completely different embouchure (flute) or reed (oboe and bassoon), since the high tones are produced not with octave keys, but by overblowing. All these various features, coupled with special playing techniques, result in the "Baroque sound," which, compared with modern instruments, is clearer and richer in overtones in the case of the oboes and bassoons and softer, mellower and more refined in the case of the transverse flute.

The wind instruments of the Baroque period were designed in such a way that they had their own unmistakable sound when used as solo instruments, but could also easily blend with other instruments of the same range, to produce a new blend of sound. Probably the best example of this is the *oboe*. (Remember: the combination of oboe and violin is the essence of the sound of the Baroque orchestra.) In addition to the standard oboes in C', there are also the *oboe d'amore* (in A) and the *oboe da caccia* (in F). Because of their special tone colors, these instruments were usually used for solos, but occasionally also doubled the middle voices of the string orchestra.

The *transverse flute* is a typical solo instrument, and there are very few orchestral works of the Baroque period in which it is used as a purely *tutti* instrument. In the most famous work composed for this instrument, the B Minor Overture, Bach achieves a unique new coloring in the orchestra when he doubles the flute with the violins *colla parte*. The special charm of the Baroque transverse flute lies in its "woody" tone and in the ongoing variation in tone color caused by switching back and forth between "open" and "forked" fingering.

The *Baroque bassoon* really sounds woody, almost "bowed" and reedy, since it has rather thin walls and the wood can vibrate. It is designed to blend ideally with the cello and the harpsichord in *basso continuo* playing, while at the same time providing clear delineation and contour for the bass.

Compositions for festive occasions called for *trumpets* and *kettle drums*. These, too, are usually incorporated into a four-voice texture and are generally only added to the oboes and violins for additional timbre. The trumpets differ noticeably from their modern counterparts, for, like the horns, early trumpets were strictly natural instruments, just a simple metal tube without valves of any kind. This tube ended in a bell and was blown through a cupped mouthpiece. The natural tones, the overtones of the fundamental which corresponded to the instrument's length, were produced by altering lip tension. Thus only the following tones could be produced on a natural trumpet in C:

(Everything sounds one tone higher on a D trumpet). Since the 11th partial f'', was too high and ". . . hovers between F and F-sharp, while rendering neither of these purely, and could therefore be called a musical hermaphrodite . . ." (Altenburg, *Trompetenkunst,* 1795), and the 13th, a'', was too low, attempts were made to compensate for these impurities either with the embouchure or by making a transposition hole to be closed by the thumb. This raised the whole instrument by a fourth; now f'' and a'' became the fourth and fifth partials and could therefore be played in tune. This construction, rediscovered by O. Steinkopf, was also used for the instruments of our ensemble, *Concentus musicus.* The shape of the tubing, either circular or straight, had always varied: "some have their trumpets built like a post horn, others like a snake, all coiled up" (Praetorius 1619). The basic structural difference between the natural trumpet and the modern valve trumpet is their different scaling, i.e. the ratio between cross-section and length. A modern C trumpet is only half as long as a natural trumpet with about the same cross-section, since the greater distance between the tones of the second and third octaves are bridged by valves. This also explains the great difference in sound, since the long air column of the natural trumpet refines and softens its tone, making it a better partner for other Baroque instruments.

The kettle drums always accompany the trumpets in both Baroque and classic orchestral writing; this practice goes back to a time when trumpeters and kettle drummers were military musicians whose fanfare provided the necessary dazzle and commanded respect for the arrival of important personages. The shape of the Baroque kettle drum of the 18th Century was unlike that of its modern descendant. Its shallow, steeply-walled kettles were covered with relatively thick skins. They were played with wooden or ivory sticks (without felt!), "which were turned [on a lathe] in the shape of a little wheel" ("welche fornen in einer Rädlins Form gedrähet"). Daniel Speer, *Grundrichtiger Unterricht,* 1687). These drumsticks did not produce the full, voluminous sound of modern drums, but one that was thin and clear, and which distinctly accentuated the trumpet chord. The drum roll, so frequently heard in Bach's music, was not done with rapid single beats, but made use of the same springy tapping as on the small drum to produce a characteristically sustained, snare-like tone.

Beyond this standard instrumentarium of the Baroque orchestra, there were other instruments which were used only for special purposes. The horns, used only for the hunt until the end of the 17th Century, began to be used in art music as well, after about 1700. At first, composers integrated typical horn motifs from hunting music into their works. But the potential of the natural horn for producing romantic-cantabile melodies was soon discovered, the tones between the natural tones being produced by "stopping," with the left hand, which created attractive changes in tone color.

The *harpsichord* was the "soul" of the Baroque orchestra. It not only assisted the musicians in maintaining their rhythm, since they usually played without a conductor, but as a continuo instrument it also filled out the harmonies, either chordally or polyphonically. However, in order to emphasize the bass line in *tutti* passages, the gamba, violoncello, contrabass and occasionally the bassoon doubled the lowest line of the harpsichord part.

The harpsichord is basically an historical instrument whose evolution ended in the 18th Century. Since by its very nature it possesses no dynamic capabilities, the player has to use the finest agogic nuances to achieve any expression and song-like quality (on this instrument, too, cantabile playing was the highest goal). The individual tone of the harpsichord has to sound so interesting and vital that the listener is content without variety of timbre. Historical harpsichords, many of which are still very playable, meet this requirement perfectly: their sound is full and clear, and they often have several sets of strings, two at the normal pitch ("eight-foot pitch") and one an octave higher ("four-foot pitch"). These "registers" are intended to provide nuances to solo and *tutti* playing (there is a louder and weaker register); the addition of the octave provides soloistic brilliance and the combination of the two eight-foot registers allows the tone to sing more fully. These combinations should be used to clarify the formal structure of the work; ordinarily, entire movements are to be played with one single registration.

This principle, which is the vital nerve of the harpsichord and of harpsichord music, was often forgotten by instrument makers and players when the harpsichord was rediscovered and reborn in this century. They tried to transfer the "accrued experience of piano manufacture" to the construction of the harpsichord, by building the instrument, which was originally closed (like a violin) in the shape of a box, like a piano: as a frame with a soundboard stretched across it. The enclosed air space, which had refined and blended the sound, was thus missing. Then, a sub-octave (16 foot) was added to the three basic registers, which only detracted from the fullness of the other registers. Having misunderstood the principle of the harpsichord's sound and harpsichord playing, the sounds of the registers were now differentiated as much as possible. The register mechanism was shifted to the pedals, which enabled the player to create a pseudo-dynamic by frequently changing registers. (This is probably necessary on these instruments because the change diverts attention from their poor sound.) These modern instruments are, oddly enough, much softer and are usually heard only as a vague, metallic noise in the orchestra. The sound of the modern harpsichords normally used today bears absolutely no resemblance to that of the original models. An old harpsichord or a first-class copy can take its place at the center of an ensemble because of its brilliant and intense sound. Along with changes in hall acoustics a shift in balance (harpsichord too soft, strings and horns too loud) is probably one of the most drastic departures from the original sound ideal...

From the standpoint of dynamics, a Baroque orchestra might well be compared to a Baroque organ, with the individual instruments and groups of instruments being used like the registers or stops of an organ. By adding or taking away different instrumental groups, the dynamic structure is modified in the continuous four-part texture. This "play of tonal groups" is used above all to clarify formal structure; it makes piano-forte effects possible, as well as rich micro-dynamics, but not the classical *crescendo*.

In general, the sound of the Baroque orchestra is much softer, but sharper, more aggressive and more colorful than that of the modern orchestra. The sound of individual instruments is much more clearly defined than in the modern orchestra, which came into existence to meet the musical requirements of the 19th Century. Similarly, the typical Baroque organ differs from the organs built during the height of the Romantic period in analogous ways.

The Relationship Between "Words" and Tones in Baroque Instrumental Music

From very early times, an attempt was made to use music to represent extra-musical programs. This marginal concern of music is broad based; the most varied types and methods intermingle and cannot always be clearly differentiated. Nonetheless, four major approaches can be identified: (1) acoustic imitation, (2) musical representation of visual images, (3) musical portrayal of thoughts and emotions and (4) music as speech. The particular fascination that such music holds is that all of this must be depicted without the use of a text, by purely musical means.

The most primitive, but perhaps most entertaining form, is the simple imitation of animal sounds by the use of specific musical instruments. This device has been used with obvious enjoyment by composers from the 13th Century on, through the English "nightingale music" around 1600 to many French, Italian and German composers, including Beethoven, Richard Strauss and even later composers. The rendering of visual images in music is decidedly more complicated. However, over the centuries, musical formulas were developed which evoke certain associations, thus building a bridge between the visual image and the music. A third category of program music is devoted to rendering thoughts and ideas musically by using more complicated associations. But here the boundaries separating program music from so-called absolute music become blurred, particularly in Baroque music. After all, Baroque music always means to make a statement, to represent and evoke at least a general feeling or *Affekt*. And finally, "speaking in tones," played a fundamental role in music from about 1650 to 1850.

The Hamburg music director and legation secretary Johann Mattheson, one of the most cultured and brilliant observers of his time, called music "the language of those who are blessed for all eternity." Several quotations from Neidthart, Quantz and Mattheson in the first decades of the 18th Century underscore just how literally he meant the term "language": "The ultimate purpose of music is to excite all the emotions through the tones and their rhythm alone, in the manner of the best speaker" (Neidthart). "Music is nothing other than an artificial language" (Quantz). "If one wants to stir others through harmonies, one must be able to express all the feelings of the heart, by skillfully combining selected sounds, without words, so that the listener is able to fully comprehend and clearly understand the thrust, the meaning, the purpose and the emphasis with all relevant segments and paragraphs as if it were an actual speech. Only then is it a pleasure! ... Instrumental melody ... endeavors to say as much without the help of words and voices as voices do with words.... Our musical structures differ from the rhetorical devices of pure speech only in their plan, themes or objects: therefore they must observe the same six elements that are prescribed for a speaker: introduction, statement, proposition, argument, refutation and conclusion" (Mattheson).

Almost all theoretical and didactic treatises from the first half of the 18th Century devote many chapters to musical rhetoric and apply the special terminology of rhetoric to music. A repertory of formulaic expressions (musical figures) was available for portraying emotions and for "figures of speech"; a vocabulary of musical possibilities, so to speak. Purely vocal forms like recitative and arioso were frequently imitated instrumentally; it was not hard to imagine an accompanying text. This final mannerist stage had been preceded by a long evolution that began with the emancipation of instrumental music. The first Venetian instrumental canzonas prior to 1600 were strongly influenced by the French chanson, although a certain motivic vocabulary, which was borrowed from one genre by the other can probably not be understood as direct quotation. Nor does the use of Gregorian or secular *cantus firmi,* which appeared especially in French and English instrumental music before 1600, usually show any connection between the text of the *cantus firmus* and its new form. I am thinking here of the *In nomine* fantasies of English viol music or the fantasies by Du Caurroy on sacred and secular *cantus firmi.* Genuine associations with meaning or action, which are a characteristic of "speaking" instrumental music, were probably first found in program music, i.e. in the musical descriptions of battles and in portrayals of nature with imitations of the hunt and of animals. These pieces are usually structured in a rather primitive way, are highly pictorial, and hardly make a *progressively developing statement.* The earliest instrumental works in which music attempts to speak on a higher plane, to make a particular statement, are probably the English *funerals* and French *tombeaux* of the 17th and 18th Centuries. Borrowing from the elegies written on the deaths of notable personages, these pieces make a clearly recognizable statement, the organization of which remained basically unchanged for more than 100 years: introduction (this person has died)—personal response (mourning)—emotional intensification to the point of despair—consolation (the deceased is enjoying eternal bliss)—concluding statement (similar to the introduction). A more or less definite repertory of figures developed at a very early stage in works of this type; the model for these *tombeaux* was undoubtedly the funeral oration organized according to the rules of rhetoric.

A strange form of virtually texted instrumental music is found in the *alternatim* practice in the mass. Here, the organ was used and accepted relatively early as a bona fide substitute for one of the singing groups in the antiphonal exchange between priest, cantors and congregation. A textless discourse is readily understood, if only because of its connection to pre-existing chorale melodies and the resulting intelligibility of "tonal discourse." Marc Antoine Charpentier went one step further in his *Messe pour plusieurs Instruments;* using a constant antiphony between the clergy and a large Baroque orchestra, he surpassed the model of *alternatim* singing. In some sections, the *cantus firmus* is actually omitted or embellished beyond the point of recognition. The "Gloria," for example, is described as follows: "The celebrant intones 'Gloria in excelsis Deo,' all the instruments answer immediately; then, 'et in terra'; 'laudamus te' (clergy), 'benedicimus te' (oboes); 'adoramus te' (clergy), 'glorificamus te' (violins); 'gratias' (clergy), 'Domine Deus' (recorders); 'Domine fili' (clergy), 'Domine Deus agnus Dei' (all wind instruments); 'qui tollis' (clergy); 'qui tollis' (all violins, oboes and flutes...)" etc.

Another form of concrete textual expression in instrumental music is the quotation. A familiar motive from a vocal work is incorporated into an instrumental work and often has a symbolic or cryptic meaning. The very basis of tonal discourse is probably related to this conscious quotation, and is at the same time its vocabulary, as it were: the repertory of figures. These figures are more or less fixed sequences of tones which were used in the 17th Century in recitative and solo singing for certain words and expressive content. Separated from their text, these motifs were then used as purely instrumental figures, but were able to evoke the original meaning or feeling in the listener by association. The content of tonal discourse was thus much more concrete than we like to think, a fact which is also documented in the sources.

It was clearly understood by instrumentalists in the 17th and much of the 18th Century that their music was always expected to "speak." After all, rhetoric with its complicated terminology was included in every school curriculum and, like music, was considered part of a proper education. And since the doctrine of the affections had been an essential component of Baroque music from the very beginning—the objective was to arouse certain emotions in the performer, in order to communicate them to the listener—there was a natural link between music and rhetoric. Even though music was virtually an international language, like pantomime or the art of gesture, various national rhythms of speech, which certainly contributed to the formation of different styles, are clearly recognized.

Theorists occasionally stress that the composer and the performer do not need to be aware that they are observing basic rhetorical principles; after all, one need not know grammatical rules to master one's mother tongue. Any violation of the rules is instinctively felt to be wrong, whether or not the rules themselves are consciously known. The matter-of-factness with which composers and interpreters assumed that their audience understood their "tonal discourse" amazes us, since both musicians and listeners today often have great difficulty with this very understanding.

This is because musical life today is fundamentally different from that of the Baroque age. We play and listen to music from four or five centuries, sometimes at one and the same concert, and we are told *so* often that true art is timeless, that we casually and without the necessary knowledge compare works from the most widely differing periods. The listener of the Baroque period, on the other hand, heard only the latest music, and since musicians of the time only played the latest music, it is clear that the nuances of this musical language were well understood by both parties.

Unfortunately, we have often been told that music which "says something" is inferior to "pure," absolute music. However, if we knew that, in fact, the music of the Baroque and, to some extent, the Classic period "speaks," if we no longer felt contempt for musical statement, we might well have a deeper understanding of and appreciation for speaking music.

From Baroque to Classicism

Even today the music of the Baroque and Classic periods is usually viewed through the eyes of the late 19th Century, and so it is played in this way, as well. To be sure, efforts have been made, and are still being made, to modernize the interpretation, for example by disregarding all performance traditions and relying exclusively on the written notation: one plays exactly what is written down and only what is written down—, and other "reform attempts" exist, as well. But basically one style of interpretation has been used for the performance of everything from the early Baroque to the late Romantic: a style that was designed for and is excellently suited to the music of the late 19th and early 20th Centuries, for Tchaikovsky, Richard Strauss and Stravinsky.

Throughout the world, attempts are being made to find a new language for Baroque music, or better, to rediscover its old language, or better still, that which we believe the old language to have been; for we cannot *know* what Baroque music sounded like, so long as no one appears from that period to either applaud or condemn our efforts. But why specifically Baroque music? It is simply that this music differs so obviously in diction, in basic musical structures, that a few musicians inevitably realized what an intolerable gulf existed between the music itself and the way in which it was being interpreted. The differences between compositions of the late 19th Century and the age of Bach are so great that different methods of interpretation are the only possible solution. Intensive study of these questions has led many musicians to adopt a new musical language for the age of Bach; a musical vocabulary that has proven to be extremely convincing. True, each and every discovery has also provoked controversy, and it will probably be some time before the matter is ultimately settled; but at least things are finally moving in the field of Baroque music performance. It is no longer thought that everything is written in stone, and the presumptuousness and arrogance of some interpreters, an attitude solely due to a lack of understanding tradition, have largely been replaced by an attitude of interested inquiry.

Oddly enough, the new approaches to interpretation which have been and are being adopted for Baroque music end abruptly with the music of Viennese classicism. Every musician and listener knows, of course, that there is a large, unmistakable stylistic threshold here. Almost no one hesitates to attribute a work to one or the other style; concert-goers will immediately hear whether a work reflects the style of Bach or Haydn. They will be aware of stylistic differences even if the works belong to the same period, for even during Bach's lifetime, there were composers in Vienna and Mannheim who composed works in the new "gallant" or Rococo style which listeners, not well acquainted with musical theory, would automatically attribute to Haydn's early period. It was during this overlapping transition from Baroque to Classicism—I am applying these concepts only to the field of music—that social and cultural upheavals took place, in the wake of which, as I have already explained, the function of music also changed. It was now expected to appeal to the uneducated classes as well. The difference between a work of the late Baroque period and one from the Classic period is that in the Classic work, melody is the primary element. Melodies had to be simple and ingratiating, their accompaniment as simple as possible. The listener was to be addressed on the level of his emotions, so that no specialized knowledge was required as was the case in Baroque music. In terms of musical substance, this turn actually represented a decline which was halted only at a later date by the masterpieces of Haydn and Mozart. Thus for the first time, music was addressed to listeners who did not need to "understand" what they heard. The prevalent view today that music does not need to be understood (if I like it, if it speaks to my emotions, if I feel something, then it is good) originated during this time as a result of this attitude.

Thus, on the boundary between Baroque and Classicism we are also on the boundary between music that is hard and music that is easy to understand. The greater simplicity of Classic music has given us to believe that there is nothing here one ought to know and understand, and this has hampered our efforts to master the vocabulary appropriate to it.

We must proceed on the assumption that Classic music was played by musicians and written for listeners who did not know the music of Schubert and Brahms, but who came rather from the "Baroque" idiom. In other words, Classic music contains a good deal of Baroque vocabulary, so everything that distinguished Classic music from the music that preceded it was—from the viewpoint of contemporaries— new, special, intriguing. This is not so for us at all. With Schubert, Brahms and all the later composers in our ears, we hear the music of the Classic period quite differently than did the listeners of that period. What was exciting and new for them has been repeated a thousand times and is old to us; moreover, it has been "surpassed" by the harmonic and dynamic innovations of subsequent periods. Having been exposed to later charms, we can no longer react innocently and spontaneously to Classic music's orginal charms. It makes no sense to try to interpret Classic music based on our understanding of the Romantic period, because this route only deprives Classic music of its true language and impact.

Since our musical concepts seem to stem from the Romantic period, it is hard for us to appreciate the need to *understand* music. If it is not immediately obvious to us it is not so interesting, not so good. But what would happen if we were to learn the vocabulary needed to understand Classic music? Perhaps this would not be so difficult, perhaps if we learned just a few basics we would hear many things in a new way. This would avoid that erosion connected with the wrong approach via Romanticism; after two hundred years, we could come to a new understanding of the music of Classicism, based on our understanding of the music of the preceding age. This approach seems to me much more natural and more effective—and once again possible.

Up to this point, we have not included Classicism in our questions dealing with performance practice, because we believed that the world of interpretation in this area was still intact; here everything was fine, no rethinking was necessary, everything could remain as it was. Unfortunately—or rather, fortunately—in recent years we have come to see that this is not so. For even though present-day interpretation of Classic music seems farther than ever from the intentions of the Classic composers, there is nonetheless a deep uncertainty and uneasiness,—a growing feeling that we are on the wrong road, that the old view, which dictated that this music must be represented *only* in terms of the emotions or *only* from the written notation, is not right for all periods. It is not far to the further insight that we must find new—or old—ways of interpreting and understanding music.

We must also recognize that listeners once had a completely different attitude toward experiencing music. They wanted to hear only what was *new,* music which they had never heard before. Composers were aware that a work could not be presented repeatedly to the same audience. There was vastly more interest in the work itself than in its rendition; critics reserved most of their comments for the piece, devoting only casual attention to its performance—whereas today usually only the details of performance are discussed and compared. The *meaning* of a familiar work is hardly touched on any longer.

Formerly, a piece was considered interesting only when new; thereafter it was put aside and for centuries served primarily as study material for later composers. No one, not even the composer himself, thought of performing it again at a later date. We know that Beethoven, Mozart and even Bach took great interest in the works of their predecessors, that they studied the techniques used by these composers, but it would never have occurred to them to perform these works as they were intended to be performed by the original composer. If a performance was desired for one reason or another, it was taken for granted that the work would be radically modernized. Mozart did this with music of Handel at the request of the avid historian Van Swieten, clothing Handel's works in authentically Mozartian garb. We would have to imagine saying: "Now wouldn't it be interesting to hear how something by Brahms would sound today? Stockhausen should write a performable score of a work, something that would be worthy of the attention of a modern audience; for, of course, it is no longer possible to listen to the music of Brahms just as he wrote it 100 years ago." That is about what the attitude of earlier audiences was toward older music. Simply reopen the concert programs of the late 18th and 19th Centuries. Every premiere, every first night up to the time of Tchaikovsky, Bruckner and Strauss, was the latest thing; these were the great events which captivated the musical world at the time—not the revivals of old works. Of course, old music was sometimes included in concert programs, too (around 1700, music older than five years was called by its proper title: "old"), but contemporary music formed the core of musical life until the end of the 19th Century.

The attitude of the 19th Century toward historical music is illustrated by the following anecdote: Joachim, the famous violinist and friend of Schumann and Brahms, found Mozart's *Sinfonia Concertante* for violin and viola in a library. He wrote to Clara Schumann that he had just discovered a musical jewel, though of course something like this could no longer be performed in public. Nonetheless, for a connoisseur it was simply wonderful to read, and perhaps they could play through it together some time. In the 19th Century, works by Beethoven and Mozart, and occasionally rather wild arrangements of Bach and Handel, were increasingly being performed. But these occasions represented only a very small segment of musical life—everything else was up to date, brand new music!

By virtue of his public performance of Bach's *St. Matthew Passion* in 1829, Mendelssohn retrieved early music from the domain of the antiquarian. With a true Romantic love for anything old, he discovered, probably quite unexpectedly, passionate music from earliest musical pre-history. The idea that such music could not only be used as a source for research, but could actually be performed again, was not possible until the Romantic period. Mendelssohn's performance of the *St. Matthew Passion* was regarded by his contemporaries as a musical sensation, an unrepeatable exception. By the way, *none* of the listeners had ever heard this work performed before, so we have reviews which describe the thrilling and unprecedented impact that this music made.

I explained above that an understanding of the music of the Classic period must be based on the preceding epoch and on the old Baroque vocabulary. Among the most important musical devices which were carried over from the Baroque into the Classic period were all manner of long and short, stressed and unstressed appoggiaturas. The long appoggiatura has a harmonic, the unstressed, short appoggiatura a rhythmical function. All appoggiaturas are written in small notes placed before their "main notes" and the musician has to know from the context what kind of appoggiatura is to be used and where. Normally it is long when placed on a consonance; it is dissonant, causing a "pleasurable pain," which is resolved by the main note in a consonance, a sense of well-being. The interpretation is largely to be found in the old vocabulary of Baroque music, for it was quite clear to a musician of that period that the dissonance itself had to be played loudly, its resolution softly. It seems quite obvious after hearing it a few times. This old principle of the appoggiatura was adopted by the generation after Bach. In his treatise on violin playing, published in 1756 but in many ways anticipating the new age, Leopold Mozart writes that the appoggiatura was used to make singing or a song more interesting and to enliven it with dissonance. No peasant, he claimed, would sing a simple country song without appoggiaturas, and to prove his point he wrote a melody with appoggiaturas which "any peasant might sing." I have shown this song to several musicians who were not peasants, but well-trained professionals,—yet none of them added these appoggiaturas. We might conclude from this that peasants of Mozart's time were more musical than musicians of today. Or at least that things which were taken for granted in the past can be completely alien to us today.

The appoggiaturas were thus adapted to the new style, although their meaning and notation were greatly altered. One of the original reasons for the notation as "appoggiatura" (German *Vorschlag* = before the beat), written as small additional notes, was that one wanted to write a *"correct" setting*, where dissonances which were "written out" in certain places would have been incorrect; the appoggiatura indicated the dissonance to be played. But as the rules of musical orthography were gradually relaxed, the tendency was to write how something was really supposed to sound. Thus many appoggiaturas came to be written as regular notes. As such, they can no longer be *seen,* although they can still be heard.

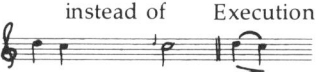

The old rules governing the interpretation of appoggiaturas now have to be applied to these written out appoggiaturas; it is especially important that a musician be able to recognize them. Countless mistakes are made in present-day performances because written appoggiaturas do not look different from "normal" notes.

Those 18th-Century treatises which discuss appoggiaturas say that it is very difficult to perform them correctly, especially when they are written like regular notes rather than as small notes above the main notes. It may even happen that a player does not recognize the appoggiatura and adds yet another one. (This is frequently done today by inexperienced musicians.) Leopold Mozart said that this is done only by "half-witted musicians." This failure to recognize appoggiaturas causes a chain reaction of mistakes in interpretation. It is hard to imagine how different a Classic work sounds when the appoggiaturas are recognized and played, as compared with when they are not. The character of a piece can be totally altered.

The most important rule in performing appoggiaturas is that the appoggiatura should never be separated from its main note. This is also quite logical. It is a dissonance which should never be separated from its resolution—as a tension should not be separated from its relaxation. And because this was so obvious, the tie which was supposed to link the appoggiatura and its resolution was only rarely indicated in the score; the composer *expected* the musician to link the appoggiatura to its resolution as a matter of course. Today a composer can no longer take this knowledge for granted, because we have accustomed ourselves to playing the *notes* and not the music which they are intended to express. A musician who has not been warped by doctrinal notions would never conceive of the idea of not connecting a resolution to its related dissonance. But when he is told by his teacher that the composer has not written a slur and that therefore the learner should not connect the notes either, he will gradually come to believe that the notes should not be tied, and, contrary to his own musical intuition, he will separate them. This has reached such a point that it is rare to hear a Mozart symphony in which these ties are correctly played. We hardly ever hear that the resolution results from the dissonance; rather, it is stressed anew and a new phrase is very often begun at this very point.

Music can lose its meaning this way, just as language can if we mix up the punctuation in a given sentence, moving commas and periods. When we then read the text, it no longer holds any meaning. In my opinion, an understanding of the appoggiatura is one of the most important links between performance practice in the Baroque and Classic periods. In the music of late Romanticism, the musician should play only what is written. But if this is done in a symphony by Mozart, where some basic things were *not* written down because contemporary musicians knew them, only a meaningless stammering will result.

Another device adopted by Classic music from the Baroque involves repeated notes. These always have a special meaning. They are forbidden in strict part-writing. In early music (prior to 1600), they appear only in onomatopoeia and when a tone is divided into syllables. Repeated notes were an invention of Monteverdi, who in the *Combattimento di Tancredi e Clorinda* consciously divided a whole note into sixteen short notes to express the emotional state of anger. From that point on, repeated notes were only used to achieve certain effects, usually having to do with heightened emotional states, in keeping with Monteverdi's original concept. Many Classic symphony movements are composed over stereotypical repeated eighth-notes in the basses, which results in a very strong feeling of excitement and tension emanating from the accompaniment. This is seldom understood today, because repeated notes are for us simply repetitions of the tone or the chord and do not express anything. In Classic music today, endlessly repeated eighth or sixteenth-notes are often played as if they were simple eighth or sixteenth-notes and not affective repeated notes, demanding tension and excitement from listener and player alike. This departure inevitably affects the interpretation. In Baroque music, similar repeated notes are frequently found in the *concitato,* which uses and continues Monteverdi's discovery in the *recitativo accompagnato.*

In addition to the types just described, another very subtle type of repeated notes has existed since the beginning of the 17th Century; it approximates *vibrato.* Like every repeated note, it is a device of expression. Italian organs of the 16th Century had a register which gave each tone a rhythmically fluctuating sound produced by two pipes, which were slightly out of tune with each other. Because of its similarity to the slightly vibrating singing voice, this register was called *voce umana.* Shortly after 1600 this sound was borrowed by string music, where it was called *tremolo* or *tremolando* and notated thus: ♩♩♩♩ It is frequently and precisely described as bow vibrato. The "pulsating" pressure of the bow is used to produce waves of loud and soft tones, although the tone should never be interrupted. The same effect is called *frémissement* in the case of wind instruments, and is a kind of rhythmic vibrato executed only by diaphragm breathing without any tonguing. This very effective device was used mainly in soft passages in the accompanying voices. It almost always suggests sadness, pain and suffering. As with most expressive devices, countless variations are possible, from almost inaudible fluctuation to staccato. Some composers try to express these by using various kinds of notation. Bow vibrato and *frémissement* were prescribed for almost two centuries by almost all composers. Unfortunately they are usually no longer recognized; the notation is misunderstood as a mere bowing instruction, forgetting that in the 17th and 18th Centuries no technical bowing instructions existed, though every sign indicated the composer's demands for articulation or enunciation.

Origin and Development of Music as Speech (*Klangrede*)

About 1600, toward the middle of Monteverdi's life, a truly revolutionary change occurred in Western music, such as had never happened before and never since. Until then, music was primarily poetry that had been set to music; sacred or secular lyrics, motets and madrigals were composed with their musical expression based on the overall mood of the poem. What inspired the composer was not the idea of transmitting the *text* as such—the spoken words—to the listener, but the textual meaning, or simply the feeling of the poetry. Thus a love poem, for example,—the words of one lover—was composed so abstractly in a polyphonic madrigal that the person speaking became an artifice. No one thought of naturalistic discourse or dialogue. Indeed, the text could hardly be understood, since the various voices were usually composed in imitation of each other, so that different words were sung at the same time. These polyphonic compositions, without their text, also formed an extensive repertoire of instrumental music; they were then simply adapted by musicians for various instruments. This vocal/instrumental music was the generally accepted basis of the whole of musical life and repertoire. It was an end stage without any discernible potential for further development: it could have gone on this way indefinitely.

But suddenly, out of a clear blue sky, musicians came up with the idea of making language itself, including dialogue, the basis of music. Such music had to be dramatic, for dialogue is by its very nature dramatic: its content is based on argument, persuasion, questioning, negation, conflict. The midwife of this idea was, of course, classical antiquity, as was to be expected at that time. A passionate interest in antiquity led to the view that Greek drama had been sung, not declaimed. In circles of lovers of antiquity an effort was undertaken to revive ancient tragedies, intending to be completely faithful to the originals. The most famous of these circles was the "Camerata" of Counts Corsi and Bardi in Florence, in which Caccini, Peri and Galilei (the father of the astronomer) set the tone as musicians. The first operas of Peri and Caccini had wonderful librettos but were rather ordinary musically; however, the ideas which underlay them led to a completely "new music"—*Nuove Musiche*—(the title of Caccini's polemical and programmatic work). They pointed the way to Baroque music, to speaking music.

To be sure, what we read about Caccini in most music reference works is quite removed from what he himself wrote. He is usually described as the master of ornamented Baroque singing; but if we study his writings, which are much more interesting than anything which has been written about him, we find that he describes quite new forms of expression; a strong aura radiating from the singer is most important to him. He recommends that coloraturas and ornamentation of all types be used *only* in those places where they reinforce verbal expression, or to compensate for a singer's lack of stage presence. (Ornaments were not invented because they are *necessary* for good singing, he says, but rather as ear-tickling for those who are not capable of performing with passionate intensity.) What was essentially new in these ideas was that a text, often a dialogue, was basically set for one voice, with the rhythm and melody of speech being followed precisely and naturalistically. The only important consideration was to render the text as clearly as possible and with the greatest expressiveness. The music had to remain completely in the background; its only task was to provide an inconspicuous harmonic backdrop. Everything which had previously been regarded as the essential musical element was rejected as being overly distracting. Only in very intense passages were the words underscored by a corresponding, often exceedingly crass musical-harmonic insertion. This new form contained almost no word repetition, in contrast to the madrigal, where words and groups of words are often repeated. In real dialogue, after all, words are repeated only if the listener has missed something, or when particular emphasis on the words is needed—a practice used in the new music, which was called monody. Caccini's colleague Galilei explained in detail how the modern composer should proceed. He should listen to how people of various social classes speak with each other in all kinds of real situations, listen to how conversations or discussions are carried out between those of high and those of low station, and note how such discussions sound! These exercises will reveal to the composer precisely what he should set to music. (This is by the way, exactly the way in which the original performance style of Greek drama was conceived.) Significantly enough, this new style was not developed by composers with classical training, but by dilettantes and singers.

Such ideas were absolutely new, and certainly must have been quite shocking. In order to grasp just how novel they were, we have to imagine ourselves alive in those days. Let us assume that we are about 30 years old, and from childhood we have never heard any music other than the wonderful madrigals of Marenzio, the young Monteverdi and the Flemish composers: highly esoteric and complex polyphonic music. Now suddenly someone propounds the notion that the way people *speak* is in and of itself music, that it is the true music. Of course, this could only have happened in Italy, where the language actually does sound melodramatic. We need only listen to conversation in an Italian marketplace or listen to Italian trial lawyers summing up their arguments to understand what Caccini and Galilei were talking about: all that is lacking are a few chords on a lute or harpsichord to complete the monody, the *recitative*. For music lovers whose madrigal dream was shattered by monody, this new music, as we have said, must have come as a shock, a shock much greater than that caused 80 years ago with the introduction of atonal music.

Caccini claimed that counterpoint was the work of the devil, that it only made music incomprehensible. The accompaniment must be so simple that one does not listen to it; dissonances should be placed on certain words only to emphasize their expression. The parts of Caccini's book *Nuove Musiche* relating to language, the melody of speech and accompaniment are critical to the development of opera and the recitative, as well as the sonata. Caccini distinguished three types of speech-song: *recitar cantando, cantar recitando* and *cantare*—or singing speech, speech-song, and singing. The first corresponds to the normal recitative, thus is more speech than song and is also extremely naturalistic. Cantar recitando, or speaking or declaiming singing, stresses singing somewhat more and corresponds approximately to the *recitativo accompagnato*. Cantare means singing, which corresponds to the aria.

We must always keep in mind the radical newness of these views, they were a bolt from the blue. Only very infrequently in the history of the arts does something absolutely new, lacking any clear precedent, emerge. (I find it noteworthy that this new departure was developed by those who believed they were reconstructing something very old, i.e. the music of the ancient Greeks.) This formulation became the foundation for the musical development which followed over the next two centuries, of what I like to describe as speaking music.

The sensational idea of speech-song only became truly interesting for our music and for us as musicians when it was taken up by a musical genius. Monteverdi was the greatest madrigal composer of his time and prior to his work in this form he had mastered the finest details of counterpoint. When he applied his superb mastery of the techniques of composition to the primitive field of musical speaking, he engendered a genuine cataclysm, musically as well as culturally. Monteverdi did not, of course, fully accept the theories and dogmas of the Caccini circle. As a full-blooded musician, he could not believe that counterpoint was the work of the devil nor that music should not be interesting because it would detract from a text. Although Monteverdi was inspired by the new ideas, he could not accept the associated dogma so he sought for new avenues of expression. When he first began to concern himself with opera around 1605, he set about to systematically develop a vocabulary for his musical dramas. In 1607, he wrote *L'Orfeo,* a year later *Ariana* (of which, unfortunately, only the famous *Lamento* is preserved) and from that time on, almost every one or two-part short piece, every duet or trio which he wrote was a kind of experiment, a small opera scene, a kind of mini-opera. In this way, he systematically worked towards his great operas. Monteverdi himself tells us just how aware he was of what he was doing. A highly educated man, a friend of Tasso and familiar with the classical and contemporary philosophers, he knew exactly why he was doing anything. With the greatest care he searched for a musical expression for every affect or emotional state, for every human sentiment, for each word, each linguistic formula.

A famous example of his systematic search is contained in the *Combattimento di Tancredi e Clorinda,* a scene composed in 1624. For this scene Monteverdi carefully selected a text with which he could express the state of violent anger. He said: "But since I could not find an example for an impassioned mental state in the music of earlier composers . . . and since I also knew that opposites move our souls the most, something which good music should also do, . . . I began with all my energy to search for a passionate form of expression . . . In the description of the struggle between Tancred and Clorinda I found the opposites which seemed right for transposing into music: war, prayer, death."

Now as a musician I must immediately ask myself: Is this true? Is it really so? Did music prior to 1623 provide no means of expressing states of great excitement? Was it perhaps not even necessary prior to this time? Supply, after all, follows demand. And so it is: the lyric art of the madrigal contains no outbursts of rage, no states of great excitement, neither positive nor negative. They were evidently not needed by the madrigal. On the other hand, they are *absolutely* necessary for dramatic action. So Monteverdi looked to Plato, and found repeated notes. He said: "I therefore investigated the fast tempos, which according to the leading philosophers originated in an excited, martial mood . . . Then I found the effect that I was looking for. To accompany words that expressed anger, I divided the whole note into sixteenths, which are individually struck."

He called his manner of expressing greatly agitated emotional states *stile concitato.* From this point on, tone repetition or "concitato" became a familiar musical device. It was still used in exactly the way Monteverdi described it in the 17th and 18th Centuries, both the term and the method. Handel and even Mozart used the same form of tone repetition. Monteverdi writes that at first the musicians objected to playing the same tone sixteen times in one bar. They probably felt insulted in being required to do something that seemed so musically senseless. After all, tone repetitions are frowned upon in strict part-writing. He first had to explain to them that this device had an extra-musical meaning relating both to drama and to the human body.

The concitato introduced a new, previously unknown element into music: a purely dramatic, physical element. This brings us to an important aspect of musical drama. It is impossible to imagine drama and dialogue without action; which includes mime, gesture and movement of the entire body. We speak with every fibre of our body. Just as the newly invented dramatic tone language of Monteverdi explained and intensified the meaning of the word, it also replicated what happens in a bodily sense. Thus Monteverdi became the first great musical dramatist to compose gesture, thereby prescribing a large part of the stage directions. In my view, true musical drama exists only when all of the above elements, including the physical, are present.

Now there are certain affective words that constantly recur in the texts of operas and madrigals. These words are linked to certain similar musical figures. Thus a musical repertory of figures was slowly formed, building on the teachings of Caccini and his friends and put into practice by Monteverdi who brought it to its peak of perfection. He went so far as to give the same words a different expression by means of differing figures. In this way, the same word took on a somewhat different meaning, depending on its context. Thus linguistic interpretation was determined to a very large extent by the composer. Not until Mozart and later Verdi do we again encounter composers who follow the same practice.

An immense vocabulary of figures each possessed of a specific meaning ultimately resulted from the work of this first generation of operatic composers, figures which were familiar to every educated listener. Thus the reverse was also possible—this repertoire of figures could be used independently, without any words: the listener makes the verbal association through the musical figure. This adaptation for instrumental music of what had initially been a vocal musical vocabulary is of the greatest importance in understanding and interpreting Baroque music. This vocabulary has its roots in the very first idea of speech-song, which Monteverdi had stylized into a high art form.

The relationship between instrumental and vocal music thus becomes crystal-clear. Here the roots of the curious dialogue-like character of "absolute" music—the sonatas, concertos of the 17th and 18th Centuries, and even symphonies composed in the Classic period—are to be found. These forms are really conceived from the point of view of speech and are inspired by either concrete or theoretical rhetorical programs.

The repertoire of figures used in monody and recitative had become so firmly established that by 1700 it was thought to provide the complete repertoire of figures for instrumental music. Bach then took this body of instrumental figures and transposed it back again into song. This interesting reversal may provide the reason that many singers find Bach difficult to sing, saying that he writes so "instrumentally". If we carefully look at the individual figures used by Bach, we clearly recognize their origin as figures of speech. This turn-about is really a further development, almost a liberation, of the figures found in monody and solo speech-song. But in Bach's hands the rhetorical components are particularly clearly expressed and are, in fact, consciously based on classical rhetorical theory. Bach had studied Quintilian and constructed his work in accordance with Quintilian's rules—so much so that they can be recognized in his compositions. For this purpose he used the greatly refined vocabulary of Italian musical discourse, developed by Monteverdi and others a century before and transposed to the German language, i.e. with greatly heightened accents. (Romance language speakers thought German sounded rather harsh and "barking," with clipped accents.) It was Bach who added the entire apparatus of counterpoint to, and integrated it with, the principles of rhetoric.

The first musical sellout almost happened with the invention of monody. Had composers dogmatically followed the rules of the "Florentines" and completely rejected the madrigal and counterpoint— a move which was actually contemplated around 1600—, music as such might have been totally destroyed. This could not happen, of course. Monteverdi himself, even after becoming acquainted with the new monodic style, did not entirely give up the composition of polyphonic madrigals. As a consequence, his works reveal an unusual stylistic diversity, even within larger compositions. The three forms of composition (singing-speaking, speaking-singing and singing) are clearly distinguished in his two late operas, but in the case of the third, singing, contrapuntal elements associated with the old art of the madrigal repeatedly appear.

In Bach's music this contrapuntal art, the so-called *prima prattica,* in contrast to the modern dramatic monody, the *seconda prattica,* had already won back so much territory that fugal and imitative style was once again accepted in secular vocal music as well. As in Flemish and Italian music before 1600, pieces were again being written in which the text phrases were not sung at the same time in all voices, but mixed, in keeping with the requirements of the movement,—though, to be sure, in each voice always on the appropriate figure. Musical vocabulary, musical drama, was now expressed quite differently, because in polyphonic writing one additional component of the overall statement, the complicated world of counterpoint, was employed in keeping with rhetorical and dramatic precepts.

The next step in this development leads to *Mozart.* Like Monteverdi, he had mastered all known technical devices, including the kind of counterpoint that had been developed during the Baroque period. In the period intervening between Bach and Mozart, the complicated music of the late Baroque, which was comprehensible only to the initiate and to connoisseurs, was radically turned aside in favor of a new, "more natural," music which was conceived of as being so simple that anyone could understand it, even those who had never heard music. These views, on which the new, post-Bach "music of feeling" was based, were, to be sure, expressly rejected by Mozart himself, when he labeled the listener who finds something merely beautiful, without understanding it, a "Papageno." He meant this in a quite pejorative way, stressing that he wrote solely for connoisseurs. Mozart considered it very important that he be understood by "true connoisseurs"; he assumed that his listeners possessed a sound musical understanding and a good basic education. He not infrequently expressed his outrage that those lacking a good knowledge of music believed themselves entitled to express critical views of music. His father was concerned that in *Idomeneo* Mozart had addressed himself too exclusively to connoisseurs: "I recommend that in your work you do not think only of the musical, but also of the non-musical public . . . Do not overlook the so-called popular element, which tickles the long ears (of the donkeys) as well." (December 1780)

Mozart had at his command all the musical tools of the late Baroque; but he could not accept the rigid form of the Italian *opera seria* as a basis for the music drama he had in mind. He adopted elements of French opera, where purely musical considerations had always been subordinated to those of language (there were almost no arias), and thus unconsciously returned to the origins of musical drama. French operas were much more directly related to the text than were the Italian operas of the 18th Century, in which grandiose arias with a schematic content constituted the major attraction. The revenge aria, jealousy aria, love aria and reconciliation aria toward the end of the last act reappeared in every opera and were practically interchangeable from one to the next; a practice which was common. French opera on the other hand had preserved the old forms of recitative, arioso and small aria which made it a more suitable candidate for dramatic reform than the Italian *opera seria*. The theory underlying this reform is found most clearly in Gluck, but in practice it was Mozart who brought the musical drama once again into its own.

We find the same principles employed by Monteverdi in Mozart's work. He is always concerned with drama, dialogue, the individual word, conflict and its resolution, not with poetry set to music. This concern is apparent not only in his operas, but also in his instrumental music, which is always dramatic. In the generation after Mozart, this dramatic, speaking element gradually disappeared from music. The reasons for its disappearance are to be sought—as already noted—in the French Revolution and its cultural aftermath, which led to consciously placing music in the service of a social and political ideology. From that time on, the listener was no longer a partner in a dialogue, but rather was inundated with and intoxicated by sound and so reduced to a state of passive enjoyment.

Precisely here lies, in my opinion, the root of our current misunderstanding of pre-revolutionary music. I contend that we understand Mozart just as little as Monteverdi when we reduce him to the merely beautiful, which is done more often than not. We turn to Mozart in order to savor, to be enchanted by beauty. In reviews of especially beautiful Mozart performances, we read again and again of "Mozartian bliss," a frequent cliché. But if we take a closer look at works about which this cliche is used, we must ask ourselves: Why "Mozartian bliss"? His contemporaries describe Mozart's music as extremely rich in contrasts, vivid, stirring, heart-wrenching; which qualities were the focus of contemporary critics' attacks on his works. How could such music be reduced, in 150 years, to "bliss," to aesthetic enjoyment? Shortly after I had read a review of such a "Mozartian bliss" performance, my students were studying a Mozart violin sonata based on a French song. It was played very beautifully, in my view with this "Mozartian bliss." Then we worked on the sonata, noticing first how very much this piece "got under our skin." It contains not only "Mozartian bliss," but the entire range of human emotion, from joy to sadness to suffering as well. Yet sometimes I wonder if I should recommend that students really work with this in mind. For when people go to a concert in order to enjoy "Mozartian bliss," and perhaps discover "Mozartian truth," it might well upset them, for they may have no desire whatsoever to hear Mozartian truth. The listening public today attends concerts to hear and experience something particular. We have discarded the attentive listening attitude, and perhaps we no longer even wish to hear what it is music has to say to us.

Is our musical culture really to exhaust itself in a wish to find in music a short moment of beauty and relaxation after a busy, stressful day? Has music nothing more to offer us?

This is, in my view, the framework in which speaking music, the dramatic, musical discourse takes place: at its beginnings, in the works of Monteverdi, it replaced the familiar world of the madrigal. At its end, following Mozart, it was largely replaced by the broad musical canvas of Romanticism and late Romanticism. In a dialogue-like, speaking music, the principal preoccupation is never with the beauty of the music; it is filled with passion, it is full of spiritual conflicts, which, though often terrible, are usually resolved. In defending himself against the charge that his music did not follow the rules of aesthetics, that it was not sufficiently "beautiful", Monteverdi once said: "All those who know music should rethink the rules of harmony, and believe me when I say that the modern composer has *only truth itself* as a guideline."

III.
European Baroque Music—Mozart

Program Music—Vivaldi: Opus 8

Much has been written about the question of "absolute" music versus program music. Even if they carry programmatic titles, Baroque concertos are usually regarded as "absolute" music, because they supposedly were created in accordance with purely musical laws and can be understood even without any knowledge of the program. In my view this is a misunderstanding of concepts which originated in the post-Berlioz understanding of program music. Quite different criteria have to be used for Baroque music in which "absolute" music cannot be distinguished from program music. Indeed, there is hardly a single Baroque work lacking a program, if one can call a dramatic event with an uncertain outcome—often, to be sure, without any concrete content and presented through the use of rhetorical devices—a program.

The marriage of words and music aims in many stylistic periods and stylistic areas at enhancing the expressiveness of the words by means of appropriate melodic figures; even gesture, the movement of the body, is expressed musically. The most important musical impulse to emanate from the Baroque period was the development, or perhaps we should say the invention, of opera. Dramatic monody, introduced around 1600, was actually conceived as a text that was sung, the music having the *sole* responsibility of intensifying the expressiveness of *speech*. Purely musical demands were rejected on the grounds that they distracted from the text, which was alone considered to be significant. Within a very short time a catalogue of musical figures had been formed, and singing had to follow the natural flow and rhythm of speech as it reflected a specific emotional state. Similar melodic and rhythmical figures, the same phrases were always assigned to the same emotional states, almost as a matter of course. These phrases were then used as building blocks, which together with the text, *but soon without a text as well,* were assumed to evoke the associations corresponding to the content of the word or phrase.

By the time of Vivaldi, this concept was already 100 years old and had in many respects degenerated. In vocal music, the original musical figures which were assumed to be logically derived from speech-song had so proliferated that the text could barely be understood; and indeed a textual reference was not even necessary, as long as the listener understood the musical language of figures. In Italy, the homeland of the Baroque, musicians had come to master this musical diction with all of the ease of born theater people, so that as early as the first half of the 17th Century, musical figures derived from vocal music were taken over by purely instrumental music, a move which turned this music into abstract, dramatic, musical discourse. Thus the greater part of Baroque instrumental music is theatrical, since natural events, mental states and emotional states are represented and brought into conflict rhetorically. Furthermore, it is often also truly dramatic, based on an abstract or concrete event, the outcome of which is disclosed only towards the end of the musical/dramatic conflict being represented by the musical diction of the Baroque.

Vivaldi wrote all kinds of theatrical instrumental music. As an Italian and opera composer, he possessed a rich vocabulary of musical figures for purely instrumental music as well. Terms such as "absolute" or "program" music simply prove to be inadequate for the object of his music. Vivaldi's music speaks, paints, expresses feelings, describes events and conflicts, and does all this not in an orderly, consecutive fashion but simultaneously and intermixed, as befits any theatrical portrayal of Italian life during the Baroque period. Vivaldi's audiences, thanks to temperament, vocabulary and opportunities to compare, understood this language intimately. Its impact must therefore have been enormous. But it is incomparably more difficult for us to understand, for we must either limit ourselves to those components which have remained comprehensible or try to hear his music anew, to follow the dialogue naively; until finally we can once again comprehend it.

Vivaldi wrote most of his numerous concertos for his own ensemble, the famous orchestra of the "Ospedale della Pietà" in Venice, composed of teen-aged girls. The Pietà was one of several Venetian hospices for orphans and unwanted children. Vivaldi had taught violin there beginning in 1704, and about 1716 was appointed "maestro dei concerti." Only the more gifted pupils received musical training, but so well were the orchestras and choruses prepared that the church concerts which took place regularly on Sundays and holy days were among the attractions of the city. Travelers wrote in glowing terms of the musicality of these girls; in 1668, Peter Tostalgo reports: "In Venice there are convents whose residents play the organ and various other instruments and also sing, so beautifully that nowhere else in the world can one hear such sweet and harmonious music. People come to Venice from all over to hear this angelic music." Vivaldi's unique institutional orchestra must have upheld the highest professional standards; indeed, we can see from the extreme demands placed on the soloists for the various instruments that these works were written for first-rate, virtuoso performers. When Vivaldi included this repertoire in the printed editions of his music, he eventually revised them drastically; if we compare the two versions, we see that the published editions, probably in order to make them more generally accessible, usually contain significant technical simplifications. His development as a composer of instrumental music was fundamentally shaped by the opportunities he enjoyed at the conservatory of the Pietà. The avant-garde and often experimental nature of his works can be explained by the fact that he had the opportunity to experiment with very extreme ideas in this setting.

The concertos published in his Opus 8, *Il Cimento dell' Armonia e dell' Inventione* (the contest between technique and inspiration) were probably not composed solely for this edition, but rather Vivaldi assembled a collection of separate compositions which could be assembled under such an extravagant title. Certainly the *Four Seasons* concertos, the heart of the collection, were not composed for this edition, although they were clearly the reason underlying the title, since they abound with truly bold ideas of every description. It is likely that Vivaldi composed these concertos long before they were published, since he writes in his dedication to Count Morzin: "Considering the long years in which I enjoyed the distinct honor of serving Your Highness as court composer in Italy, I blush to think that until now I have presented no proof of my profound esteem. Thus I have resolved to have this volume printed in order to lay it most humbly at the feet of Your Highness. I beseech Your Highness not to be surprised when you find among these few weak concerti the *Four Seasons* which so long ago found the benevolent favor of Your Highness; please believe me, that was the reason why I found them worthy of being printed, (although they are essentially unchanged) because now, in addition to the sonnets, precise explanations for all of the things contained therein have been added. I am confident that you will judge them as if they were new." The first printing of this monumental collection was done by Le Cène in Amsterdam in 1725.

Sometime previously, Vivaldi had received, in addition to many other positions and honorary appointments, the title of "Maestro di musica in Italia" to Count Wenceslaw Morzin, which most likely involved sending compositions to the Bohemian count as well as managing the Count's orchestra on his visits to Italy. Vivaldi reminds the Count of the pleasure that the latter had derived "so long ago" from the *Four Seasons*. Thus these pieces were already several years old when they were first printed. The two concertos for violin *or* oboe ("Questo concerto si può fare ancora con l'Hautbois") Nos. 9 and 12, were undoubtedly composed as oboe concertos; as all of the other concertos would be unplayable on the oboes, since they exceed the upper and lower limits of its range and because double stops are required. This grouping cannot be coincidence. Vivaldi probably included the oboe concertos in this collection of violin concertos in order to offer the buyers of the volume some easier pieces to play on the violin.

The *Concentus Musicus* uses the printed edition by Le Clerc et Mme. Boivin of Paris, which appeared immediately after the first edition as a source for performance of these concertos, because it seems to us especially reliable as a carefully revised, almost error-free edition. After various experiments, we settled on the organ to play the basso continuo, which is in fact called for in the carefully marked bass part ("organo e violoncello"). Its gentle speech retains the many subtle tone colors of the string instruments, which is not the case with the crisp attack of the harpsichord sound. On the other hand, harmonic fillers can be heard with particular clarity. The nature of the bass part clearly indicates that Vivaldi intended a harpsichord, at least for the long movement of the *Fall* concerto, for the part carries the notation "Il cembalo arpeggio". Therefore we use a harpsichord in all movements of this concerto. The deployment of the continuo instruments is not clear from this bass part, but we can gather from Vivaldi's treatment of the bass elsewhere that the contrabass plays only in *tutti* passages. Only the slow movement of *Winter* has, in the continuo part, a separate page for a cello; therefore the usual bass part is played by the organ and contrabass. In addition to the figuration, "tasto solo" or "tasto solo sempre" are frequently indicated for this part. The slow movements of the two oboe concertos (Nos. 9 and 12), as well as of the violin concerto No. 10, are printed on two staves, so that the continuo players could read along with the solo part, even when it is ornamented. (This tells us something about the practice of accompanying.)—There are numerous remarks in the viola part ("alto viola"), which expand and clarify the programmatic sonnets: *Concerto I,* second movement: "Largo, si deve suonare sempre molto forte, e strappato" (this should always be played very loudly and aggressively) and "Il cane chi grida" (a barking dog); third movement: "Allegro Danza Pastorale." *Concerto II,* first movement: "Languidezza per il caldo" (languishing in the heat), *Concerto III,* first movement: "Ballo e canto de'Villanelli" (dance and song of the peasants), in measure 41 "L'Ubriachi" (the drunkards); second movement: "Dormienti Ubriachi" (the sleeping drunkards); third movement, in measure 83: "Scioppi e cani" (gunfire and dogs). "Tempo impetuoso d'Estate" (stormy summer weather) is written in all parts of the third movement of the *Summer* concerto.

In attempting to come to grips with the Italian tempo markings of the 17th and 18th Centuries, it must be kept in mind that most of these words (e.g. allegro, largo, presto) were and are part of the Italian vernacular and were used by Italian composers literally, rather than as musical terms. Thus allegro means merry, cheerful, rather than fast; only when the particular nature of gaiety requires a certain tempo does allegro indirectly become a tempo indication. In general these marks should be understood as indications of emotional states, with the absolute tempo deriving from the context. Numerous ⌢ and marks which are strewn throughout the movements indicate a rhapsodic style of playing, with frequent rubato and agogic accents.

Vivaldi provides numerous directions for performance and technical execution. The dynamics are very subtly indicated, and one must assume that numerous intermediate levels remain undesignated. In this work Vivaldi uses molto forte, forte, piano, più piano and pianissimo. It should be noted that the dynamics are not called for at the same time in all voices. In the slow movement of the *Spring Concerto,* for example, the solo violin plays at a normal middle volume (no indication marked), while the two ripieno violins play "sempre pianissimo" or very softly, and the viola is instructed to play "molto forte" (very loud). In the slow movement of the *Winter Concerto,* the viola plays pianissimo, the solo violin at normal volume, the ripieno violins pizzicato without any indication, the bass sempre piano and the violoncello sempre molto forte! Dynamics like these conclusively show that Vivaldi utilized sound in a extraordinarily impressionistic way. The articulation, or the bowing and accentuation in playing, was so familiar to musicians of the time that the composer did not bother to write any detailed indications when the part was to be played *normally,* i.e. in keeping with familiar practice.

Vivaldi used a large number of different articulation signs and some ornamentation signs especially in passages which could easily be misunderstood and variously played. He placed slurs over groups of two to eight notes; bow vibratos of varying degrees ⌒ ⋯ ⁀, a + sign for trills, mordents etc. and a sign ∿ that can also be combined ∿ ∿ ∿ ∿ and probably represents something between the vibrato and the trill, about like a quarter-tone trill. All unmarked passages had, of course, to be articulated in keeping with the accepted rules, using all the bowing techniques, including sautillé and jeté. In similar passages in other concertos Vivaldi called for these bowings by using either words or symbols, and thus we know where they were employed at that time.

The Italian and French Styles

In the 17th and 18th Centuries, music was by no means the international and universally accessible art form which it aspires to be and could be today thanks to modern modes of travel and communication. Independent styles developed in various cultural centers, evolving further and further away from their common beginnings in the course of successive generations.

However, communications were sufficiently well developed in those days that the various regional musical styles were at least in broad outline widely understood. Traveling virtuosos disseminated the playing techniques of their homelands to those living in other countries while music lovers in the course of their travels had the opportunity to hear and compare different musical styles and idioms in their native setting. A kind of competition thus developed between musical nations, which further underscored the distinctness of these national styles. This centuries-old interaction was made particularly interesting by stylistic features which migrated from one area to another, due in part to purely musical influences, in part to "turncoats" i.e. composers who lived in a stylistically alien country and attempted to blend the musical traditions of their old and new homelands.

The reason for the development of such clearly distinct, sometimes downright antithetical national styles cannot be simply attributed to a lack of communication. In such cases differences in style would not have separated so completely and "coincidentally" along regional lines. There must also have been reasons having to do with the character, mentality and temperament of whole peoples. The theatrical and individualistic orientation of the Baroque led to an unfolding, indeed, to a veritable cultivation of the personality, the individual with all his peculiar traits, and by extension to a cultivation of the national characteristics of various peoples. This sense was felt and expressed in very concrete ways—by reckless disregard of anything "different." Obviously, this differentiation was sharpest between those two nations which had the most clearly defined and delineated national characters and between which the greatest rivalry existed—geographically and intellectually, politically and culturally: Italy and France.

These stylistic differences evolved ever more clearly in the 17th Century and were based above all on the differing temperaments of the Italians and the French: the former extroverted, loudly proclaiming joy and pain, spontaneous, emotional, lovers of formlessness; the latter controlled, cool, thoroughly rational, lovers of form. The Italians were essentially the creators of Baroque style. Its theatricality, its superabundance of forms, its fantastic and bizarre elements completely suited their nature. The roots of Baroque *music* are therefore also found in Italy.

French music of this period, on the other hand, can be felt almost as a reaction to the eruption of this musical volcano.

As a result, Baroque music was either Italian or French. The contrast between these two musical idioms was regarded at that time as insuperable, and even from the perspective of three centuries later it appears obvious that we can still comprehend the way in which the controversy arose. Vieuville wrote in 1704: "You know as well as I that in France there are now two factions in music, one of which greatly admires the Italian taste . . . They are extremely autocratic and condemn French music as the most tasteless music in the world. The other party, which is loyal to the taste of its fatherland and has a deeper insight into the musical sciences, is vexed that decent French taste is despised even in the capital city of the kingdom."

The gap between the parties was so great that the musicians of either nation felt only scorn for the other; string players trained in the Italian style refused to play French music and vice versa. They were in fact unable to play it, since the stylistic differences affected all the finer points of playing technique, as well as the formal differences in the works themselves. Since music at that time was understood as discourse, one could not "speak" musically in a language which one had not mastered—and which one disliked. The French musicians were indignant about the Italians' free use of ornamentation: "Such was not the taste of Lully, that lover of the beautiful and the true . . . he would have banished any violinist from his orchestra who wanted to ruin his ensemble by adding all kinds of tinkling ill-conceived, unharmonic figures. Why does one not require them to play the various parts as they have been set?"

It was first thought that a fusion of the two styles was impossible. Composers of other countries, particularly Germany and England, were forced to decide which style, which manner of writing, they preferred. Despite efforts undertaken at the end of the 17th Century, primarily by the Austrian composers Muffat and Fux, to merge the two styles, even to reconcile them in a formal sense, the synthesis of the so-called "mixed style" did not occur until the 18th Century.

Italian Baroque music with its emphasis on concerto and opera used every form of exuberant sensuality and fantasy to the limits of the wildest imagination; its musical forms were magnificent and sumptuous. The sound of the strings dominated; but based on the model of the sensuous Italian singing voice. Rich embellishments were improvised *ex tempore* by imaginative interpreters, which precisely suited the spontaneous and extroverted Italian national character. It is interesting that of all musical instruments, the violin was regarded as *the* Italian instrument as well as *the* Baroque instrument *par excellence*. No other instrument is better adapted to the extroverted music-making of the Italians. The violin is as well suited for brilliant soloistic virtuosity as sweeping adagio playing—the two pillars of Italian music. Thus Italian Baroque music is conceived primarily for string instruments. The wind instruments are used less frequently, and then only to achieve special effects and provide a partner in dialogue for the strings. All Italian schools of string playing originated in Monteverdi's circle; he was himself a violinist. The fantastic elements in his style were therefore a basic component of Italian string music from the beginning. Via Carlo Farina, Biagio Marini and others, this path led to the important string schools of Bologna, Rome and Naples.

On the other hand, the French manner of composition was characterized by concise, clearly discernable forms, the tightly formulated instrumental character piece or "pièce," extreme simplicity and brevity of movements, and also by opera, but in a form completely different from that of the Italians. In fact, we are dealing here largely with dance music, the forms of which were related to the rational, linear forms of French palace and garden architecture. The clear, strict form of the dances was perfectly suited to the stylized music of this nation.

Oddly enough, it was an Italian, Jean-Baptiste Lully, who brought French music to its ultimate perfection, one which was internationally regarded as a legitimate alternative to Italian music. To be sure, Lully had completely acclimated himself to France and had only added a dash of Italian fire to French music. He rigorously defined the playing method of the strings with extremely stringent directions. Bowing was strictly regulated, down to the last details, so that it was said that a thousand French musicians could *sight-read* a piece of music as one man, using uniform bowing!

There was a fundamental difference in the ornamentations which had to be used in the two styles as well. The players were expected to vary an adagio in the Italian style, giving their imagination free rein, especially in the repeats. There were very few rules; a plentitude of ideas was everything. In French practice on the other hand, this approach was frowned upon as being undisciplined. No free improvisation was allowed; rather, musicians depended upon a codex of ornamentation which was very complex and which had to be applied ingeniously as possible at appropriate places. Thus there was a repertory of countless small embellishments which had to be executed with painstaking precision, as well as a strict set of rules governing their usage. This order in the midst of apparent clutter, this absolute formal transparency even in the most luxuriant movements, confers on French Baroque music its meaning, its grace. It is a highly cultivated pleasure for those who listen astutely to its clever and highly intellectual artistic offerings—an entertainment, as it were, open to those with similar outlook and education. In contrast, Italian music was regarded as vulgar and undisciplined: "One can say that Italian music is like a charming but painted concubine . . . who always wants to show off, without knowing why . . . French music can be compared to a beautiful woman whose natural and unaffected grace attracts hearts and glances; who only has to show herself to offer immediate pleasure, and who need not feel any competition from the affectations of a wanton coquette..."

Italian opera found no place in France. Rather an indigenous music drama accompanied by dance evolved, called the "ballet de cour." From these beginnings Lully developed the typical French opera in the second half of the century. It differs from its Italian counterpart above all in a marked stress on formal aspects. The airs are short, sung dances in very strict form, separated by meticulously rhythmic recitatives. The accompaniment for the airs and recitatives is virtually always the same, only harpsichord and cello. One can understand how an Italian listening to such an opera might come to think it was all recitatives while waiting longingly for an aria, which would never come, however. (In this context we mention the comment of the Italian prima donna Faustina, who, listening to a French opera, "after having sat quietly for half an hour, is said to have cried out: 'For God's sake, when does the aria begin?' ") It is to the many richly instrumented choral movements and the numerous instrumental dance movements which the listener must look for diversity. The music in any single act was not interrupted; one short piece follows directly upon the previous one. In Italian Baroque opera, on the other hand, every recitative group (freely declaimed) is followed by a long aria, so that the audience was always in a position to express its approval or disapproval loudly and intensely.

This Italian/French polarity runs through the entire history of Baroque music. In 1773, Burney writes in his *Musical Journey:* "If French music is good and its expression natural and pleasing, then Italian music must be bad. Or vice versa; if Italian music has everything that an unspoiled, astute ear can desire, it cannot be supposed that French music would afford the same degree of enjoyment to such an ear. The real truth is that the French cannot stand Italian music; they pretend to accept and admire it, but this is pure affectation." Burney's views seem somewhat harsh, for again and again we have French accounts expressing genuine enthusiasm for the Italian music clearly beyond mere affectation. A kind of longing for the emotional effusiveness of the South led the French to envy and admire the Italians. Two famous attempts to transplant Italian Baroque to France attest to this admiration, although they foundered on a fundamental misunderstanding: Louis XIV's invitation to Bernini in 1663 to assist in building the Louvre, and his invitation to Monteverdi's successor Cavalli to compose an opera on the occasion of the royal wedding in 1660. Neither artist received acceptance or understanding, and both returned to their homeland embittered. Lully's achievement in creating a genuine national opera for the French must therefore be all the more highly respected.

For us, who approach this music 250 years later, the extraordinary polarization which so irreconcilably separated these two styles is no longer easy to understand. The centuries have obviously erased the differences to some extent, which could in part be due to the fact that we play and listen to music today much less intensely than people did then. The very harsh judgments of contemporary critics, the militant reaction of the public at that time, must have had a more substantial basis than today's pallid performances can support. Perhaps we too should commit ourselves, proclaiming our loyalty to one or the other musical party in order to be able to render this music in a credible way.

Austrian Baroque Composers—
Attempts at Reconciliation

Without a doubt, one of the strangest aspects of music history is the concentration of the most potent style-setting and creative forces in particular countries or regions at particular times. For no apparent reason, centers of world-wide significance develop, sometimes here sometimes there, only to disappear after but a generation or two of the greatest creative force, their energies spent. Almost every European country enjoyed at one time or another, sometimes more than once, a "golden age" of music. These musical centers did not necessarily coincide with the major political centers of their times, although such a relation often existed. For example, Flemish music flourished around 1500, coinciding with the great expansion of political power and pomp at the French court of Louis XII and at the Holy Roman court of Maximilian I.

We can find numerous reasons for these shifts in musical centers. As a musician who does not regard music as a timeless, isolated art, but rather in its historical context, I have endeavored to ascertain to what extent these shifts had an impact on music itself; whether they were the cause or the effect of developments in the history of music and whether they paralleled shifts in the centers of the other arts.

We no longer subscribe to the old thesis of a serial sequence in the different arts, since each historic style finds its expression in all of the arts *simultaneously*. This is clearly inevitable, as any art form is a direct expression of the intellectual climate of its times.

European nations, however, differ greatly in intellectual outlook and values. The English, French, Germans, Spaniards and Italians all think differently, express themselves differently, react differently. In the course of historical transitions, new and abrupt intellectual directions emerge. These directions find the greatest sympathy in those nations to whose mentality they most closely correspond. If all the components of a movement in art, of an historic style, are in harmony with the natural characteristics of a given people, then this people is bound to assume leadership of the movement in question.

The transition from the late Renaissance to the Baroque demonstrates this kind of change in leadership in a particularly telling way. Within one or two generations, the Flemish, who until the Baroque led musical development, were replaced by the Italians. The theatricality of the new age, the emergence of the individual personality—of the soloist—the pathos and individual expression, which were displayed in a downright exhibitionistic way, corresponded in ideal fashion with the Italian mentality. The Baroque found its purest expression in the architecture and music of Italy. Italy became the role model for all other countries. Like the Flemish before them, Italian artists were invited to serve as music directors, soloists and composers throughout Europe.

Thus, at 17th-Century German courts, either Italian musicians, or at least those who had been trained in Italian methods and who regarded the French style with extreme reservation, if not outright hostility, received appointments. A greater contrast can hardly be imagined! Italian instrumental music was dominated by the sonata and the concerto, which basically consisted of sweeping virtuoso allegro movements and grand cantabile adagios, in which soloists were expected to demonstrate their creative fantasy through elaborate ornamentation. The short French dances and the strictly defined manner of playing required for their performance must surely have seemed strange to musicians who had been schooled in these free forms. Around 1700 many a nobleman wishing to convert his musical ensemble to the French style met with stiff resistance; Italian musicians refused to play the French music, and this refusal was probably based less on a spirit of defiant stubbornness than on the actual impossibility of being able to play both well.

In countries other than France and Italy, the personal taste of the respective ruler dictated which music would be performed. At the court in Vienna, the Italians of course dominated the musical scene. The emperor felt such enmity towards France that he would not tolerate hearing the French language spoken, while the sensuous Italian music was better suited to the Austrian mentality than the rational French music. The result was that for several generations, only Italian musicians, singers and composers could make a name for themselves in Vienna. The rise of Schmelzer and Fux, two native Austrians, to the highest positions in the imperial music establishment must be regarded as a minor miracle as the Italian court musicians naturally wished to keep "their" ensembles as free of foreign influence as possible. Austrian, German, Bohemian and French composers were, however, occasionally able to obtain appointments at small courts or with the Jesuits. Unusually talented performers, such as the harpsichordist Wolfgang Ebner, the violinist Heinrich Schmelzer and the composer Johann Joseph Fux, were included in the court chapel only upon the emperor's specific wish.

The fact that Vienna was, already in the Baroque period, a first-rate musical center is probably due to the passionate enthusiasm for music of a handful of Hapsburg emperors. In the case of Leopold I, the quintessential Austrian Baroque emperor, this enthusiasm was carried to the point of fanaticism. Although he was emperor for almost 50 years, this remarkable man was anything but a ruler by nature. Since he was frail and weak, had a powerful brother (who became Emperor Ferdinand IV) and was deeply pious, he was educated for a religious career. But the sudden death of his brother forced him into the role for which he was ill prepared. Nonetheless, or perhaps for this reason, his reign was extremely fruitful, despite some discord, and no less successful than that of his magnificent counterpart Louis XIV of France, who enjoyed an equally long reign. Leopold had no taste for military ventures: a splendid concert was more important to him than victory in battle. His generals complained that he had no money for the army, though he spent huge sums for his opera company. Since life at the court was played out more or less publicly, members of the landed gentry imitated the customs and fashions of the mighty—thus many of the smaller French and German courts parroted the life style and the architecture of the palace and gardens in Versailles. In Austria and Bohemia, the imperial passion for music was similarly imitated. Even the minor nobility maintained court orchestras composed of musicians who enjoyed permanent appointments. Abraham A Santa Clara wrote in 1679: "The resounding trumpets and the music arising everywhere from the palaces and courts of the nobility made such a pleasant noise at all times that one would have thought the heavens must have a hole through which blessings fall in abundance on the city of Vienna."

The most splendid music resounded every Sunday in the many Viennese churches as well as in the convents and monasteries of lower Austria, both ecclesiastical and secular Baroque dwellings. The Austrian and Bohemian archives are filled with such an immense amount of music, particularly from the reign of Leopold, that it is hard to imagine how it could all have been performed, and considering the enormous number of scores lost over the succeeding centuries the amount of music written and performed is staggering. The amount of music required for 52 Sundays a year plus the music played during the week at music-loving courts, provides some sense of the enormous demand for new music. Burney reports of Vienna in his *Musical Journey* (1772): "This country is really very musical . . . This penchant is explained to some degree by the music school at the Jesuit college in every Roman Catholic city, but other reasons can also be adduced; among these it should be remembered that there is hardly a church or monastery in Vienna where a musical Mass is not performed each morning; . . . sung by singers and accompanied, in addition to the organ, by at least three or four violins, violas and basses; and because the churches are very full every day, this music, even if it is not the most beautiful, must to some extent train the ears of the city's residents." At that time every trained musician was able to compose music that was correct, at least in terms of craftsmanship. No one can, after all, live with a steady diet of true masterpieces. As the Salzburg *Hofkapellmeister* Georg Muffat expressly demanded, serious works had to be alternated with easily understood, simple pieces, so as not to overtax the listener.

Leopold I himself was not only a passionate listener but also a fair composer. He wrote masses, oratorios, dances, German songs and a large number of interludes to be interpolated into the compositions of his court musicians. He often contented himself with inventing the melodies and leaving the setting and instrumentation to his court musicians Berthali and Ebner. Although the Austrian state treasury was always empty, often even in debt, the Italian musicians of the *Hofkapelle* received princely compensation. They were in every respect the predecessors of today's well-paid musical stars. Gottlieb Eucharius Rinck, a captain in the imperial army, notes of Leopold I and his court orchestra: "The Emperor is a great musical artist . . . If there is anything in the world that brings joy to the Emperor, it is a piece of good music. Music gives him happiness, relieves his cares, and one can say that nothing gives him more pleasure than a well-ordered concert. This fondness is especially evident in his living quarters. He is accustomed to changing residence four times a year, from the palace in Vienna to Laxenburg, from there to the Favorita and then to Ebersburg, in each of which is a valuable spinet on which the Emperor whiles away his leisure hours. His court chapel is probably the best in the world, which is no surprise, since the Emperor himself interviews every prospective member basing his judgment solely on merit, not favoritism . . . One can judge from the number of experienced artists how dearly they must have cost the Emperor. Many were raised to barons and received incomes commensurate with their rank . . . The Emperor attends each concert by his incomparable orchestra, from which he derives such great pleasure and listens with such infinite concentration he appears to be hearing it for the very first time . . . If a particular passage particularly pleases him, he closes his eyes in order to listen with even greater attention. His ear is so keen that among fifty musicians he can identify the one who bowed incorrectly."

In addition to the court chapel in Vienna, there were several others in the Hapsburg lands, constituted in keeping with the personal taste of their patron. All enjoyed the special attention of the Emperor. The most important of these belonged to the Prince Archbishop of Olmütz, Karl Count Liechtenstein-Kastelkorn. This wealthy prince of the church had built a colossal summer residence in Kremsier. His musical performances ran to solo music, so he engaged the best soloists available, including many Austrian and Bohemian musicians. Most were composers as well, and since the orchestra was composed of real virtuosos, a profusion of orchestral and chamber music was written and performed which was clearly distinguishable from any other music being written at that time. The Emperor was so enthusiastic about this orchestra that he made several trips each year to Kremsier in order to revel in the music. The imperial composers wrote particularly demanding music for the "Liechtenstein Orchestra," since such music could best be realized by this group. To lead this unique ensemble, the archbishop had engaged the remarkable violinist and composer, Heinrich Biber. While the

Olmütz-Kremsier ensemble was clearly indebted to Biber for its most important works, Biber's development was, on the other hand, inconceivable without the stimulation he received from that orchestral body. For example, he wrote a large number of quite important trumpet solos for the first trumpeter, Pavel Vejvanowsky, who later succeeded Biber as orchestra director. In addition, there were superb trombonists, basoonists and flutists. The string instruments were acquired from Jacobus Stainer in Absam, the best instrument maker of his age.

The Archbishop of Salzburg also kept a superb court chapel, as did many other aristocrats. All built magnificent palaces including marble-lined halls, so that the music enjoyed not only an architectural equivalent, but also an acoustically ideal space.

Naturally enough, Italian music could not maintain its purity in a city like Vienna, which had always been a melting pot of the most varied styles. Leading figures from every musical center came together here in the course of the centuries on what was to some extent neutral ground. Flemish and Italian, English and French musicians could all be heard in the city. Thanks to Vienna's proximity to the Slavic and Magyar worlds, Eastern musical traditions were present as well. In addition to Italian and French music, Hungarian, Bohemian and Austrian folk music was constantly performed, so that each style ultimately influenced and enriched the others. By the 17th Century, a typical Austrian style emerged, in which elements of these other styles were fitted to the Italian form.

Because of the close political ties of the Emperor to Italy, opera, the great musical-dramatic novelty of the early 17th Century, was introduced into Vienna, where it immediately found an enthusiastic and cultivated home. In the 17th Century, Vienna became one of the outstanding centers of Italian opera. Almost all the significant opera composers worked in the city at one time or another. A great deal of purely instrumental music was incorporated into their operas, for in addition to the dance interludes, the music for which was written by specialist ballet composers, instrumental interludes and instrumental concertos were inserted as well. Although the ballet interludes usually imitated French models, a number used regional melodies, as is evident from titles such as "Steyermärker Horn," "Gavotta tedesca," "Styriaca," "Bohemian Bagpipes" and others. The instrumental interludes were, however, written by the Italian opera composers themselves. They were called "sonata," and were usually in five parts, particularly those of the older composers. Their form was derived directly from the old Italian *canzon da sonar*. These polyphonic "sonatas" are not to be confused with the Classic sonata for a solo instrument. At the time of Leopold, then, the stylistic antipodes in instrumental music were the French suite and the Italian sonata. The differing nature of these two forms, elsewhere irreconcilable, was successfully synthesized in Austria into a fascinating new entity by ingenious composers such as Georg Muffat, Fux,

Schmelzer and Biber.

Georg Muffat is particularly interesting today because he wrote extensively on all questions of style and interpretation in the prefaces he supplied for his compositions. His unusual career led him to become a first-rate expert and representative of the leading musical styles. He studied in Paris under Lully, moved from there to the Viennese court under the patronage of Leopold I and then went to Salzburg as court composer to the Archbishop. He described himself as the first German "Lullist." The Archbishop of Salzburg sent him to Italy to further perfect his knowledge and skills. While there he wrote concerti grossi in the manner of Corelli, writing in his preface to these compositions these beautiful words: "I have tried to moderate the profound Italian emotions with French charm and gaiety, so that the former is neither too dark nor pompous while the latter is not too free and riotous. This is a fitting symbol for the high virtue and character of Your Grace . . . I received the initial idea for this meaningful combination some time ago in Rome—when I was studying the Italian style on the clavier under the world-famous Bernardo Pasquini, where I heard with great pleasure and wonder several beautiful concerts, carefully produced with a large number of instrumentalists by the great artist Archangelo Corelli."

In his dedication to the *Florilegium primum,* he wrote: "Just as the primary attraction of a garden lies in the diversity of its plants and flowers, and just as the excellence of great heroes appears to consist of the coalescence of various virtues which join for the common good; thus I deemed that for the most humble and fitting service of Your Lordship, not one kind, but rather the best taken from the various nations is fitting. From Your Gracious Lordship, and from Your courts and undertakings I fear nothing, nor of encountering assaults by malicious or feeble minds, who judge iniquitously, simply because I have taken my beginnings with those most experienced masters in this art in France and thus entertain feelings of sympathy towards that nation that are quite extraordinary. In these times of war with France, I might be judged unworthy of a benevolent reception by the Germans . . . The weapons of war and their motives remain alien to me; the notes, the pages, the charming sounds of music inspire me, and since I blend the French style with the German and Italian, I wage no war. But perhaps my music will help establish the sought-after harmony of the people, and dear peace . . ."

Muffat was thus the first to consciously join the two divergent styles as a symbol of European reconciliation. The daring of this undertaking is manifest, given the bitter political hostility between Louis XIV and Leopold I which could easily have deepened the "cultural enmity" between two such different peoples.

Muffat was obviously familiar with the difficulties that violinists trained in other traditions had with the French style of bowing: he wrote that they should not "consider this new method of no value, just because they are not accustomed to it." He is enthusiastic about the French manner of playing: "In the ballets the violins are played in the manner of the famous Johann Baptist Lully . . . so that something more charming or more beautiful could hardly be imagined."

The French style is obviously dominant in the *Florilegium,* a collection of ballet suites with programmatic titles, even though Italian elements are used extensively in the overtures and in several dance movements, adagios and allegros. The French style clearly predominates in the concerti grossi, which were composed in Italy, over the Italian, though a vigorous and conscious fusion of both styles is evident. Muffat's concerti grossi are indebted to those of Corelli, although they contain movements from the French suite which are occasionally worked out with Italian exuberance. He prescribes the ornamentation in minute detail, even the bowing. He wished to use French oboes, which had just been invented, as solo instruments "if anyone has already mastered them," and suggests almost unbelievable adaptations and transpositions.

Following Muffat's pioneering work, nearly all Austrian composers wrote sonatas and suites in both the Italian and French styles, unlike their Italian and French counterparts who cultivated one style or the other. To be sure, they primarily adopted the forms, for their themes usually depended upon German, Hungarian and Bohemian elements. As a consequence of this exposure to the universe of European styles, the native musicality of the Viennese and the Austrians in general gradually resulted in a distinct style which harmoniously incorporated such diversity. From its beginnings the very strong folkloric tradition of Austria, Hungary and Bohemia played an important role in this synthesis but became an especially significant element once local masters such as Schmelzer and Fux assumed leadership of the Court Chapel. From this point on, we can say that truly Viennese and Austrian music was composed.

Johann Joseph Fux introduced new popular sounds into the well-groomed preserves of the imperial Hofkapelle. The early history and musical development of this peasant's son from Styria has been lost. At about age 30, he turned up in Vienna as a fully trained musician, working primarily as an organist. The Emperor heard him play at the home of a Viennese nobleman and in 1698 named him "Hofkompositeur," a title especially created for him. He later joined the Imperial Court Chapel and in 1715 was named its director by Charles VI. The low regard in which Fux is held today is unjust, considering his great merits. This poor estimate is probably due to the fact that his *Gradus ad Parnassum* became the leading theoretical work on counterpoint (based upon which subsequent Viennese composers, including Beethoven, developed their technical expertise). Generally it is and was believed that a theorist is incapable of being a full-blooded musician. Even today a musician who can clearly and forcefully express himself on the subject of music is written off as a "dry" theoretician; audiences want to see their artists surrounded by a magic aura, a role in which intellectuals do not comfortably fit. Fux thought of himself in quite a different light: "For as soon as I had attained only the slightest use of my reason, I fairly burned with desire and focused all my thoughts and senses on music. I am still inflamed with the desire to learn such; it has a hold on me, even against my will, as it were, so that music sounds in my ears day and night, so that I do not for a moment doubt the truth of my inner calling..."

The fame Fux enjoyed during his lifetime as a composer is certainly well-justified. He mastered all the different styles of his age. He learned from the Italians their instrumental and operatic style; through Muffat he became acquainted with the French style of Lully and his successors. Moreover, he maintained a special love for native Austrian folklore and music, so that Styrian Ländler and other folk dances appear over and over again in his dance movements. Fux handled this rich palette like a master; his instrumental music is of the greatest naturalness and vitality, his church music is sublimely artistic in the strict contrapuntal style, while his operas are sumptuous Baroque works in the Italianate manner.

Fux's major instrumental work is his *Concentus musico instrumentalis* written in 1701, which he dedicated to Leopold's son, Joseph I. All the forms of instrumental music of the time appear in this collection of suites. It features French dance forms, as did all suites of the time, but these are transformed by typical Austrian modifications. In addition, some purely Italian instrumental movements are interposed.

Heinrich Schmelzer was one of the most interesting and original musicians of his age. His father was an army officer, so the young composer grew up in military encampments. He probably received regular instruction on the violin, as well as gaining his first musical impressions in a military setting. The Polish, Hungarian, Croatian and Bohemian soldiers of the Austrian army undoubtedly included some self-taught folk musicians, of whom a handful must have been superb natural virtuosos. Throughout his life, Schmelzer retained a profound concern for folk music, and most of his early works reflect impressions received in military camps. Before he had reached the age of 20, his violin technique must have been quite remarkable, for he was appointed as a violinist in the imperial court orchestra. It was not long before his special talents attracted the attention of the Emperor. He was soon requested to write ballet interludes for virtually all the operas which were presented. Leopold held him in such high esteem that in 1679 he appointed him *Hofkapellmeister,* the first non-Italian to hold this position. Several of his works found in the Kremsier archives are so extremely demanding both technically and musically that Schmelzer must certainly have written them for the virtuosos of this Kapelle. The form of all of these one-movement sonatas follows the Italian style. The individual sections in various meters are not separated by complete breaks, but rather flow without interruption into each other. Occasionally the form is concluded with a reprise.

Heinrich Ignaz Biber was born in 1644 at Wartenberg in Bohemia. Almost nothing is known of his musical background. We assume that he studied both composition and violin with Schmelzer. His style of playing and his violin technique are hard to imagine without an intimate knowledge of Schmelzer's manner of composition. Biber's obvious preference for the forms and elements of folk music also appears to have derived from Schmelzer. In any case the two musicians were in close contact for some years; Schmelzer often accompanied the Emperor to Kremsier where he composed a number of works for the soloists there. He probably played his scordatura sonatas for two violins in Kremsier with Biber himself. For his part, Biber frequently visited Vienna, where, like Schmelzer, he was finally raised to the nobility by Leopold I.

Biber made arrangements for the archbishop to purchase an entire set of string instruments for his orchestra from Jacobus Stainer, whose instruments he preferred above all others. As a consequence we know a great deal about Biber's concept of sound. Just why Biber left Kremsier to settle in Salzburg is uncertain—but it was not with the approval of his lord. In any case, the Court Chapel in Salzburg was also extremely capable and, what was perhaps even more important to Biber, Georg Muffat, its director, was an interesting and stimulating composer. Biber became Muffat's assistant Kapellmeister.

The presence of the violinist, the instrumental virtuoso, can be heard in almost all of Biber's compositions. Most of his works contain large or smaller violin solos, which the composer undoubtedly wrote with himself in mind. But even in the vocal works and pieces for wind instruments, the hand of the practical musician is always clearly present in his virtuosic mastery of the fine points of instrumentation as well as his unerring instinct for effect. Yet Biber never fell victim to the curse of most virtuoso composers, sacrificing everything, including the musical statement, to audience appeal. There is hardly a sacred or secular work by Biber that does not combine the most profound musical substance with a brilliant, effective manner of composition.

His *Animal Sonata* includes imitations of the sounds of the nightingale, cuckoo, frog, hen, rooster, quail and cat. Oddly enough, even a musketeer's march is incorporated into a violin sonata that is brimming with life and the exuberance of spring. Despite all the clever details and the humor, Biber found it completely appropriate to dedicate this sonata "to the greater glory of God, the Virgin Mary and St. Cecilia." Evidently, even at the court of a Baroque period Archbishop, the hereafter could be thought of as very merry and earthy.

We can summarize by saying that while the Italian taste initially dominated in Vienna, a new and characteristic style evolved which combined Italian and French styles with the natural musicality of the Austrians.

Telemann—The "Mixed" [Eclectic] Style

Georg Philipp Telemann was above all the composer who brought about a fusion of the Italian and French styles in northern Germany. Telemann was far and away the most famous composer of his time. In today's historical outlook we hardly think of the artist as a practitioner who must satisfy the voracious appetite of his contemporaries for art to meet the needs of their daily lives. Some all too quickly resort to the pejorative term "Vielschreiber," with which they casually disparage the overwhelming creativity of many a Baroque artist. Obviously not all of these thousands of pieces of music can be masterpieces, nor were they ever intended to be. They were written for a particular purpose, which they more than adequately fulfilled. We cannot do justice to a composer like Telemann if we compare him to his great contemporary Bach and continue to refer to the "erroneous judgment" of his contemporaries: the shallow "Vielschreiber" of high renown vs. the great cantor, who was completely misunderstood. It goes without saying that connoisseurs recognized Bach as the greatest living composer, although his works were not widely disseminated since he allowed so little to be printed. In addition, as a cantor in Leipzig, he wrote music intended primarily for Sunday church services, music which he did not publish. In contrast, Telemann exhibited an extraordinarily dynamic and outgoing personality. Wherever he went, he had a great impact on musical life, founding performing ensembles and devoting himself unflaggingly to the printing and distribution of his works. Telemann had written his first opera by the age of 12; he played the recorder, violin and harpsichord, acquiring almost all his musical knowledge and expertise by virtue of his own efforts, for he never received thorough musical instruction. As a student in Leipzig he founded a high-quality collegium musicum with which Bach later performed many of his instrumental concertos. Thanks to a series of professional appointments, as *Hofkapellmeister* in Sorau and Eisenach and as music director in Frankfurt and finally in Hamburg, he was able to familiarize himself with a wide variety of musical styles. In Sorau he wrote many French overtures and in Silesia he became acquainted with Polish folk music, which he frequently used in subsequent works.

Telemann's urbane nature, his tremendous energy and his preëminent talent were bound to bring him universal acclaim. In 1730 he traveled to Paris, where he was warmly received not only by the most famous instrumental virtuosos, but also by the French audiences. His style was imitated by many German and French composers. Telemann constantly tried to introduce new elements into his compositions; he was never satisfied simply clinging to an "accepted" style, but was rather always at the forefront of stylistic developments. Even at the age of 80, he put younger musicians to shame with his ultra-modern works written in the style of the Viennese-Mannheim school. Telemann was at home in all styles, possessing a supreme mastery of both the French and the Italian modes (regarded at the time as virtually contradictory) in their purest forms as well as all the intermediate stages in their coalescence. Since he evidently had a special preference for unusual sounds and sound combinations, he wrote music for every conceivable type and combination of instruments. Any ensemble, no matter how exceptional its makeup, can find suitable literature among Telemann's works.

Instrumentation, experimenting with particular colors and technical methods, creating new sounds by the combination of different instruments, was, until late in the Baroque age, primarily the responsibility of the interpreter. As late as the 17th Century, printed music often contains the instruction "zum Singen und Spielen, auf allerhand Instrumenten" (for singing and playing on all manner of instruments). Of course, not just any instruments could be combined: there were unwritten laws stipulating which instruments were suited to each other and which were not. By and large, however, the musical fabric of a composition was determined only at the time of performance and only for a particular performance. Played at another location, the same piece might sound quite different, yet this freedom to interpret was perfectly in keeping with the plan of the composer. The score of a work was an abstract design which indicated the substance of the music, though not its actual realization. The Kapellmeister performing the work had to "arrange" it in accordance with the resources available to him, i.e. he had to decide what parts were to be played, what was to be sung, where ornamentation was to be added, and many other questions as well. This freedom was gradually restricted as composers called for very specific combinations of sounds. Until late in the 18th Century, however, traces of the old freedom still remain, as is evident in many instrumental designations such as "violin or flute, oboe or violin, bassoon or violoncello, harpsichord or fortepiano."

The three great contemporaries, Bach, Handel and Telemann, were the first to search out the idioms of the new musical language that would lead from the Baroque to classicism. They were well aware of this role and indeed discussed the fact that their efforts were breaking new ground. Handel was less interested in instrumentation than in melody and together with Telemann, explored the limits of its rules. Bach and Telemann went the furthest in their constant search for new avenues of musical expression. Once and for all, for themselves and for posterity, they embodied the boldest musical dreams of their predecessors, which had on rare occasions been realized under especially favorable conditions. Their musical palette encompassed a richness which remained unequaled for 200 years, and was then achieved only in a totally different way. Telemann enjoyed ideal circumstances for his experiments and comparisons: his career as Kapellmeister and composer took him to far-flung corners of Europe, giving him the opportunity to hear the best folk musicians as well as the most renowned virtuosos. He wrote of himself: "I had the good fortune of getting to know the most famous musicians in various countries, whose skill undoubtedly implanted in me the desire to do my composing with the greatest care possible." All these impulses are reflected in his compositions, and because he played several string and wind instruments from a very early age, it was a simple matter for him to adapt his works to the technical capabilities of the various instruments. Virtuosos were shown to their best advantage and played his music with great enthusiasm.

Instrumentation was always an important aspect of composition in Telemann's judgment; here, too, he was far ahead of most of the composers of his generation, in whose works many instruments could be simply interchanged. While still very young, he chose a manner of composition which, because of its attention to playing technique and to precise characterization of the individual instruments, was capable of maximizing the tonal and technical properties of each instrument: "I came to know the diverse natures of the different instruments, which I myself did not neglect to refine with as much diligence as possible. I continue to discover how necessary and useful it is to be able to distinguish among these in their most essential aspects, and maintain that no one can find joy and success in composing who lacks this knowledge. A precise knowledge of the instruments is also necessary for composing. Because otherwise, one might have to say that

    The violin is treated as if it were an organ,
    The flute and oboe as if they were trumpets,
    The gamba comes along as if it were the bass,
    Only with a trill here and there.
    No, no, it is not enough for the notes to sound,
    That you know how to write according to the rules:
    Give each instrument whatever suits it best,
    Then the players will be happy and you will have your pleasure as well.

        (Die Violine wird nach Orgel-Arth tractieret
        Die Flöt' und Hautbois Trompeten gleich verspühret
        Die Gamba schlentert mit, so wie das Bässgen geht
        Nur dass noch hier und da ein Triller steht.
        Nein, nein, es ist nicht gnug, dass nur die Noten klingen
        Dass du der Reguln Kram zu Marckte weist zu bringen.
        Gieb jedem Instrument das, was es leyden kan
        So hat der Spieler Lust, du hast Vergnügen dran.)

Many of Telemann's works are conceivable with no other instrumentation than that called for by the composer. For example, in a *Concerto à 6. Flaute a bec et Fagotto concertato,* he uses the recorder, which was well established as a solo instrument, as a dialogue partner for the bassoon, which until then had been used with very few exceptions only as an orchestral bass instrument—and he handles this instrument so masterfully that it instantly becomes an equal partner.

A *Concerto à 4 Violini senza Basso,* i.e. for four melody instruments, is a logical continuation of the solo literature for a single instrument without bass so popular at the time; Telemann wrote many such sonatas and suites for one or more violins or flutes. The four violins are treated as complete equals, the intention being to simulate a competition in which each instrument tries to outdo the others, with melody and bass functions shifting from one violin to the next. The apparent disadvantage of having four instruments of the same range is exploited by Telemann to create harmonically daring tone-colors.

The *Overture in F Major* for two horns and string orchestra is another example of Telemann's technique of composition and treatment of instruments. This, too, represents a blending of widely differing traditions of an entirely different nature. The form of a French overture (suite) is fused with the concertizing principle of an Italian concerto. It was during Telemann's lifetime that the horn, which had previously been used exclusively for the hunt, was recruited for use in art music. It is interesting that the first itinerant horn virtuosos, who always travelled in pairs, were without exception Bohemian huntsmen. Thus, in the earliest works for horns, hunting motives predominate. The two horns were always played together, as though they were a single instrument; the dialogue thus takes place between them and the string orchestra. The slow movements of the suite do not follow the usual pattern of the horn music of the period. Here, perhaps for the first time in music, Telemann took advantage of the particular suitability of the sound of the horn for lyrical romantic melodies. Any other composer would have used the horn only in the fast outer movements and had them rest in the slow movements. However, Telemann obviously wanted to demonstrate the horn's *cantabile* potential, since he positioned three slow movements between the brisk hunt-like outer movements.

The wind instrumentation in several of Telemann's "Darmstadt" overtures is very interesting. Ordinarily, *two* obbligato oboes are used with the first violins, or individually with the first and second violins, which creates an intensification and coloration similar to that obtained by adding registers on an organ. Occasionally there are trios: small solos for the two oboes and bass. The bassoon does not have its own part at all—it simply moves with the cellos and contrabasses. It may occasionally play the bass line for oboe solos, though this is not indicated in the parts, but rather was determined ad hoc by the performer. At other times, Telemann calls for a complete wind quartet: three oboes and bassoon. In this instrumentation, the registration-like character is obviously preserved, with the third oboe playing the viola part, insofar as it lies within its range. Moreover, this instrumentation offers the opportunity for an equal alternation with the strings; the wind choir now has four voices, as does the string orchestra. This scheme results in a particular type of scoring in which the dialogue now takes place not only within two homogeneous sounds, by means of alternations of motives and figures, but also between basically different groups of sounds. Given the period's approach to polychoral music, hall acoustics and disposition of instruments, such groupings required that the wind and string choirs be placed separately, possibly each with its own continuo instruments.

Some 20–30 years earlier, Georg Muffat had made some very interesting suggestions and comments regarding the possibilities of music written in this way. He leaves the distribution of the parts largely to the interpreter; describes the performance with the smallest instrumentation (omitting the middle voices), and the preferred performance employing the largest possible orchestra. "But if you have even more musicians at your disposal, you can use more first and second violins in the large choir, but also both middle violas, and the bass at your discretion, embellishing the latter with accompaniment by the harpsichord, theorboes, harps and other such instruments: but the little group, which is known by the term concertino, should be played by your three best violinists with no doubling, accompanied only by one organ or theorbo." He also writes that these two "choirs" can be positioned apart from each other. After all, separate continuo instruments (organ or theorbo) only make sense given this kind of spatial separation.

In several of Telemann's suites, the wind instruments are opposed to the strings idiomatically and as soloists. This involves not only a dialogue between two equal sound groups (such dialogue does occur in places), but also solo writing, in which the winds are given soloistic prominence from the outset by means of idiomatic wind figures. This was by no means common during Telemann's lifetime, when the oboe part could only very rarely be distinguished from a string part. The opening of the "Darmstadt" suite in C Major, for example, is characteristic in its emphasis on the unusual and special. In this case the strings are completely silent which must have created a striking and surprising effect at a time when a tutti was expected. (Fifty years later, Mozart describes a similar reaction at the opening performance of his "Paris" Symphony.)

Ultimately this "contest" between the Italian and French styles was to enrich Western music for it brought about the so-called "mixed [eclectic] style" which characterizes 18th-Century German music. The great German composers, when writing French suites or Italian sonatas and concertos, included elements of the "other" style. The German tradition acted as a catalyst in this fusion of styles.

Before closing it should be noted that a strictly German style in the specialized field of organ music had developed. An unbroken series of teachers and students leads from the Dutchman Sweelinck (1562–1621) via H. Scheidemann (1596–1663) and J. A. Reincken (1623–1722) to J. S. Bach. The special feature of this German organ style is a fondness, derived from old Dutch polyphony, for complex part writing, which ultimately led to the formal development of the fugue.

Baroque Instrumental Music in England

Baroque music, a festive reveling in sounds and virtuoso treatment of broken chords, theatrical, brilliant, spectacular—all these attributes are justifiably aspects of our contemporary understanding of this music, even though they do not completely do justice to it. The term "Baroque music" in the minds of most means the Italian and perhaps also the French music of this period, since these two countries were the pace setters in the style. The no less important German and Austrian Baroque music also relates to these two styles, since each individual work is clearly related to either one or the other. One hardly thinks of English Baroque music, since it has remained in the background, despite valiant efforts to revive it in recent years.

Our age relishes the spectacular, the large-scale production which makes the current apparent renaissance of Baroque music all too easy to understand. However, English Baroque music does not fit the criteria of this renaissance, since the former is based on totally different values and so offers neither the stimulating drive nor the musical lustre of typical Baroque music. Their island geography permitted the British to largely isolate themselves from European trends and develop their own patterns of producing and consuming art. Whatever the exchanges, they remained relatively minor.

During the Baroque age, when what mattered most in music was its effect, the British were much more concerned with content, with the depth of the musical statement. English Baroque music is not concert music which provides virtuosos with a vehicle to display their talents, but rather very subtle and most profound music for a small circle of devotées. England surely boasts no fewer music enthusiasts than Italy or France, perhaps more, but they did not require the stimulating backdrop of a public setting in order to enjoy music. Musical life was thus contained primarily in countless small circles of people who possessed genuine knowledge and ability. The English kept to the soft and delicate instruments of the gamba family as long as possible: the beauty and subtlety of its sounds were incomparably more important to them than sheer volume. They wanted to listen actively, intensively. For this reason, the larger portion of English music of the 17th Century is chamber music. In certain respects, English musical life during this age can be compared with that of Austria at the end of the 18th Century. Even though there was a very active Austrian concert life, nonetheless very important musical events were taking place in chamber music, especially the string quartet. In this as well, large audiences were not involved; this was music cultivated in private circles, where the meaning of the musical statement was more highly valued than its effect. So it comes as no surprise that in both countries composers created their greatest masterpieces in the genre of chamber music. This is also the reason for the limited popularity of English music which, like chamber music from the Classic period, eschews empty display and therefore, like it, is relegated today to the musical sidelines.

John Cooper (1575–1626) and William Lawes (1602–1645) are two of the most typical and most important composers of the great century of English music. Indicative of the misplaced regard accorded anything foreign or exotic, a trait wholly inappropriate at any time and in any place, John Cooper, having gained several years of experience in Italy, took the name Giovanni Coperario on returning to England, in order to pass as an Italian and so gather greater popular appeal. This behavior becomes particularly grotesque when we compare Cooper's works with those of contemporary Italians, when we see how independently he worked Italian influences into purely English forms, and when we note how superficial the first Italian trio sonata attempts are compared with those by Cooper written during the same period. This assimilation of or independence of national styles can be discovered in a few other cases as well. At the beginning of the 17th Century, several Italian composers (e.g. Ferrabosco, Lupo) moved to England to seek their fortune. Within a very short time they were writing *purely English* music; musically speaking, they had become Englishmen. By way of contrast, Cooper merely brought an Italian name home with him.

Cooper's foremost student was William Lawes, one of the greatest composers of the 17th Century. Charles I, for whom he wrote the greater portion of his many works, loved his music and held him personally in high esteem. Following Lawes death in the battle of Chester, any number of poets and composers wrote Laments on his death, for he was universally recognized as a great master musician. His music is characterized by an unbelievable richness of ideas, a modern and original tonal language, which had never before been heard, and stirring depth of expression.

Henry Purcell (1658–1695) is the last in the series of major composers from the great age of English music. His work seems to imply that he was aware of his role. Thus one of his earliest known works is a cycle of fantasies for three to seven gambas, in which he quotes themes by Dowland, among others. The forms of these fantasies are thoroughly traditional: they could have been written 70 years earlier, yet they are excitingly modern. These works are undoubtedly intended to mark the conclusion of a great epoch, but at the same time they point the way to the future. Purcell wrote them in just a few months at the age of 22; they are the only works he wrote for this combination of instruments. In them he exploits the technical and musical resources of the gamba to their very fullest and in all their nuances.

All of Purcell's later compositions must be understood in relation to these early works: on the one hand, the way in which he again and again uses modern dance forms, tone painting, or even the French overture form, all unmistakably anglicized or "refined", and how, on the other hand, he resorts to the old English fantasy, with its grandiose, long, wide-ranging harmonic developments.

Although the great age of English music ends with Purcell, George Frideric Handel, who spent the greater part of his musical life in England, must be regarded as the last English Baroque composer. Here, too, it is interesting to note how greatly the specifically English musical climate formed his style of composition. Handel's works are truly a continuation of Purcell's œuvre, without which they are inconceivable; nor could they have been written anywhere else on earth. No Baroque composer wrote more memorable melodies than Handel, which is undoubtedly due to Purcell's influence. My statement at the beginning of this chapter on English Baroque music is no longer true of Handel. Even Purcell, after all, had used large Baroque gestures in several of his works.

Concerto Grosso and Trio Sonata in the Works of Handel

George Frideric Handel was the first great man of the world among the composers of his age. From the beginning of his musical career he enjoyed uninterrupted success as a composer and fascinating organ virtuoso and improviser. He invariably composed a work for a particular occasion, for a particular location and for a public well known to him. Much of his enormous success rests on the fact that he created his musical statements in a "language" which the public understood, and like a first-rate orator he pegged his thoughts to the level of his audience, so his works reflect the correspondence between composer and listener. Handel remained thoroughly aware of the chief obligation of the artist: to command the listener's attention in such a way that as a result of listening to the music, he becomes a different, better person.

Handel had thoroughly mastered all the musical styles of his period. At the age of 18, he was a violinist, harpsichord player and composer with the Hamburg Opera; at 23, he travelled to Italy, the undisputed center of Baroque musical life, where he entered the circle of Cardinal Ottoboni, a great patron of the arts. There he worked with the leading Italian composers Corelli and Scarlatti, absorbing their methods of composition. Thus he was well-rounded, a genuine practitioner who himself was able to play whatever he composed. His education, his talent for languages and his good taste in all the arts (in England, he assembled an important collection of paintings) sharpened his native skill of reading the public's pulse. From his time in Hamburg, Handel had been counted among the marvels of international music. Following his stay in Italy, 1706–1710, and his successes there, competition was keen among German courts to engage the services of this new superstar. Handel was well aware of and took advantage of the going rates for his services. He was one of the few pre-Classic composers who achieved a measure of social and economic success. His cooperative posture with publishers assured his works a broad distribution and consequently a secure income for him. Thus it is not surprising that many of Handel's compositions, some in different versions and instrumentation, can be found in a variety of contemporary printed editions.

Handel was discovered by 19th-Century music lovers even before Bach, and traditionally commanded a greater following in concert life than Bach. Thus a Handel style developed in England and moved to the continent. Even a cursory glance at the music reveals considerable differences in the great oratorical works of the two contemporaries. Bach's music is much more finely elaborated, his middle voices, especially, are much more lively and participate more independently in the musical event than do Handel's middle voices, which are largely filler. On the other hand, Handel uses longer melodic arches in the upper voices. In general the parts in Bach's music are elaborated in much greater detail, all ornamentation is written out, leaving no room for improvisation. Handel, on the other hand, gives the sweeping line precedence over the detail which is often only suggested or left to the interpreter, as is the ornamentation of cadenzas and da capos. The preëminence of the melodic in Handel as compared with the complex polyphonic fabric in Bach provides us with the key to a meaningful interpretation.

After Handel's works were revived, which happened surprisingly soon after his death, it became increasingly apparent that their monumental aspects could readily be emphasized. Handel's broader style of composition lent itself particularly well to a tonally sumptuous interpretation. To the extent that such interpretation represented what in later generations was described as "Baroque," and perhaps because of Handel's powerful image as a man of affairs, this Handel style gradually gained recognition and was regarded as correct. Although a misconception of the Baroque quest for grandeur and the fact that Handel's major works were not written at the height of the Baroque period should give us pause, nonetheless, the Handel style is both plausible and convincing in purely musical terms. The monumentality of sound achieved in 19th Century performances was imposed directly on the substance of the music itself. Tempos were drawn out; the broadly chordal aspects were emphasized so much that a primitive harmonic monumental style resulted, which the listener can enjoy in comfortable relaxation. This style of performance was soon regarded as the very embodiment of Baroque music: enormous masses of sound which created a kind of innocent festive atmosphere with magnificent and very simple harmonic sequences.

The relatively simple construction, the dominance of the melodic, the accompanying function of the middle voices, clearly pointed toward Classicism. Their acceptance was equally clearly based on social factors, whether the composer was aware of this or not. Music history has repeatedly revealed that music aimed at an educated clientele is esoteric, complicated, complex and depends upon ingenious part writing— written in a secret code, as it were, based on the educational level of the initiate. Music intended to please the "people," on the other hand, is primarily melodic, for one voice with accompaniment; in short a kind of music addressing itself to the emotions. The musical life of England during the age of Handel was much more liberal and popular than that of the continent and so is reflected in Handel's music. The audiences for his operas and oratorios were the common people whom he successfully reached.

Any performance of Handel's works should involve the sensible application of accepted principles of performance practice at the time as to articulation, instrumentation, tempos, dynamics and ornamentation.

The surprising result will be the emergence of a lean, resilient music. In precisely this way, the dominance of melody appears meaningful; dull pathos is replaced by a clear, easily comprehensible statement. As of its own accord, the music approaches the early Classic composers, even Mozart. The power of these works lies in their musical substance, not in the number of performers. For his *Messiah*, Handel used a choir of 27 singers and a correspondingly small orchestra. (Large orchestras were used only for open-air performances or on very special occasions.) There is no reason to assume that he regarded the small forces for which he composed as a temporary or makeshift solution. Indeed, many musical details can be realized only with a small ensemble. The clear articulation of small note values, the essential characteristic of the tonal language of the period, is particularly important in Handel's coloraturas and other musical vocabulary. All contemporary treatises stress the importance of accentuating these smaller and smallest phrases which are likened to the words and syllables of language. Through trial and error, new dimensions are immediately revealed to the musician and listener, but we also learn that this kind of articulation can only be realized with small ensembles. If larger choruses and orchestras are used, everything becomes blurred, or the stresses appear extremely exaggerated and superimposed. The same is true of the tempos: if we select a traditionally brisk tempo, we definitely need a small and flexible musical apparatus. An ideal blend of sound without loss of clarity and transparency can only be obtained on instruments of the period. The goal of interpretations worked out in this way is a modern Handel style. The listener must once again become active, for he will neither be fed a pre-fabricated, bland pap, nor sumptuous sounds. The music then no longer streams from the podium, with the listener appreciatively allowing it to wash over him, but only comes about when interpreter and listener collaborate in an active understanding of musical discourse. It seems to me, therefore, that the interpretation that corresponds most closely to historical conditions is not only the most appropriate for the work, but also the most modern.

Like his organ concertos, Handel's concerti grossi are primarily composed as interludes, overtures, entr'actes for oratorios, cantatas and operas, which does not at all imply that they contain music of lesser importance. On the contrary, it is documented that the audiences at performances of Handel's oratorios were particularly interested in the organ concertos played between the parts, and that they often listened more attentively to the concertos, which were played during intermissions, than to the main work of the evening.

The twelve concerti grossi of Opus 6 were composed in quick succession between September 29 and October 30, 1739. This swift method was not at all typical of Handel, who usually borrowed from a variety of earlier compositions when he composed a new opus. (Here, too, we find individual movements which have been taken from other works, but much fewer than in any comparable work). Consistent design and generally similar instrumentation characterize the twelve concertos from the outset: only the strings and a chordal continuo instrument are obligatory. To be sure, Handel added wind parts to a few of the concertos, but they are always ad libitum and can be omitted without loss of substance. They do, however, clearly indicate the approach Handel took when expanding his instrumentation. They are therefore models which could easily serve for some of the remaining concertos.

In these concerti grossi, Handel did not follow any of the strict formal patterns customary at that time. He had three models to choose from: first, the old church sonata form with its slow-fast-slow-fast sequence of movements (in which a slow movement could be reduced to a few introductory measures); second, Vivaldi's modern Italian concerto form: fast-slow-fast, with a long, independent slow movement; third, the French orchestral suite with an introductory overture and numerous dance movements. However, Handel developed a different sequence of movements for each of his concertos by combining these formal patterns as he best saw fit.

Handel seems to prefer to conclude stimulating virtuoso concertos with an innocent and light dance movement, preferably a minuet. This does not at all correspond to our notion of an "effective" conclusion aimed at evoking enthusiastic applause. Apparently the listener was not to be dismissed in a state of excitation, but rather to be returned to a state of equanimity after having been led though the most varied emotional affects of the music. This recovery and calming effect, the ordering of the emotions after enthusiasm and arousal, are part and parcel of the composition. Certainly, Handel wanted to greatly move and please his listeners, to touch them to the quick; but thereafter he undertook to reconcile and dismiss his audience with a feeling of equanimity.

The original title of the first printing by Walsh in 1740, which Handel supervised, reads: "**TWELVE GRAND CONCERTOS IN SEVEN PARTS FOR FOUR VIOLINS, A TENOR VIOLIN, A VIOLONCELLO WITH A THOROUGH BASS FOR THE HARPSICHORD. COMPOS'D BY GEORGE FREDERICK HANDEL. PUBLISHED BY THE AUTHOR. LONDON...**"The oboe parts of which we spoke earlier are omitted here, as is the figuring in the solo violoncello part—which certainly implies a second continuo instrument. Handel evidently chose the simplest version and thus the easiest to sell, because the various possibilities of performing such concertos had been clearly understood since the time of Corelli and Muffat: every musician could modify the instrumentation in keeping with his own resources and those of the hall where the performance was to take place.

Since Handel's concerti grossi are closely related to those of Corelli, the "inventor" of the concerto grosso, their performance practice was probably also very similar. Fortunately, in Georg Muffat we have a reliable witness who described Corelli's style and imitated it in his own works. Muffat had heard Corelli's early concerti grossi in Rome, under the direction of the composer himself, and as a result was inspired to compose similar works: "The beautiful concertos in the new genre which I enjoyed in Rome have greatly encouraged me and given me a number of ideas." He then describes the various ways they can be performed: "One can play them only *a tre*..." (in compositional terms, this is especially true of Handel's concertos, which are conceived as trio sonatas: the viola part was only added later. As a result, it is sometimes an essential element in the composition, while at other times it seems to be out of place, jumping about in a contrapuntally most illogical manner, filling any remaining gaps in the texture). "They can be played *a quattro*," with tutti and soli simply being combined. "If they are to be played as a full concertino *a tre* with two violins and violoncello," contrasted with the "concerto grosso," the tutti orchestra, then the violas are doubled "in suitable proportions," i.e. according to how many first and second violins are available. The concertos can therefore be played by orchestras of any size, from the smallest to the largest, which was precisely Corelli's practice. In the title to his 1701 concerti grossi, Muffat again writes that the pieces can be played with a small orchestra, "but much more agreeably if they are divided into two choirs, a small one and a large one." One should also play the concertino, the solo trio, "accompanied by an organist with no doubling," i.e. it should have its own continuo instrument, which in turn explains Handel's figuring of the continuo cello part in the autograph and other sources. Even the inclusion of oboists (ad libitum) is mentioned by Muffat: "but only if there are some who can play the French hautbois sweetly." Under some circumstances he is willing to entrust to them, together with a "good bassoonist," the solo trio. This extreme flexibility aimed at an optimal interpretation in terms of the forces and hall available remained an essential feature of the concerto grosso genre. In other words, along with the form, the performance practices were also passed on from Corelli to Handel and beyond, so that for several generations, "concerto grosso" meant both a particular type of instrumental music and a method for performing it.

This brings us to the very important question of positioning performers. Contemporary sources frequently mention choirs (in this context, instrumental groups) that were set up at great distances from each other, sometimes on opposite sides of the room. If the concertino (the solo trio) is played by the first players in the orchestra—which is unfortunately a frequent practice today—many effects, which are clear from the score and thus intended by the composer, are lost. This happens in Concerto I, in the second half of the measure in each of the first three measures, where both solo violins play the same notes. This distribution of voices makes no sense at all if everything is played from within the orchestra. However, if the concertino is moved to a separate position, it is heard as a dialogue-like reaction to the tutti. But even the normal interplay between ripieno or full orchestra and concertino requires a separation to achieve its full effect.

Having experimented with various positionings in concert, we have reached the conclusion that the effects called for by the composition have the greatest impact when the concertino—with its own continuo instrument—is placed to the right rear, i.e. positioned both to the side and further away from the audience than the ripieno.

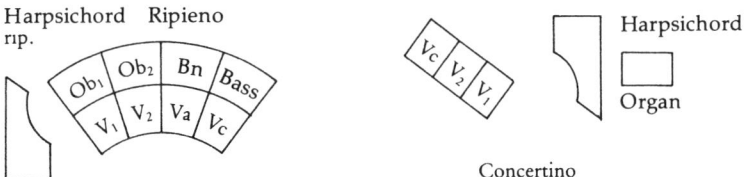

In this positioning, the dialogue between continuo and ripieno becomes clear, and the *sound arrangements* found in certain movements, e.g. Concerto Two; fourth movement, measures 27–40 and similar passages; Concerto Five, fourth movement, etc., finally make sense in performance. Furthermore, those movements in which concertino and ripieno play together also acquire a very compelling and unique coloring, because the entire tonal arsenal of the continuo instruments is added, and because the upper voice is heard not only from the left, as customary, but also from the back and far to the right. This results in an unusual spatial effect.

The continuo can be treated differently from concerto to concerto, even from movement to movement: two harpsichords, one for the ripieno and one for the concertino, and possibly an organ and one or more lutes should be used, in as many different ways as possible.

As to the role of the winds: we know that Handel, like many other composers of his time, as well as his English predecessors such as Henry Purcell, often used oboes and bassoons without specifically indicating their use in the score. Their presence evidently depended upon the size of the orchestra and the number of available musicians. In Concertos I, II, V and VI, one can keep to Handel's wind parts. According to Handel's principles, the oboes and the bassoon should give fullness and contour to a large ripieno, providing brilliance to the coloratura in virtuoso passages by their prompt attack on first and last notes. In complex divisions or embellished passages they would make the movement clearer by playing the unornamented bass part. In accordance with these principles, one could also have one or two oboes and a bassoon play in Concertos III, IV, V, VIII, IX and XII. Concertos VII and XI appear to have been written solely for strings.

I would like to say one more thing about a characteristic of Baroque notation which has received less than adequate attention, and which Handel especially, frequently used: the combination of several measures to form one large measure. This practice chiefly determines articulation and phrasing. Unfortunately, this form of notation, which is very graphic for the player, is suppressed in almost all modern editions, making it impossible to ascertain just how the composer himself notated the work. This combination means that the "usual" meter, e.g. 3/4, is shown by the time signature, but bar-lines are drawn only every four bars, occasionally irregularly. Some scholars believe that this was done only for the sake of simplicity, allowing passages with very small note values to be more easily accommodated; I am firmly convinced that it is a specific type of notation, which belongs in the score and should not simply be mentioned somewhere in the critical apparatus. Seventeen movements are notated like this in these concertos.

Handel's Concerti Grossi, Op. 3 are, in contrast to Op. 6, also known as "Oboe Concertos." This name was assigned in the 19th Century in order to distinguish them from the Concerti Grossi Opus 6, which were regarded as "string concertos." Since that time, our knowledge of these works and their performance practice has changed, so that these designations have lost their meaning. The "oboe concertos" are works with extremely varied scorings in which almost all the instruments also make solo appearances: recorders, flutes, oboes, violins, violoncello. The "string concertos" also use oboes and a bassoon to color the tutti sound and to achieve clearer contours.

At this point let us consider Handel's *trio sonatas,* a form very closely related to the concerto grosso. As in works by both Corelli and Handel, the concertino, the solo group of the concerto grosso, consists of two violins (or two wind instruments in the concertos for winds), and continuo. The concerti grossi are thus formally expanded, concertante trio sonatas. The trio sonata is the most characteristic form of Baroque chamber music, flourishing from the beginning of the 17th to the middle of the 18th Century. It is very rewarding to study its origin and development and to observe the musical and cultural transformations evident in this small genre.

In the 16th Century, completely independent instrumental music first began to emerge. Its forms were derived from the French and Italian chansons and madrigals and from popular dance music as well. They were expanded by typical idioms of whatever instruments were used. These instrumental "canzone" or fantasies had from three to five voices, with all voices equal in imitative movements.

Around 1600, as the soloist, the individual musician, began to dominate the field in contrast to the vocal and instrumental groups of previous centuries, the style of the polyphonic instrumental movement changed as well. The outer voices, upper voice and bass, became more important, while the middle voices were gradually reduced to filler which provided accompaniment for the other voices. The number of voices was very often increased to six, but this was not a real increase, since the upper voice of the old five-part movement was merely divided. These upper voices were once again equal: they had a completely new and thoroughly Baroque task, that of "concertizing" with and against each other, of entering into a dialogue.

The Baroque age viewed music as "a discourse in tones." The soloist developed his "recitation" in accordance with the rules of rhetoric. Dialogue, a contest between speakers, is naturally the most interesting form of discourse. This is the principal reason that, particularly in Baroque music, two or even more soloists are often called for. Take the six-part instrumental piece with two concertizing upper voices (very common in the music of Brade, Scheidt, Monteverdi) mentioned above: If the accompanying middle voices are omitted (which in any case act as a continuo), and only the thorough bass accompanies the two soloists, the result is a trio sonata. This is exactly how the first trios were structured. The first authentic trio sonatas appeared in the ballet and canzone collections of the first decades of the 17th Century.

Two forms were strictly distinguished from each other at a very early stage: the dance suite coming from the ballet, later sonata da camera, and the sinfonia or sonata, sonata da chiesa, derived from the instrumental canzona. Around 1700 both of these forms were again intermixed. Chamber sonatas were given introductory movements which actually belonged to church sonatas, while minuets or gigues were occasionally added to church sonatas. (This development in time led directly to the classical sonata form). The trio sonata is very closely associated with the violin. Italian violin composers of the 17th Century, including Marini, Uccellini, Pesenti, Cazzati, Legrenzi, Corelli and Vivaldi all wrote trio sonatas, particularly for two violins and basso continuo (harpsichord with a violoncello doubling the bass line). Trio sonatas were written in other countries as well, but either they adhered so closely to Italian models that they must be regarded as part of the same development, or else they attempted to introduce new stylistic elements into this Italian type, for example the *Pièces en Trio* by Marin Marais or the trios of Couperin. These French works confronted the Italian style with a completely different tradition. Here it was not the aspect of dialogue that was critical, but the fact that the two upper voices were "stating" the same thing together, in extremely refined and articulated "language." The French composers did not share the preference of their Italian colleagues for the violin, and so in their trios they frequently used wind instruments, flutes and oboes, as well as gambas. But it was the German composers of the 18th Century who were masters of the so-called "mixed taste," in which elements of both the Italian and French styles were blended. This "mixed taste" largely characterizes the trio sonatas of Bach, Telemann and Handel, where the resulting stylistic diversity is balanced by the personal style of the composers. Thus it was that the trio sonatas of that late period blended all the diverse elements which had characterized this varied genre over the course of its 100 year history. These included special forms of the church and chamber styles, the special characteristics of Italian and French musical expression, and the use of a wide variety of instruments.

What an Autograph Can Tell Us

It is a widespread error to believe that for a musician the notes, the graphic appearance of the music simply indicates the tones to be played—how fast, how loud, with what kind of expressive nuance. Above and beyond their purely informational content, the notational picture, both of the single voice and especially of the full score, possess a suggestive power, a magic that no sensitive musician can resist—whether he wants to or not, or is even aware of it. Although this power emanates from printed music, it is much stronger in the case of a manuscript and naturally is strongest of all in the autograph, the composer's original handwriting. For every musician, writing notes is the graphic depiction of a vivid musical event that takes place in his mind. Thus it is only natural that the emotional content communicates itself in the gesture of writing: it is quite impossible to jot down a stirring allegro passage or some tense harmony with nice, neat little note heads. The expression of such a passage must somehow manifest itself through the written notation, and this is inevitably communicated to the performing musician without his even being aware of it. For this reason, it is of the greatest importance that we become acquainted with the work we are performing in the original, i.e. the autograph, or at least in a good facsimile reproduction. The influence this has on the execution of a piece of music can be very great, whether due to conscious or subconscious insights or simply because of the magical aura emanating from the manuscript.

The facsimile of the original score of Handel's *Jeptha* provides us with a stirring and inspiring insight into Handel's working method; it also yields many specific clues for performance, such as can never be derived from a printed score. Handel was still composing in the traditional method which at that time was 150 years old, writing the outer voices first, i.e. the bass as foundation and one or two upper voices. At this stage, he sometimes also wrote down instrumental ideas, such as the entrance of new instruments, and sometimes the vocal and instrumental middle voices, especially in passages where they are treated contrapuntally. He left the staves for the other voices empty for the time being. In the recitatives, he simply wrote the text under the upper of the two staves provided, for they had not yet been composed. Again and again, a reference to the progress of the work is found at the end of a page, e.g. "begun 21 Jan."—"finished 2 Feb. Act 1"—"completed 13 Aug 1751"—etc.

It is clear that *this first stage of composition* was the essential process of composition for Handel; thereafter the work was "completed," or given its final form. This way of proceeding was by no means unique to

Handel; it was the old academic approach to composition. Many 17th and 18th Century compositions, especially those of Italy and France, were handed down only in this form, which seems incomplete to our way of thinking. The "completion," the rounding out of the full orchestral or vocal score, was simply not an essential part of the composition, but rather the responsibility of the performers. A clear difference existed between "work" and "execution." This qualitative distinction can also be clearly seen in Handel's scores, in that he writes "finished" after finishing the composition and only after the *second stage of work*—in which he composes the middle voices, makes cuts or adds, lengthens or repositions arias, makes textual alterations, composes the recitative—does he write "complete." In Handel's case, these stages of composition can be recognized rather easily by two different patterns of writing: meticulous, well-organized and carefully arranged in the first, dashed off in the second. Moreover, in the score of *Jeptha,* Handel's progressive eye trouble, which forced him to interrupt his work several times, evidently made it so difficult for him to write that his music manuscript looks completely different prior to and after the crisis; in the sections written after February 13, 1751, it is obvious that he had to hold the page very close to his eyes to see what he was writing. Because of this, the extent of the changes, cuts and rearrangements in the second stage of this composition can be easily recognized. By studying these procedures, we observe again and again that Handel composed movements, then evidently did not consider them best for the place in question, whereupon he crossed them out and replaced them with another piece, either discards from other compositions, parts of existing compositions, or newly composed. Deleted pieces seldom disappeared completely: usually they appeared in a new context in a different work. These reconstructions, despite considerable differences such as replacement of the text or transposition to a different register, always retained their basic emotional affect. Indeed, we see that the musical ideas usually achieve their greatest impact in the final form. (This approach is closely related to what Bach does in similar situations where, to our amazement, we also observe that the later, rewritten, i.e. "parodied" version is artistically more compelling.)

In incorporating excerpts from older works, Handel did not hesitate to use compositions by other masters as well, if the emotion expressed was especially pertinent. Here, for example, he transcribed a significant passage from the first and second violin parts of Pergolesi's F Minor Concertino as obbligato violin parts in the chorus "Doubtful fear . . ." (m. 54–63), giving great urgency to the homophonic invocation "Hear our pray'r." Of course Handel made this interpolation in the first stage of his work; we can see from the manuscript that the two violin parts had been written first.

Jeptha's aria "Waft her, angels, through the skies . . ." clearly reveals the composer's struggle to achieve a final form of the score. Beyond the basic idea, nothing much seems to be left of the first stage of work, except the first four introductory measures; we observe that Handel rejected individual measures, even entire pages, corrected, deleted again . . . With all its deletions, the piece fills seven pages, of which just over three were finally used.

Among the most important lessons that can be drawn only from the manuscript are the numerous corrections of tempo markings: Handel originally wrote *larghetto* above Iphis' aria "Tune the soft melodious lute," but later crossed this out and wrote *andante*. At that time "tempo" markings signified both a description of emotional affect and formal instructions: larghetto is not only faster than largo, it also has a different quality. Andante is not only a particular composition technique—in a relatively steady tempo—above a walking bass, but also, among other things, a warning to avoid choosing a tempo that is too slow. There are many such examples. Some information about tempo and phrasing can be derived from the hand-written time signatures, bar-lines and symbols indicating rests. Like many composers of the time, including Bach, Handel wrote bar-lines of different lengths and frequently set them at intervals of several measures, which allowed larger contexts to be instantly visible. (Unfortunately, this very practical method is usually ignored by present-day editors.)

The longer we study these questions, the clearer it becomes that from the viewpoint of performers, the composer's manuscript cannot be replaced by the most beautiful print or the best edition. Aside from the suggestive power of the manuscript, which no print can duplicate, the manuscript also provides much concrete information, which we need to obtain directly wherever possible, and not from long-winded critical reports.

Dance Movements—The Suites of Bach

As a musical concept, "suite" means a series or "set" of pieces, usually dances. Bach himself never called his suites by this name, but used the name of the weighty introductory movement, the "overture," as the title of the work as a whole. Nonetheless, these compositions are genuine suites, and number among the last works of this venerable genre.

At the beginning of what would become mainstream Western music, which can be dated from the emergence of true polyphony in the 12th Century, dance music was performed by professional players; it was strictly folk music, and it would have been unthinkable to speak of it in the same breath with learned sacred and secular art music. The circles of the two genres rarely intersected, only when minstrels were occasionally pressed into service for performances of religious works in church, a practice which was frowned upon by church authorities. Despite this strict separation, it was inevitable that the genres would influence each other. Minstrels played dance tunes for peasants and princes alike, so that their virtuosity and musical forces penetrated into the upper social spheres directly involved with secular and sacred art music. Yet before long, traditional folk dances were performed in polyphony, artistically interweaving the various voices, since even here one did not wish to do without the opulent sounds of art music. Unfortunately, we do not possess a good sense of the dance music of this period, as it was not written down, but passed on, with minor fashionable modifications, from one generation of minstrels to the next.

At a very early date, various dances were divided into two kinds: the *Springtanz* or *Nachtanz* (jumping or following dance) and the *Schreittanz* (stepping dance). Minstrels played the same tune for both, but in different rhythms: first a measured pace, then in a fast and fiery fashion. The *Schreittanz* was often executed in duple and the *Nachtanz* in triple meter. This pair of dances can be regarded as the germ which grew into the suite.

Naturally enough, the musical style of the dances always followed the current fashion. Moreover, certain dances climbed the social ladder, developing from crude peasant forms into fashionable court dances, only to drop out of fashion once again as other, newer dances moved into aristocratic circles. The first dance collections were published in the 16th Century. The dances were usually arranged according to type. In Attaingnant's dance books of 1529 and 1530, for example, all dances of the same type are grouped together. The musicians themselves had to select and arrange "suites," often matching a *Nachtanz* to a particular *Schreittanz*.

Despite their strict separation, art music was constantly and greatly enriched by the inexhaustible spring of original dance music. In the long run, art music could not afford to disregard such a vital source and competitor. Gradually, even the most respected composers began to write dances. To be sure, a distance, or more precisely, a difference in status, between the composers of dance music and those of sacred and secular art music lingered. (Even in the 17th Century, the ballets of the Paris opera were composed by a dance master, those of the Viennese opera by a "ballet composer," Heinrich Schmelzer, who also wrote "serious" music.) Once the great composers had taken possession of this powerful and inspiring treasure, they began expanding its individual forms, stylizing them into artistic structures which barely resembled the original dance. Thus, alongside music which was intended to be danced to, a number of collections emerged which were no longer intended for the dance, but were meant to give pleasure as purely instrumental music to listeners and players alike. In the preface to his *Terpsichore* of 1612, Praetorius writes that "all kinds of French dances are played by French dance masters in France and can be used at princely banquets and other convivial gatherings for recreation and amusement." From the very beginning, this concert-like dance music bore the festive stamp of court life.

Playing the short dance movements was naturally affected by the lack of connection between them. Linking movements by theme was occasionally tried, but offered no solution. A suitable opening piece had to be found in order to give the suite in its entirety a valid and complete form. For some years a more or less suitable part of the dance sequence was placed at the beginning of the suite. This might be a strutting *pavane*, for example, which dropped out of fashion at the beginning of the 17th Century, or a serious *allemande*, which was rarely danced after the middle of the 17th Century (Mersenne), although it remained one of the most popular suite movements. In the second half of the century, free introductory movements were finally tried. The Englishman Matthew Locke, for example, selected the fantasia for his consort suites for four viols, while the Austrian Heinrich Biber chose the Italian *sonata* for his *Mensa sonora* (1680).

During the 17th Century, in addition to ancient dance music and the suite made up of stylized dances and intended for concert performance, a second form of purely instrumental music developed: the sonata for several instruments. It developed out of various forms of vocal music and was intended primarily for use in church. Its adagios and allegros were freely invented music, with no relationship to the dance. As direct descendants of the imitative style of the old Flemish school and of the age of Palestrina, they were normally written fugally, i.e. the individual voices took up the same motive in succession and participated as equal partners in the piece. The two primary forms of instrumental music, the suite and the sonata, symbolized the polarity of secular/sacred or courtly and church music. However, the sonata also played a role in the development of the suite into a unified musical form. It could be used as an introductory movement of full and equal importance, to give cohesion to the richly varied dance sequence.

In the France of Louis XIV, the suite received its final shaping as the brilliant showpiece of courtly-secular music. The inspired court composer Lully formed from the old "ballet de cour" a specifically French form of opera, in which ballet played a major role. His operas were interspersed with widely varied dance movements, which in their day were as famous as popular street songs. Arranged in suites, these opera dances were played before the king and in the palaces of the nobility. Although Lully never composed actual instrumental suites, his opera suites became a model for the "French suite," which his students and imitators spread throughout Europe. Since Lully's opera suites were introduced by the overture of the opera, the key problem of this genre was solved at the same time. The overture, a creation of Lully, provided the French orchestral suite its final shape.

In the earliest French operas, instrumental movements derived from the festive dance pairs, *intrada-courante* or *pavane-galliarde*, were usually played. In his overtures, Lully joined a slow opening section, a fugal middle section—interspersed with solos (usually oboes)—and a slow, concluding section, which takes up the opening theme again. For the opening and closing sections he used the *allemande* with its dotted rhythms, which had already proven its usefulness as an opening movement. However, since the form of this dance could not be further expanded, he added a fugal Italian sonata between its two parts. This ingenious idea, the "French overture," the contrasting introductory movement of the suite, took the shape it was to maintain for decades. The newly devised suite was a genuine product of the French spirit, with the greatest possible freedom of the whole, concisely stated and strict and clear in its elaboration of details. No other musical form offered such unrestricted freedom to shape the overall work. The composer could incorporate almost any musical idea into the suite, and it was up to the interpreter to arrange the individual movements. Rules were never spelled out for the sequence of movements; indeed, even in its final form the French suite may be a collection, e.g. by the court gambist Marais, in which several movements of the same type are found which would be selected in keeping with the occasion and mood. However, this freedom was counterbalanced by extreme strictness and precision in the form of the individual movements. These were kept as short as possible, their melodic structure reduced to the utmost simplicity. They resembled witty *bons mots* which permitted not a single extraneous word. Le Blanc wrote in 1740: "the imitation of the dance in the arrangement of tones, in which phrases are joined together like intertwining steps in the formal dance, the symmetrical arrangement of measures, all this has shaped that creation known as the *pièce,* which represents poetry in music" (in contrast to the prose of the sonata). "The entire ambition of the French nation is directed toward...that subtle symmetrical division, which shapes the musical figures in a *pièce,* like those ornamental shapes of boxwood hedges which comprise a garden in the parterre of the Tuileries."— Parallels can also be found in the furniture of the Louis XIV period with its clean geometric lines, its smooth surfaces richly decorated with the finest inlaid work. For even in the simplest and shortest minuets and gavottes, individual tones and tone combinations are ornamented with a myriad of embellishments. But these embellishments were not improvised, as was customary in Italian music. On the contrary there was a long list of trills, mordents, slides and others, which had to be introduced in certain places, which were precisely prescribed by some composers, including the most complicated tremolos and glissandos.

The "Lullists," as Lully's students called themselves, exported the French orchestral suite to other European countries as well. Only Italy, whose mentality was much too alien to this genre, remained untouched by this wave. It met with special interest in Germany where life at court imitated the style of Versailles, including the new French music. This led to interesting conflicts between the representatives of various styles. The "eclectic style" (*Vermischte Geschmack*) was formed from French, Italian and German instrumental music with their most important forms: the suite of the Lullists, the concerto and the polyphonic style. This manner of writing was not simply a conglomeration of styles. The composer was free to select the most suitable style as the primary form and to introduce other elements as well. Thus the "overtures" of Bach, which are written primarily in the French style, also incorporate many features of other styles, in a typical Bach synthesis.

The pieces appearing in the suites of Bach are derived from traditional forms. But having already been transformed into free concert movements, they were only loosely related to their danced prototypes. Their names served primarily to identify their origin in a particular dance type. Mattheson writes: "An allemande intended for dancing and one for playing are as different as night and day." We must therefore think of the tempo and character of each movement as being easily modified, even though each dance movement retained its characteristic features. The history of these dance movements is sketched briefly below.

The *allemande* does not occur in any of Bach's orchestral suites as an expressly named form; however, the slow sections of all four overtures are, strictly speaking, nothing but stylized allemandes. In the 16th Century, the tempo of this dance was rather fast, its melody simple and song-like. Since the allemande was rarely danced by the 17th Century, the composer could use his imagination freely. Like most dances, it grew ever slower in the course of its history. By the beginning of the 18th

Century, the allemande had become an artistically-wrought, festive piece. Walther describes it in 1732 in his lexicon. The allemande "is in a musical partita (suite) at the same time the proposition out of which the other suites (the following movements) flow; it is composed in a dignified and stately manner and must be executed accordingly." In Walther's time both German and French allemandes were either sharply dotted or flowed in running 16ths. Both of these rhythms can be found in the slow parts of the Bach overtures. There are frequent, charming overlappings, when several voices maintain the dotted rhythm while the upper voice or the bass, for example, plays running 16ths. This is especially clear in the overtures to the first and fourth suites, while in the second and third suites, the dotted rhythm dominates in all the voices.

The *courante* is an old court dance. By the 18th Century, it was used only as an instrumental movement and no longer danced. Prior to this time, two distinct forms of the courante had developed. The Italian version was notated in 3/4 or 3/8 time and characterized by a fast, even rushing movement in 16th or 8th notes. The much slower French version was usually in 3/2 time, but frequent ingenious shifts of accent make it difficult for the listener to identify the meter (3/2 or 6/4 time). Both forms occur in the works of Bach. The courante of the first suite is purely French. Mattheson described it perfectly: "the passion or emotional state which should be expressed in the courante is sweet hope, for there is something heart-felt, something yearning, but also something joyful to be found in this melody. These are all pieces which give rise to hope." Mattheson demonstrates these three elements using a courante with a melody so similar to Bach's that one could just as well use the latter's as an example.

The *gavotte* was originally a French peasant dance that, in the course of the 16th Century, was also danced in aristocratic circles, a fact which led to its musical refinement. For several centuries it remained a popular court dance, finally dropping out of vogue in the 19th Century. It is still danced in some parts of France. Its character is one of measured gaiety; joy which never loses self-control. Gavottes "are sometimes treated gaily, but sometimes slowly as well" (Walther). Their upbeat, which consists of two quarter notes, restrains any headlong start. Many gavottes in Marais' gamba suites bear the tempo and expression instructions "legèrement," "gracieusement" or "gay." The gavotte was frequently used as a basis for larger forms; the rondeau of the B Minor Suite is actually a "gavotte en rondeau." The gavottes of all four Bach suites are quietly cheerful pieces.

The *bourrée*, too, was and is a French folk dance which, like the gavotte, was included in 16th-Century collections of courtly dances. All the older descriptions portray it as being very like the gavotte, although its tempo is said to have been faster. This is a joyous and vigorous dance. With its upbeat, which consists of a quarter or two eighth-notes, the bourrée might be said to begin with a brisk leap.

The most famous of the French courtly dances was undoubtedly the *minuet*, and during the reign of Louis XIV it was danced frequently at court. Lully was the first to include it in his operas. The minuet came to be regarded as fit for aristocratic society in the 17th Century, but it was originally a lively folk dance in Poitou, a region of southwestern France. Even as a court dance, it was rather fast and jolly at first (Brossard 1703), but with increasing refinement it gradually became more measured and slow. Saint-Simon gives us a concrete reason for this development: the aging king Louis XIV issued a decree that called for the minuet to be played more slowly, since it had become too difficult for him to dance faster: a practice which was copied all over France. In the *Encyclopédie* of 1750, it is described as "restrained and noble." It was danced with short formal movements and bows and with elegant restraint. This serene elegance is also reflected in the concertante minuets of the early 18th Century, for which Mattheson (1739) demands "no affect other than a moderate gaiety." Quantz writes: "A minuet is to be played lightly, marking the quarters with a heavy but short bow stroke."

The *passepied* is a fast form of the minuet which was very popular, especially in England as the paspé, in the works of Purcell. Most passepieds are in 3/8 time, with two bars often being contracted into one of 3/4 time (hemiola), giving the piece particular rhythmic appeal. Quantz gives us an exact description of how these hemiolas are to be played, i.e. "short and with detached bow." The passepied was usually characterized by jumping eighths; "it comes very close to being frivolous," observes Mattheson. Bach's passepied in the first suite is only distantly related to this model. It is certainly much faster than the minuet in the same suite, but it by no means jumps.

The *forlana* is a wild folk dance which was probably introduced in Venice by Serbo-Croatian immigrants. During the 18th Century it was the most popular dance among the simple Venetian people. In art music, it was used only to portray the wild revelry of the common people, e.g. during the pre-Lenten carnival season. The stereotypical dotted rhythm and the repetition of short musical phrases underscore the ecstatic frenzy of this dance. Türk writes in 1798: "Forlana means a dance in 6/4 time which is very common in Venice among the simple folk. This cheerful dance calls for very rapid movement."

The best example of a fast dance gradually becoming a slow one is the *sarabande*. It probably developed in Mexico or Spain, becoming known in Europe around 1600 as an extravagant, erotic dance song. Initially banned—singers of the sarabande in the Spain of Philip II could count on long prison sentences—, the sarabande was danced with exuberant abandon at courts in France and Spain by the first half of the 17th Century. While in England it long remained a fast and fiery dance (Mace said in 1676: "Sarabandes are in fast triple time, but are lighter and more playful than courantes"), in France it was transformed by Lully into a graceful, measured dance by the middle of the century. From that time on, it became ever more stately and ceremonial in France, and in this manner it was adopted by the German composers. Mattheson: "The sarabande expresses no passion other than reverence." Walther calls it "a solemn melody especially popular among the Spaniards."

The origin of the *polonaise*, which was to become so popular in the 18th Century, is somewhat unclear. To be sure, "Polish dances" of all types had been popular throughout Europe, since the 16th Century, although they bore no similarity whatever to the typical polonaise rhythm. The polonaise spread only at the beginning of the 18th Century, when it attained its final form: a proud stepping dance which was usually played when members of a festive group entered a hall and took their places for a social event. It begins with a stressed downbeat, which emphasis gives it "open-heartedness and quite a free nature" (Mattheson).

The *gigue* was probably derived from the jig, an English folk dance. It was rarely danced on the continent, but developed early as an instrumental movement. Although as early as the Baroque period its name was believed to have been derived from "geigen" or fiddle, this interpretation is viewed with some scepticism today. The first gigues appear among the English virginalists of the Elizabethan age, and in "Much Ado about Nothing," Shakespeare calls them "hot and hasty, ... fantastical." The gigue had thus always had a genuine allegro. It was adopted into the suite repertoire by the French harpsichord virtuosos of the 17th Century, Chambonnières, d'Anglebert, Louis Couperin and others. Lully formed the first orchestral gigues in dotted rhythm for his opera ballets, while the Italian composers around Corelli developed their own form in running 8ths for their chamber sonatas. Like the courante, there were two forms of the gigue: the French in hopping, dotted rhythm, and the Italian in virtuoso running eighth notes. Both forms used a fast, forward-moving tempo. The gigues "are distinguished by a hot and hasty zealousness, a temper that soon passes" (Mattheson). In only very few of his gigues did Bach decide clearly in favor of one or the other of the two types.

Throughout their operas, French composers had interspersed small dance-like movements, the names of which describe either their function in the ballet music or a particular characteristic of the piece. Being unencumbered by any model using a fixed sequence of movements or relationship between movements, the orchestral suite proved ideal for accommodating such character pieces, outside opera as well. This freedom was put to good use, so that elements of program music, which until then had appeared only in rare exceptions were able to freely unfold in art music. Thus various types of imitations found their place as suite movements, including the ringing of bells, the blaring of trumpets, asthmatic groaning, garrulousness, the clucking of hens, caterwauling, and others.

The *badinerie* and the *rejouissance* are particularly popular names for movements of this type. The first means something like "flirting" or "dalliance." It is interesting that certain forms developed around such names and reveal a great similarity to each other. This may have to do with the fact that at that time, it was taken for granted that ideas could be taken from other composers and re-worked, such borrowings not being considered plagiarism. Rejouissance "means joy, gaiety and occurs in overtures, since cheerful pièces are frequently called by this title" (Walther). It is thus simply a word coined to mean "happy ending."

In 16th-Century France and England, serious songs with homophonic instrumental accompaniment were called *airs*. From their beginnings, a particular kind of instrumental piece developed in England, in which the upper part played a sweet and ingratiating melody. At the time of Bach, "air" was a generic term for any piece of music written especially for instrumental pieces. Thus in some of his suites Telemann called all the dances "airs," somewhat akin to the use of the word "movement." But the term was ordinarily used to describe slow pieces with a pronounced, song-like upper voice. "Aria is used to refer to any kind of melody, whether produced vocally or instrumentally" (Walther); "this instrumental aria is . . . played on all types of instruments, and is usually a short, singable, simple two-part melody . . ." (Mattheson).

French Baroque Music—Excitingly New

One of the most rewarding experiences a musician can have is coming to know a new previously unknown piece of music. This experience is completely independent of the age of a work; it can be just as exciting to hear or to play a piece from the 17th or 18th Century for the first time as it is to work with a new composition by one of our contemporaries. For the musicians in the Concentus Musicus, our encounter with Rameau's *Castor et Pollux* was just such an experience. We had all of course been aware of the historical significance of Rameau's theoretical writings. Some of us were also familiar with his chamber music, his compositions for the harpsichord, and one or the other of his cantatas. We also knew that Rameau, like most of his contemporaries, considered his operas among the most important and significant achievements of the 18th Century. Nonetheless, it was a true adventure to encounter something completely unexpected. Even in our wildest dreams we could not have imagined that such grandiose music, absolutely revolutionary for its time, existed in those library volumes.

This brought to mind the transitory or timeless nature of musical masterpieces. Often it is pure chance that some works become famous, well-known, played everywhere. Certainly, there is the "unerring" judgment of history, which separates the wheat from the chaff, but in order to enter into this contest in the first place, a work must first be rescued from the archives in which it may have languished in obscurity for several hundred years, and performed. The fact that French music was rather isolated from the mainstream of European musical life in the 18th Century and even later, may explain Rameau's fate. France was the only country closed to the international language of Italian Baroque music, to which France counterposed its own, completely different musical idiom. It may be that French music remained a kind of foreign language for other Europeans, its beauty revealed only to those willing to take the trouble to cultivate it intensely and devotedly. It is no different for musicians. While Italian Baroque music moves us immediately, even in a faulty rendition, French music must be intensively studied before the musician and the listener can penetrate its core, its statement. It may well be this difficulty which has delayed the renaissance of the great works of Rameau.

During the first orchestra rehearsals for *Castor et Pollux*, we had to remind ourselves at every step of the way that this music had been composed in the 1730s, at the very time Handel and Bach were writing their masterpieces! The absolutely new quality of Rameau's musical language must have been overwhelming during its own age. It is the language of Gluck and in many ways of the Viennese classicists, whose music Rameau anticipated by at least 40 years. We would have thought it impossible that a single composer could invent such a completely new way of treating the orchestra and instrumentation. Rameau has no predecessor here; even his harmonies are remarkable, fascinating. His non-French contemporaries considered many of his dissonances and harmonic developments shocking and ugly—yet there were several older French and English composers who occasionally wrote similar avant-garde harmonies.

We had the same reaction that Debussy describes in his review of a performance of *Castor et Pollux,* namely, almost everything previously ascribed to Gluck had existed earlier in a musically perfect form. Before reading Debussy's essay, we were struck by the parallels between Gluck and Rameau from the very first moment. But what does it mean if musical "parallels," in this case *innovations* of the disposition of sound in musical drama (which were thought to have originated in the 1770's, at a time when things evolved more slowly than they do today) actually had been completely worked out 40 years earlier? Rameau was ahead of his time, and this may well have been the "fatal flaw" in his music.

French Opera: Lully–Rameau

Rameau's operas were the first great masterpieces of the genre to be written in France in the 18th Century; they are also one of the high points of French music in general. These works, which went unrecognized and almost unknown for so long outside of France, hold a strange position in the history of music.

At the beginning of the 17th Century, Italy had become the generally recognized center of European music. The extroverted Italian temperament and ardent southern imagination had given a musical dimension to the new "Baroque" spirit. Monteverdi and his students created a completely new kind of musical drama: the first operas.

The preëminence of the text, of the dramatic expression, over the music, was stressed—a position anticipated in theoretical writings. Nonetheless the nature of the Italian language and the Italian temperament were so musical that music, because of the great power of the abstract medium, came to dominate the text, until finally the libretto simply became a vehicle to showcase the music. This tendency inheres so markedly in the relationship between text and music that any dogma holding music to be merely the handmaiden of the word eventually had to be discarded. Thus at regular intervals in the course of its almost 400-year history, attempts have been made to return this fascinating genre to its origins.

Through the efforts of the Italian Jean-Baptiste Lully, the typical French opera or "tragédie lyrique" was formed, in clear contrast to the Italian opera. In 1646, when only fourteen years old, Lully moved to Paris. At the age of 20 he became the director of the royal instrumental music and by age 39, undisputed ruler of French musical life. Clearly he had adapted himself in a very short time to the French character, which is so fundamentally different from the Italian. Through diligent study he had transformed himself into a superb composer of dance music which played such a major role in French music. Now, together with the poet Quinault, he created the French version of the new genre of opera. The recitative, the ritornello-like preludes to the ariosos, and above all the musical components of overture and chaconne were all borrowed from Italy. But due to the completely different musical traditions of France and the very specific character of the French language and French poetry, these forms were reshaped into a completely new musical genre.

Although Lully incorporated elements of Italian instrumental music into the French operatic overture, he used them in an ingenious yet strict formal design, which established a model for the French overture for 100 years to come. Almost the same was true of the chaconne; Lully shaped this old instrumental dance, based on variations on a repeated bass figure, into the grandiose finale of an act and typically the entire opera as well. These chaconnes could be sung by a chorus or played by the orchestra, but their form was precisely defined. The old French preference for ballet also had to be taken into account in this new form of music drama. Accordingly, all of Lully's operas include numerous dance movements of a wide variety, most of which were purely orchestral pieces, though some were also sung. These ballet interludes soon followed a definite order, so that each act had to end with a kind of "play within a play," a so-called "divertissement" which, like the English "masque," was only loosely connected to the main plot.

The drama itself was based on the recitative, just as in Italian opera. Although Lully took this kind of spoken song from Italy, he tailored it to the French language, thus giving it a completely different character. The Italian recitative was performed with complete rhythmical freedom. Its performance followed spoken language in free, realistic declamation; a few dry harpsichord or lute chords were the foundation for the melodious flow of natural speech. French opera libretti, on the other hand, make conscious use of grand, strictly enunciated language, the rhythm of which was precisely pre-determined by the verse form, usually alexandrines. Lully studied the melody and rhythm of language by having famous tragedians recite passages in his presence so their language could model his recitatives. This relationship was later reversed—great actors studied the recitative performance of singers. Lully thus turned speech into recitative by giving it precise rhythms and demanded that it be performed this way. Other forms of singing, above all the aria, were treated quite differently in France and in Italy. If in that southern country the intention was to provide the vocalist with an opportunity to demonstrate his or her voice (and after the middle of the 17th Century in bel canto or bravura style), in France the aria was completely subordinated to the course of the action, so was less clearly differentiated from the recitative.

In this way Lully, the man from Italy, created a completely independent French version of the music drama drawing upon the material of the new Italian opera and the old French ballet, a version which for quite some time remained the only alternative. French opera combined all the forms of dramatic/musical expression: song, instrumental music and dance. The overall form of the "tragédie lyrique," as the serious opera was then called in France, was also laid down once and for all by Lully and Quinault in an obligatory format: a mythological action, the course of which *had* to be directed through the constant intervention of the gods, was interrupted in each of the five acts by a "divertissement"—an interlude of light dancing and singing often unrelated to the plot—, in which the all-important theatrical machinery, flying devices and fireworks could be staged and ballet presented. These interludes gave the composer the opportunity to use all the French dance forms, all kinds of dance-like airs, without having to pay much attention to the dramatic action. The musical and dramatic climax was provided by the obligatory "tonnère," a thunder storm hurled down by the gods in the final act. Every composer was expected to prove himself by the way in which he handled this set piece.

Song was treated quite differently in France than in the other European countries, which were vocally oriented to the Italian bel canto. France was the only country in Europe in which Italian singers, especially the castrati, were not overwhelmingly in evidence. The division of voice ranges also differed in French opera. Women's roles were sung either by sopranos or mezzo sopranos, depending on the nature of the part (the range in both cases extended from c' to g''). Male roles, both solos and in the choruses, were sung by "haute-contres" (extremely high tenors who probably also sang falsetto [c–c']), "tailles," (low tenors or high baritones), and basses.

Jean-Philippe Rameau (1683–1764) was an accomplished and well received composer when he wrote his first opera at the age of 50. In his first decades, he was an organist at various provincial theaters; at the age of 40 he travelled to Paris, where he lived for the rest of his life. Although he lived a very modest and secluded existence, he attracted the attention of several wealthy patrons. The tax agent Le Riche de la Pouplinière took him into his home, invited him to work with his private orchestra and promoted his cause at court. Rameau was inordinately critical of his own work; his wife reported that during the first 40 years of his life he almost never discussed his work. Once he discovered opera in his old age, nothing else existed—in his last 20 years, he wrote close to twenty works for the stage.

His first opera, *Hippolyte et Aricie,* was a tremendous success, although it set off one of those controversies for which French opera was so notorious and all of which involved Rameau's work in one way or another. As a French composer, Rameau was firmly rooted in the tradition of Lully. He considered himself a Lullist, even though he was not, as he himself stated, capable of being a "slavish imitator." Nonetheless, he was reproached for having betrayed Lully's French opera. It was claimed that he introduced Italian harmonies, diminished seventh chords, etc., so that his work was destructive of French traditions. The opposing parties called themselves "Ramists" and "Lullists." The controversy quickly escalated and became greatly heated. Rameau represented the French side in the so-called "guerre des bouffons." He represented the old tradition, defending it against the followers of an Italian "bouffonist" group, which had performed Pergolesi's *La Serva Padrona* as an intermezzo between the acts of one of Lully's operas. This quarrel pitted the principles of French music against those of Italian. The principal adversary of Rameau and French music was Jean-Jacques Rousseau, who, in his famous *"Lettre sur la musique française,"* vigorously condemned French music, including that of Rameau, while extolling the virtues of Italian music. Rameau's friends were ultimately victorious, as demonstrated by the warm reception accorded the second version of *Castor et Pollux* in 1754. Twenty years later the quarrel broke out anew. This time it was Gluck, not Rameau, and once again it was a question of the differences between French and Italian opera. The vehemence with which these "battles" were carried out was even reflected in private lives. People making social calls were asked if they were "Gluckists" or "Piccinnists," in order to determine whether they could be accepted in a particular social circle.

Despite Rameau's clear traditionalism, we can understand the aversion felt by the "Lullists," for in addition to the accepted forms, to which he closely adhered, Rameau discovered, even invented, an entire repertoire of completely new expressive devices, which he used for the first time in music. He wrote what might be described as old French operas that sounded like the most modern, avant-garde music. In Rameau we may well discover the link that was missing for so long between the Baroque and the Classic. His harmonies are rich and daring, anticipating developments that would come only decades later. In studying the instrumentation of the large orchestral pieces (overtures, chaconnes), of the choruses and above all of the accompanied recitatives, we encounter many genuine inventions. The winds, which were used in Baroque music only after the fashion of organ stops or for solos, are often placed under the string orchestra as independent harmonic support or as sustained pedal tones. Various emotions could thus be portrayed simultaneously in a credible and understandable way. It was thought that this technique had originated only 30 years later with Gluck. In order to heighten the progress of the dramatic action, he introduced many stages between the accompanied aria and the secco recitative. Accompanied recitatives of all types and—for the time—incredibly colorful instrumentation and harmonic usage produced sounds which had never been heard before. His wind writing is obbligato for long passages and each instrument is handled completely idiomatically. This is especially true of the bassoons, which are used not simply to reinforce the bass.

In this way, Rameau was able to create extremely naturalistic onomatopoetic effects, especially in the accompanied recitatives. "Imiter la nature," to imitate nature, was a fundamental principle of French musical aesthetics in the 18th Century. In the "tonnère" of Act V of *Castor et Pollux,* thunder, lighting, tempests, and generally disturbed nature are expressed by wild tremolos and runs for strings, austere wind chords and accentuated sustained notes. This ominous, stormy scene is transformed by almost romantic sound painting into a serene, sunny landscape: of the six wind instruments which had represented thunder and lightning, a single melodic flute remains; the skies clear and Jupiter floats gently and gracefully down. The independent and purely coloristic treatment of the bassoons is also radically modern. Rameau was the first to lead this instrument up to a'. Almost all the achievements of the Classic period thus seem to have their roots here. Recalling that this opera was written in 1737, at the time Bach and Handel were composing their oratorios and cantatas and the Mannheim innovations were only in their infancy, we can begin to understand what an enormous impact Rameau's genius had on music history.

Castor et Pollux was enthusiastically received by contemporary audiences. In his *Essai sur la Musique,* de la Borde wrote: "This wonderful opera has gone through a hundred performances without any diminution in applause or in the enthusiasm of its audiences; it equally delights the soul, heart, reason, eyes, ears and imagination of all Paris." *Castor et Pollux* was revived by the Parisian Schola Cantorum around 1900, a performance which Debussy attended and reviewed. He instantly recognized the parallels with Gluck: "Gluck's music is inconceivable without the work of Rameau... In individual details, there are so many similarities between the two that one is justified in claiming that only by appropriating the most beautiful creations of Rameau was Gluck able to secure for himself a lasting place in French theater." He describes the opening of the first act: "After an overture, the sighing voices of a chorus of mourners are raised in honor of the dead Castor. One is immediately caught up in this tragic atmosphere... These are people who weep like you and me. Then Telaïre appears, and one hears the sweetest, most moving lament that ever poured forth from a loving heart...". The opening of the second act: "The aria of Pollux, 'Nature, Amour,' speaks to us so personally and has such a unique structure that time and space disappear and we feel as if Rameau were living among us so we could thank him for his work...". And of the last scene in this act: "Hebe, the goddess of youth, dances at the head of the heavenly delights... Never has the gentle emotion of rapture found such perfect expression. Blinded by this supernatural world, Pollux must call on all of his Spartan fortitude to escape the enchantment and remember Castor (whom I myself forgot for some time)."

In contrast to instrumental music, which was usually notated rather accurately, operas were written down only sketchily. This is true of the Italian operas of Monteverdi and Cavalli as well as of the French operas of Lully and his successors. Many orchestral parts have been preserved, particularly in the case of Parisian performances, so that scores of some works can be reconstructed. It is of course very difficult to gauge the composer's input from these parts; in many cases, they were probably written by the musicians themselves or by talented arrangers, perhaps from the "workshop" of the composer himself. Most of Rameau's operas have also come down to us this way. There are two printed scores of *Castor et Pollux,* one of the first version of 1737, one of the second version of 1754, both in outline form only. The overture is notated in only two lines, with simple indications of instrumentation. The words "violons," "hautbois," "bassons" or "tous" sometimes occur in the allegro part; flute and oboe parts are occasionally written out, the middle voices never. However, the dynamics are indicated very precisely, even with intermediate values. A five-part score with two violas, which conveys a very authentic impression, can be reconstructed from the orchestral parts used for the first performances. The quality of this material leads me to believe that the middle voices and the details of instrumentation also derive from Rameau, or at least were supervised by him. The few instructions in the printed score-outline are painstakingly carried out in these parts. There also exists a series of adaptations which were evidently not approved by Rameau, since their instrumentation deviates too greatly from his instructions, but which show nonetheless how much latitude was accorded at that time to the performer. For example, there is a score in which, in addition to the flutes, oboes and bassoons, horns are also used, which was certainly not intended by the composer; in the same version, Rameau's bassoon solos are assigned to the violas, etc.

Aside from the score and its instrumentation, the question of improvisation and ornamentation has to be addressed for every Baroque opera. Here the French were much stricter than the Italians; they permitted absolutely no improvised ornamentation, only the precisely codified "agréments" of instrumental music. To be sure, they demanded an extremely sophisticated and well thought-out execution. Every single case demanded a decision about the type of ornamentation most suitable, before or on the beat, a long or short appoggiatura, with or without support, etc. Rameau notes: "No matter how well-executed an ornament might be, if that 'certain something' is missing on which everything else depends . . . too much or too little, too early or too late, longer or shorter in the 'delayed tones' (suspensions), the increasing or decreasing volume of tones . . . in a word, this ultimate precision . . . , if missing just once, then all ornamentation becomes boring . . ." These ornaments passed from instrumental music to vocal music, even to the choruses.

Rameau stands at the end of a development which began with Lully almost 100 years earlier. Even though he was a modern, even trend-setting composer in every regard, he still saw himself as the guardian of French operatic tradition. He retained the "divertissement" and even the "tonnère," and held that a lack of realism in the scenes with the gods was an essential feature of true opera. Yet, like no composer before him and only very few since, he opened up completely new pathways for traditional form.

Reflections of an Orchestra Member on a Letter by W. A. Mozart

Letter from Paris, July 3, 1778: "I have had to compose a symphony for the opening of the Concert Spirituel. It was most successful... I was very nervous at the rehearsal, for never in my life have I heard a worse performance. You have no idea how they twice scraped and scrambled through it... I would gladly have had it rehearsed again, but as there was so much else to rehearse, there was no time left... The symphony began... and just in the middle of the first Allegro there was a passage which I felt sure must please. The audience were quite carried away—and there was a tremendous burst of applause. But as I knew, when I wrote it, what effect it would surely produce, I had introduced the passage again at the close—when there were shouts of 'Da capo.' The Andante also found favour, but particularly the last Allegro, because having observed that all last as well as first Allegros begin here with the instruments playing together and generally unisono, I began mine with two violins only, piano for the first eight bars—followed instantly by a forte; the audience, as I expected, said 'hush' at the soft beginning, and when they heard the forte, began at once to clap their hands."

June 12: "I have been careful not to neglect le premier coup d'archet—and that is quite sufficient."

July 9 concerning a conversation with le Gros, the manager of the Concerts Spirituels: "the symphony was highly approved of—and le Gros is so pleased with it that he says it is his very best symphony. But the Andante has not had the good fortune to win his approval; he declares that it has too many modulations and that it is too long. He derives this opinion, however, from the fact that the audience forgot to clap their hands as loudly and to shout as much as they did at the end of the first and last movements. For indeed the Andante is a great favourite of mine and with all connoisseurs, lovers of music and the majority of those who have heard it. It is just the opposite of what le Gros says—for it is quite simple and short. But in order to satisfy him (and, as he maintains, some others) I have composed a fresh Andante—each is good in its own way—for each has a different character. But the last pleases me even more." [Quotes from *The Letters of Mozart and His Family* translated by Emily Anderson. Macmillan 1966]

The first excerpt is taken from one of Mozart's most beautiful letters, written during the night following his mother's death. In the opening, he tries in a moving way to prepare his father for this fateful blow by describing his mother as very ill. Immediately following comes a fresh, carefree description of the premiere performance of the "Paris" Symphony. Although this juxtaposition seems almost shocking to us today, death was a familiar companion for the deeply religious people of Mozart's time.

The Paris orchestra, for which the symphony had been written, was quite large for that period. In addition to the strings, it included transverse flutes, oboes, clarinets, bassoons, horns, trumpets and kettle drums. Nonetheless, the sound of this orchestra was quite different from that to which we are accustomed today. The string instruments at that time had a much softer, and better defined sound. Horns and trumpets were twice as long and had a smaller bore than today, thus they produced a lean, but aggressive and brazen sound, above all the trumpets. There were no valves, so only natural tones could be played. The woodwinds were softer as well, and the timbre of each instrument was more distinct than today. On the whole, an orchestra of this period must have sounded much less massive, even in the *forte,* than a modern orchestra of the same size. The sound was more colorful and less round and uniform than today. There was no conductor; the concert master, seated at the head of the first violins, gave the cues. Mozart's description of the performance of the symphony is particularly interesting, because this valuable testimony by the composer describes not only the effect on the audience, but also the careful *planning* to achieve this effect. Mozart studied the programs of the *concerts spirituels* in order to create as strong an impact as possible by the clever application of his capacity for invention and fantasy. It is unfortunate that Mozart's words describing the effect of this symphony are not printed on the first page of the conductor's score. These comments would be of inestimable value to conductors who are concerned with faithfulness to the work but do not happen to have this letter handy.

The symphony begins with the entire orchestra in forte-unisono. This "premier coup d'archet," the sudden forte entry of all of the strings, was a famous feature of the *Concerts Spirituels* and was expected at the opening of each symphony. What almost mischievous pleasure Mozart derived from this effect in the finale! Instead of the anticipated forte entry—the "coup d'achet" was also expected at the beginning of the final movement—the first and second violins play very softly in a filigree duet, only to relax the artificially enhanced tension eight measures later by means of a liberating forte-unisono of the entire orchestra. Unfortunately, I can think of very few performances in which this effect is fully realized.

What kind of a passage is it in the first movement, which "carried away the audience" and evoked "a tremendous burst of applause"? It is a delicate spiccato passage in the strings in octaves, with flutes and oboes playing long chords, above a pizzicato bass. Most performances gloss over this passage, of which Mozart, even as he was composing it, knew precisely "what kind of an effect it would have." Today's listener is aware of nothing unusual in this place. Yet earlier composers could expect an attentive and informed audience, which noticed each new idea, each effect in instrumentation, each unusual harmonic or melodic feature, and which passionately expressed its approval or disapproval. The public of today concentrates its interest not on the composition, but on its execution, which, to be sure, is judged with a high degree of expertise.

His remarks about the audience also deserve particular attention. Mozart is not at all surprised that the audience applauds between the movements, or even while the musicians are still playing; in fact he seems to count on it. This spontaneous applause reassured the composer that he was understood. Indeed, part of the music was probably lost at first hearing in the lively reaction of the audience, so that repeats may have served a dual purpose. There is no loud applause after the intimate andante, of course. The original andante, which Mozart preferred to the other movements, is not known at all today, although he considered it the equal of the others—"each is good in its own way." The reaction of the audience demonstrates quite clearly just how far-reaching are the changes which have occurred in the way music is played and listened to. At that time, people wanted to be surprised by something new, something they had never heard before. The listener gladly allowed himself to be moved to outbursts of excitement when a gifted composer succeeded in a particularly effective flash of inspiration. No one was interested in what was already known; the stress was on novelty and *only* on novelty. Today, on the other hand, we are interested practically *only* in what is known and what is all too well known. As musicians, we feel quite keenly that this desire to listen only to what is known is carried too far, for example when we play Beethoven's Seventh Symphony several times for the same audience in a very short time. Or we find quite embarrassing the audience's, and sometimes even the conductor's, lack of interest in unfamiliar works of the present or of the past.

This leads to another, unfortunately distressing thought, which Mozart's letter also evokes. Mozart complains bitterly and with desperation that too little time was devoted to his symphony. "As there was so much else to rehearse, there was no time left." Certain passages in the "Paris" Symphony (for example, the difficult violin duet at the beginning of the finale) pose problems even for a modern orchestra, problems which cannot be solved by simply playing through the work twice. If a Mozart or Haydn symphony is not one of the three or four most commonly performed, it is condemned to a miserable Cinderella existence. The conductors spend most of their rehearsal time on the big concluding piece of the program, usually a work that every musician knows backwards and forwards, and finally, at the end of the last rehearsal, the Mozart symphony is played through all too rapidly. This symphony is included at the beginning of the program simply to warm up the orchestra, as it were, since "it is very easy anyway." Thus the work, which actually deserves to be the musical focus of many a program, is played casually before an apathetic audience.

Almost no one doubts that Mozart was one of the greatest composers of all time. In actual practice, however, we pay almost no attention to many of his works, while other works, whose lesser quality is candidly admitted, are preferred. Is this really due only to the louder volume of the latter?

From the perspective of the orchestra, therefore, treatment of Mozart's works is a somewhat sad story. Many of his most magnificent accomplishments are rarely performed. In this respect, one of the greatest geniuses known to mankind has still not received his due.

Discography (Selection)

Nikolaus Harnoncourt

JOHANN SEBASTIAN BACH

Johannes-Passion, BWV 245
Equiluz, van t'Hoff, van Egmond,
Wiener Sängerknaben,
Chorus Viennensis,
Concentus musicus Wien
LP 6.35018 (3 LPs) EK
DMM
MC 4.35018 (2 MCs) MH TIS
Grand Prix du Disque

Johannes-Passion—Excerpts
Equiluz, van t'Hoff, van Egmond,
Wiener Sängerknaben,
Chorus Viennensis,
Concentus musicus Wien
LP 6.41069 AH

Matthäus-Passion, BWV 244
Soloists: Wiener Sängerknaben,
Esswood, van Egmond,
Schopper, King's College Choir,
Cambridge
Concentus musicus Wien
LP 6.35047 (4 LPs) FK
DMM
MC 4.35047 (3 MCs) MR TIS
Premio Della Critica Discografica
Italiana, Edison-Preis

Mattäus-Passion, BWV 244,
Arias and Choruses
Concentus musicus Wien
LP 6.42536 AH

Matthäus-Passion, BWV 244,
Arias
Concentus musicus Wien
LP 6.41136 AQ
MC 4.41136 CQ

Mass in B Minor, BWV 232
Hansmann, Iiyama, Watts,
Equiluz, van Egmond
Concentus musicus Wien
LP 6.35019 (3 LPs) FK
DMM
CD 8.35019 (2 CDs) 2A
Deutscher Schallplattenpreis,
Grand Prix du Disque

Missa 1733, Kyrie—Gloria
Hansmann, Iiyama, Watts,
Equiluz, van Egmond, Wiener
Sängerknaben,
Chorus Viennensis,
Concentus musicus Wien
LP 6.41135 AQ

Christmas Oratorio, BWV 248
Esswood, Equiluz, Nimsgern,
Wiener Sängerknaben,
Chorus Viennensis,
Concentus musicus Wien
LP 6.35022 (3 LPs) FK
DMM
CD 8.35022 (3 CDs) 2B

**Die Weihnachtsgeschichte aus
dem Weihnachtsoratorium,**
BWV 248
Soloist: Wiener Sängerknaben,
Esswood, Equiluz, Nimsgern,
Wiener Sängerknaben,
Chorus Viennensis,
Concentus musicus Wien
LP 6.42102 AQ

THE CANTATAS
First complete recording with
authentic instruments. Complete
texts and scores included.
40 albums.
Erasmus-Preis.

Motets
Singet dem Herrn ein neues Lied,
BWV 225; Der Geist hilft unserer
Schwachheit auf, BWV 226; Jesu,
meine Freude, BWV 227; Fürchte
dich nicht, BWV 228; Komm,
Jesu, komm, BWV 229; Lobet
den Herrn, BWV 230
Bachchor Stockholm
Concentus musicus Wien
LP 6.42663 AZ
DMM DIGITAL
MC 4.42663 CY CrO$_2$
CD 8.42663 ZK
Deutscher Schallplattenpreis
Caecilia-Preis

Der zufriedengestellte Äolus
Zerreisset, zersprenget,
zertrümmert die Gruft, BWV 205
Kenny, Lipovšek, Equiluz, Holl,
Arnold-Schönberg-Chor,
Concentus musicus Wien
LP 6.42915 AZ
DMM DIGITAL
CD 8.42915 ZK

ORCHESTRAL WORKS
**Brandenburg Concertos
Nr. 1–6**
Concentus musicus Wien
LP 6.35620 (2 LPs) FD
DMM DIGITAL
MC 4.35620 (2 MCs) MH

**Brandenburg Concertos
Nr. 1, 2, 4**
Concentus musicus Wien
LP 6.42823 AZ
DMM DIGITAL
MC 4.42823 CX
CD 8.42823 ZK

**Brandenburg Concertos
Nr. 3, 5, 6**
Concentus musicus Wien
LP 6.42840 AZ
DMM DIGITAL
MC 4.42840 CX
CD 8.42840 ZK

**Suites Nr. 1, BWV 1066;
Nr. 2, BWV 1067**
Concentus musicus Wien
LP 6.43051 AZ
DMM DIGITAL
MC 4.43051 CY CrO$_2$
CD 8.43051 ZK

**Suites Nr. 3, BWV 1068;
Nr. 4, BWV 1069**
Concentus musicus Wien
LP 6.43052 AZ
DMM DIGITAL
MC 4.43052 CY CrO$_2$
CD 8.43052 ZK

Suites Nr. 1–4
Concentus musicus Wien
LP 6.35046 (2 LPs) DX
MC 4.35046 (2 MCs) ME TIS
Deutscher Schallplattenpreis
Grammy

Harpsichord Concerto Nr. 1,
BWV 1052; Sinfonia from the
Concerto, BWV 1045
(Fragment); Double Concerto, BWV 1060
Herbert Tachezi, Harpsichord,
Alice Harnoncourt, Violin,
Jürg Schaeftlein, Oboe,
Concentus musicus Wien
LP 6.41121 AS TIS

Harpsichord Concerto Nr. 1,
BWV 1052; **Nr. 10,** BWV 1061
Gustav Leonhardt, Anneke
Uittenbosch, Herbert Tachezi,
Harpsichord,
Concentus musicus Wien
Leonhardt-Consort/Leonhardt
LP 6.42488 AQ
MC 4.42488 CQ

Musical Offering, BWV 1079
Concentus musicus Wien
LP 6.41124 AZ
DMM
MC 4.41124 CY CrO$_2$
Edison-Preis

Sinfonia, Movements from the
Cantatas, BWV 18, 21, 29, 31, 35,
42, 49, 244
Concentus musicus Wien
LP 6.41970 AQ

**Chamber Music—Vol. 1
Violin Sonatas,** BWV 1014–1019
Alice Harnoncourt, Violin,
Nikolaus Harnoncourt, Gamba,
Herbert Tachezi, Harpsichord
LP 6.35310 (2 LPs) FX

**Chamber Music—Vol. 2
Flute Sonatas**
Leopold Stastny, Frans Brüggen,
Flute, Herbert Tachezi,
Harpsichord, Alice Harnoncourt,
Violin, Nikolaus Harnoncourt, Cello
LP 6.35339 (2 LPs) FX

**Chamber Music—Vol. 3
3 Gamba Sonatas**
Concentus musicus Wien
LP 6.35350 (2 LPs) FX

Violin Concertos—Vol. 1
Concerto for Two Violins,
BWV 1043; Violin Concertos,
BWV 1042, BWV 1041
Alice Harnoncourt and Walter
Pfeiffer, Violin,
Concentus musicus Wien
LP 6.41227 AZ
DMM
MC 4.41227 CY CrO$_2$
CD 8.41227 ZK

Violin Concertos—Vol. 2
Concerto for Violin, BWV 1056; Concerto for Oboe d'amore, BWV 1055; Concerto for Violin, BWV 1052
Concentus musicus Wien
LP 6.42032 AW TIS

Violin Concertos
BWV 1041, 1042, 1043, 1052, 1056, 1060
Alice Harnoncourt, Walter Pfeiffer, Violin, Jürg Schaeftlein, Oboe,
Concentus musicus Wien
LP 6.35610 (2 LPs) DX

Magnificat, BWV 243

Georg Friedrich Händel:
Utrecht Te Deum
Palmer—Lipovšek—Langridge
Wiener Sängerknaben,
Arnold-Schönberg-Chor,
Concentus musicus Wien
LP 6.42955 AZ
DMM DIGITAL
MC 4.42955 CY CrO$_2$
CD 8.42955 ZK

HEINRICH IGNAZ FRANZ BIBER

Schlachtmusik, Pauernkirchfahrt Ballettae, Sonate
Concentus musicus Wien
LP 6.41134 AS TIS

Requiem, Sonata St. Polycarpi à 9, Laetatus sum à 7, Dreikönigskantate
Wiener Sängerknaben, Soloists: Equiluz, van Egmond,
Concentus musicus Wien
LP 6.41245 AQ

JOHANN JOSEPH FUX

Concentus musico instrumentalis . . . 1701
Sernade à 8, Rondeau à 7, Sonata à Quattro
Concentus musicus Wien
LP 6.41271 AQ

GEORGE FRIDERIC HANDEL

Alexander's Feast
(Cäcilien-Ode, 1736)
Palmer, Rolfe-Johnson, Roberts,
Bachchor Stockholm,
Concentus musicus Wien
LP 6.35440 (2 LPs) EK
DMM
CD 8.35440 (2 CDs) ZA

Belshazzar, Oratorio
Tear, Palmer, Lehane, Esswood,
Concentus musicus Wien
LP 6.35326 (4 LPs) GK
Edison-Preis

Giulio Cesare Highlights
Esswood, Alexander, Murray,
Concentus musicus Wien
CD 8.43927 ZK

Jephtha
Hollweg, Linos, Galle, Esswood, Tomaschke, Sima,
Concentus musicus Wien
LP 6.35499 (4 LPs) GK
DMM
MC 4.35499 (3 MCs) MR
CD 8.35499 (3 CDs) ZB
Deutscher Schallplattenpreis

Ode for St. Cecilia's Day
Palmer, Rolfe-Johnson,
Bachchor Stockholm,
Concentus musicus Wien
LP 6.42349 AZ
MC 4.42349 CY CrO$_2$
CD 8.42349 ZK

Messiah
Gale, Lipovšek, Hollweg,
Kennedy, Stockholmer Kammerchor,
Concentus musicus Wien
LP 6.35617 (3 LPs) FR
DMM DIGITAL
MC 4.35617 (3 MCs) MU
CD 8.35617 (3 CDs) ZB

Concertos
Concerto F Major, Concerto D Minor, Concerto G Minor, Sonata à 3 F Major, Concerto D Major
Concentus musicus Wien
LP 6.41270 AW TIS

Alexander's Feast-Concerto— Concertos for Organ, Oboe, Violin
Alice Harnoncourt, Jürg Schaeftlein, Herbert Tachezi
Concentus musicus Wien
LP 6.43050 AZ
DMM DIGITAL
MC 4.43050 CY CrO$_2$
CD 8.43050 DIG ZK TELDEC

Concerti grossi, op. 3
Nr. 1, 2, 3, 4a, 4b, 5, 6; Oboe Concerto Nr. 3
Concentus musicus Wien
LP 6.35545 (2 LPs) EX
DMM
CD 8.35545 (2 CDs) ZA

Concerti grossi, op. 6,
Nr. 1–12
Concentus musicus Wien
LP 6.35603 (3 LPs) FR
DMM DIGITAL
CD 8.35603 (3 CDs) ZB

Organ Concertos, op. 4 & op. 7
Herbert Tachezi, Organ
Concentus musicus Wien
LP 6.35282 (3 LPs) FK
CD 8.35282 (3 CDs) ZB

Water Music—Complete
Concentus musicus Wien
LP 6.42368 AZ
DMM DIGITAL
MC 4.42368 CY CrO₂
CD 8.42368 ZK

Trio Sonatas
Sonata B Minor for Traverso,
Violin and B.c., op. 2, 1b;
Sonata D Minor for 2 Violins and
B.c., op. 2, 3; Sonata D Minor,
Oboe, Violin and B.c.; Sonata
F Major for Recorder, Violin, and
B.c., op. 2,5
Frans Brüggen, Recorder, Alice
Harnoncourt, Walter Pfeiffer,
Violin, Herbert Tachezi, Harpsichord
LP 6.41254 AQ

Utrecht Te Deum
J. S. Bach: Magnificat,
BWV 243
Palmer, Lipovsek, Langridge,
Wiener Sängerknaben,
Arnold-Schönberg-Chor,
Concentus musicus Wien
LP 6.42955 AZ
DMM DIGITAL
MC 4.42955 CY CrO₂
CD 8.42955 ZK

JOSEPH HAYDN

The Creation
Gruberova, Protschka, Holl,
Arnold-Schönberg-Chorus
Wiener Symphoniker

The Seasons
Blais, Protschka, Holl,
Arnold-Schönberg-Chorus
Wiener Symphoniker

CLAUDIO MONTEVERDI

L'Orfeo, complete recording
Berberian, Kozma, Hansmann,
Katanosaka, Rogers, Equiluz,
Egmond, Villisech,
capella antiqua, München,
Concentus musicus Wien
LP 6.35020 (3 LPs) FK
CD 8.35020 (2 CDs) ZA
Deutscher Schallplattenpreis,
Edison-Preis

L'Orfeo, excerpts
Berberian, Kozma, Hansmann,
Katanosaka, Rogers, Equiluz,
Egmond, Villisech,
capella antiqua, München,
Concentus musicus Wien
LP 6.41175 AN

L'Orfeo
Il Ritorno d'Ulisse in Patria
L'Incoronazione di Poppea
Complete recordings with
original instruments
Concentus musicus Wien
LP 6.35376 (12 LPs) JY

L'Incoronazione di Poppea,
Complete recording
Donath, Söderström, Berberian,
Esswood, Langridge, Equiluz
Concentus musicus Wien
LP 6.35247 (5 LPs) HD
Deutscher Schallplattenpreis
Grand Prix du Disque, Premio
Della Critica Discografica
Italiana
Art Festival Prize, Japan
Grand Prix du Disque, Canada

Lettera amorosa—Lamento
d'Arianna—Disprezzata
Regina—A Dio, Roma from
"L'Incoronazione di Poppea"
Cathy Berberian, Mezzosopran,
Concentus musicus Wien
LP 6.41930 AW TIS

Cathy Berberian sings
Monteverdi
Arias from L'Orfeo,
L'Incoronazione di Poppea, Madrigals
and Songs
Concentus musicus Wien
LP 6.41956 AQ

Vespro della Beata Vergine
Marian Vespers, 1610
Hansmann, Jacobeit, Rogers,
van't Hoff, van Egmond,
Villisech, solos by Wiener
Sängerknaben, Monteverdi Chor,
Hamburg,
Concentus musicus Wien
LP 6.35045 (2 LPs) DX
Grand Prix du Disque

Combattimento di Tancredi e Clorinda—Lamento dell ninfa
Schmidt, Palmer, Hollweg
Concentus musicus Wien
LP 6.43054 AZ
DMM DIGITAL
MC 4.43054 CY CrO$_2$
CD 8.43054 ZK

WOLFGANG AMADEUS MOZART

Idomeneo, Complete recording
Hollweg, Schmidt, Yakar, Palmer,
Equiluz, Tear, Estes, Mozart-
orchester & Chor des
Opernhauses Zürich
LP 6.35547 (4 LPs) GX
DMM DIGITAL
CD 8.35547 (3 CDs) ZB
Prix Mondial du Disque
Caecilia-Preis
Preis der Deutschen Schallplattenkritik

Mass in C Minor, KV 427
Laki, Equiluz, Holl,
Wiener Staatsopernchor,
Concentus musicus Wien
LP 6.43120 AZ
DMM
MC 4.43120 CY
CD 8.43120 ZK

Thamos, König von Ägypten,
KV 345
Thomaschke, Perry, Mühle,
van Altena, van der Kamp,
Niederländischer Kammerchor,
Collegium Vocale, Concertgebouw
Orchestra
LP 6.42702 AZ
DMM DIGITAL
MC 4.42702 CX
CD 8.42702 ZK
Preis der Deutschen Schallplattenkritik

Requiem, KV 626
Yakar, Wenkel, Equiluz, Holl,
Wiener Staatsopernchor,
Concentus musicus Wien
LP 6.42756 AZ
DMM DIGITAL
MC 4.42756 CX
CD 8.42756 ZK

Serenade Nr. 7 D Major, KV 250
"Haffner Serenade"
March D Major, KV 249
Staatskapelle Dresden
LP 6.43062 AZ
DMM DIGITAL
MC 4.43062 CY CrO$_2$
CD 8.43062 ZK DIG

Serenata Notturna, KV 239
Notturno, KV 286

Symphony Nr. 25 G Minor,
KV 183,**Symphony Nr. 40,**
G Minor, KV 550
Concertgebouw Orchestra,
Amsterdam
LP 6.42935 AZ
DMM DIGITAL
MC 4.42935 CX
CD 8.42935 ZK

Symphonies Nr. 29 A Major,
KV 201;**Nr. 39 E-flat Major,**
KV 543
Concertgebouw Orchestra,
Amsterdam
LP 6.43107 AZ
DMM DIGITAL
MC 4.43107 CY CrO$_2$
CD 8.43107 ZK

Symphony Nr. 33 B-flat Major,
KV 319, **Symphony Nr. 31 D Major,**
KV 297 ("Paris")
Concertgebouw Orchestra
LP 6.42817 AZ
DMM DIGITAL
MC 4.42817 CX
CD 8.42817 ZK

Symphony Nr. 34 C Major,
KV 338, **Symphony Nr. 35**
D Major, KV 385 ("Haffner")
Concertgebouw Orchestra
LP 6.42703 AZ
DMM DIGITAL
MC 4.42703 CX
CD 8.42703 ZK

Symphony Nr. 38 D Major,
KV 504 ("Prague"), **Symphony
Nr. 41 C Major,** KV 551
("Jupiter")
Concertgebouw Orchestra
LP 6.48219 (2 LPs) DX
DMM DIGITAL
MC 4.48219 CY CrO$_2$

Symphony Nr. 40 G Minor, KV 550,
Symphony Nr. 25 G Minor, KV 183
Concertgebouw Orchestra
LP 6.42935 AZ
DMM DIGITAL
MC 4.42935 CX
CD 8.42935 ZK

"Posthorn Serenade", KV 320,
Marches D Major, KV 335,
Nr. 1 and 2
Peter Damm, Posthorn,
Staatskapelle Dresden
LP 6.43063 AZ
DMM DIGITAL
MC 4.43063 CY CrO$_2$
CD 8.43063 ZK

Gran Partita, Serenade Nr. 10
B-flat Major, KV 361 (170a)
Wiener Mozart-Bläser
LP 6.42981 AZ
DMM DIGITAL
MC 4.42981 CX
CD 8.42981 ZK

**Concerto for 2 Pianos and Orchestra
Nr. 10 E-flat Major,**
KV 365 (316a); Chick Corea:
Fantasy for two pianos; Friedrich
Gulda: Ping-pong for two pianos
Friedrich Gulda, Chick Corea,
Clavier, Concertgebouw
Orchestra
LP 6.43961 AZ
DMM DIGITAL
MC 4.43961 CY CrO$_2$
CD 8.43961 ZK

Piano Concertos Nr. 23 A Major,
KV 488, **Nr. 26 D Major,** KV 537
("Krönungskonzert")
Friedrich Gulda, Piano,
Concertgebouw Orchestra
LP 6.42970 AZ
DMM DIGITAL
MC 4.42970 CY CrO$_2$
CD 8.42970 ZK

Horn Concertos Nr. 1-4
Hermann Baumann, Naturhorn,
Concentus musicus Wien
LP 6.41272 AZ
DMM
MC 4.41272 CX
CD 8.41272 ZK

Organ Works
Adagio and Allegro (Adagio)
F Minor for a mechanical organ
KV 594; Epistle Sonata F Major,
KV 244; Veroneser Allegro, KV 72a;
Leipzig Gigue in G, KV 574; Fantasia
F Minor, KV 608; Epistle Sonata C Major,
KV 328; Andante F Major, KV 616
Herbert Tachezi, Organ, Members of
Concentus musicus Wien
LP 6.41117 AH TIS

MOZART AND ANTONIO SALIERI

Der Schauspieldirektor
Prima la Musica, Poi le Parole
Alexander, Hampson, Holl
Concertgebouworkest Amsterdam
CD 8.43336 ZK

ANTONIO VIVALDI

**Il Cimento dell'Armonia e
dell'Inventione**
12 Concertos op. 8: The Seasons,
La Tempesta di Mare, Il Piacere,
La Caccia
Concentus musicus Wien
LP 6.35386 (2 LPs) EK
DMM
MC 4.35386 (2 MCs) MH
Grand Prix du Disque

**Concerti à cinque,
à quattro, à tre**
Frans Brüggen, Recorder,
Jürg Schaeftlein, Oboe,
Otto Fleischmann, Bassoon,
Alice Harnoncourt and
Walter Pfeiffer, Violin,
Nikolaus Harnoncourt, Cello,
Gustav Leonhardt, Harpsichord
LP 6.41239 AW TIS

**Concerto for Oboe A Minor;
Concerto for Traverso, Oboe,
Violin, Bassoon and B.c. G Minor;
Concerto for Bassoon E Minor;
Concerto for Strings G Minor**
Concentus musicus Wien
LP 6.41961 AW TIS

JOHANN DISMAS ZELENKA

**Hipocondrie—Sonata for
2 Oboes, Bassoon and B.c.;
Overture à 7 concertanti**
Concentus musicus Wien
LP 6.42415 AW

Addendum to the 1995 Edition
Available CDs (Selection)

All Harnoncourt's recordings are released on the Teldec label; in the United States they are sold through Warner Classics USA.

Chamber Orchestra of Europe
Beethoven
   Die Geschöpfe des Prometheus
   Symphonies 1–9
   Violin Concerto, Romances
Mendelssohn
   A Midsummer Night's Dream
   Symphonies 3, 4
Mozart
   Concert Arias
   Symphonies 38–41
Schumann
   Concertos for Piano and Violin
   Symphonies 3, 4

Concentus musicus Wien
Bach
   Arias and Choruses for Boys' Voices
   Brandenburg Concertos
   Cantatas
   Choruses
   Christmas Oratorio
   Complete Harpsichord Concertos
   Johannes-Passion
   Magnificat
   Mass in B Minor
   Matthäus-Passion
   Motets
   Orchestral Suites
   Thomas Hampson Sings Bach Arias
   Violin Concertos
Handel
   Concerti grossi
   Hallelujah—Famous Handel Choruses
   Messiah
   Organ Concertos
   Samson
   Theodora
   Utrecht Te Deum
   Water Music, Two Organ Concertos
Haydn
   Piano Concerto 11
   The Seven Last Words of Christ on the Cross
   Stabat Mater
   Symphonies 6–8, 30, 31, 45, 53, 59, 60, 69, 73

Monteverdi
   Combattimento
   L'Incoronazione di Poppea
   L'Orfeo
   Il ritorno d'Ulisse in patria
   Vespro della Beata Virgine
Mozart
   La finta giardiniera
   Great Mass in C Minor
   Horn Concertos
   Litanies
   Lucio Silla
   Masses K. 66, 139, 257, 317, 337
   Requiem
   Sacred Arias
   Serenades
   Symphonies 12, 19, 23, 24, 27
   Vespers K. 321, 339
   Works by Leopold and Wolfgang Amadeus Mozart
Music at the Court of Mannheim
Music at the Imperial Habsburg Court
Pergolesi
   Stabat Mater
Purcell
   Dido and Aeneas
Rameau
   Castor et Pollux
Telemann
   Darmstadt Overtures, Suites
   Tafelmusik
   Der Tag des Gerichts, Ino
Vivaldi
   Four Seasons
   Gloria

Concertgebouw Orchestra
Bach
   Matthäus-Passion
Haydn
   Symphonies 68, 93–104
Mozart
   Così fan tutte
   Die Entführung aus dem Serail
   Don Giovanni
   Idomeneo
   Le nozze di Figaro

Overtures
Piano Concertos 23, 26
Symphonies 25, 26, 28, 29–41
Die Zauberflöte
Schubert
Symphonies 1–9
Strauss, Johann II
Blue Danube
Die Fledermaus

Opernhauses Zürich
Monteverdi (by the Monteverdi Ensemble)
L'Incoronazione di Poppea
L'Orfeo
Il ritorno d'Ulisse in patria

Mozart
La clemenza di Tito
Die Entführung aus dem Serail
Idomeneo
Die Zauberflöte

Staatskapelle Dresden
Mozart
Marches K. 249, 335
Serenades K. 250, 320

Wiener Symphoniker
Haydn
The Creation
The Seasons

Index

A Santa Clara, Abraham, 151
Agricola, Martin, 109
Altenburg, Johann Ernst, 115
Anderson, Emily, 196
d'Anglebert, Jean-Henri, 186
Attaingnant, Pierre, 180

Bach, Carl Philipp Emanuel, 37, 56
Bach, Johann Sebastian, 12, 14, 16, 26, 41, 43, 52, 53, 67, 69, 71, 86, 88, 89, 93, 95, 111–112, 122, 133, 183
　acoustics of St. Thomas Church, 83
　arrangements of his music, 125
　B Minor Overture, 114
　"Bach bow," 109
　Brandenburg Concertos, 82, 84, 112
　compositions for gamba, 105, 106
　counterpoint, use of, 134
　Die Kunst der Fuge, 31
　Mass in B Minor, 44
　St. John Passion, 88
　St. Matthew Passion, 44, 125
　suites, 180–187
　and Telemann, 159
　trio sonatas, 175–176
　use of dots, 45–46
Baillot, Pierre-Marie-François, 25
Barberini, Cardinal, 85
Bardi, Giovanni, Count, 129
Bartok, Béla, 69
Beethoven, Ludwig van, 86, 87, 88, 93, 118, 124, 155, 198
Berlioz, Hector, 23, 29
Bernini, Gian Lorenzo, 147
Berthali, Antonio, 152
Biber, Heinrich Ignaz Franz, 109, 152–153, 154, 157, 181
Böhm, Theobald, 74–75, 88, 94
Brade, William, 175
Brahms, Johannes, 15, 16, 17, 25, 69, 123, 124
Brossard, Sébastien de, 185
Bruckner, Anton, 15, 125
Burney, Charles, 147, 151
Buxtehude, Dietrich, 105

Caccini, Giulio, 129–131, 133
Cavalli, Pier Francesco, 147, 194
Cazzati, Maurizio, 175

Chambonnières, Jacques Champion, 186
Charles VI, Emperor, 155
Charpentier, Marc-Antoine, 120
Cherubini, Luigi, 25
Cooper, John, 166
Coperario, Giovanni. *See* Cooper, John
Corelli, Arcangelo, 85, 109, 154, 155, 171–172, 174, 175, 186
Corsi, Jacopo, Count, 129
Couperin, François, "Le Grand," 175
Couperin, Louis, 186

Debussy, Claude, 189, 194
Denner, Johann Christoph, 74
Des Prez, Josquin, 16
Du Caurroy, François-Eustache, 119
Dufay, Guillaume, 16

Ebner, Wolfgang, 150, 152
Einstein, Albert, 12
Engramelle, Père, 112

Farina, Carlo, 109–110
Ferdinand IV, Emperor, 150
Ferrabosco, Alfonso, 166
Fontana, Giovanni Battista, 108
Forkel, Johann Nikolaus, 56
Forqueray, Antoine, 105
Forqueray, Jean Baptiste, 105
Frescobaldi, Girolamo, 53
Furtwängler, Wilhelm, 14, 72
Fux, Johann Joseph, 145, 150, 153, 155–156

Galilei, Vincenzo, 129–130
Ganassi, Sylvestro di, 104
Gandolf, Max, Archbishop, 154
Geminiani, Francesco, 34
Gluck, Christoph Willibald, 135, 188–189, 193, 194

Haas, Johann Wilhelm, 74
Handel, George Frideric, 55, 56, 57, 93, 112, 124, 160, 167, 168–176, 177–179
　arrangements of his music, 125
　and Classic composers, 170
　concerti grossi, 170–175

and Corelli, 171–172
Jeptha, 177–179
Messiah, 170
rediscovered in nineteenth century, 168–169
transcriptions, 178
trio sonatas, 174
Haydn, Franz Joseph, 85, 93, 106, 122–123, 198
Hiller, Johann Adam, 37
Hindemith, Paul, 46, 111–112
Hotteterre, Jacques, 74–75

Ionesco, Eugène, 68

Joachim, Joseph, 125
Joseph I, Emperor, 156
Josquin. *See* Des Prez, Josquin

Kepler, Johannes, 61
Kreutzer, Rodolphe, 25, 26, 109

La Borde, Jean Benjamin de, 194
La Pouplinière, le Riche de, 192
Lasso, Orlando di, 67
Lawes, William, 166
Le Blanc, Hubert, 33, 105, 182
Le Clerc, Jean, 141
Le Gros, Joseph, 196
Legrenzi, Giovanni, 175
Leopold I, Emperor, 150–151, 152, 154, 156, 157
Liechtenstein-Kastelkorn, Karl, Count, 152
Liszt, Franz (Ferencz), 23
Locke, Matthew, 181
Louis XII, King, 149
Louis XIII, King, 105
Louis XIV, King, 105, 147, 151, 154, 182, 183, 185
Lully, Jean-Baptiste, 37, 145, 146–147, 154, 155, 182–183, 186, 190–195
Lupo (Italian composer), 166

Mace, Thomas, 185
Mahler, Gustav, 28, 49, 95
Marais, Marin, 105, 175, 182, 184
Marenzio, Luca, 130
Marini, Biagio, 108, 146, 175
Marteau, Henry, 109
Mattheson, Johann, 118–119, 183, 184, 185, 186, 187
Maximilian I, Emperor, 67, 79, 149
Mendelssohn, Felix, 93, 125

Mersenne, Marin, 109, 181
Monteverdi, Claudio, 12, 28, 50, 52, 54, 59, 60, 67, 77, 86, 88, 89, 110, 134, 135, 136, 146, 175, 194
Ariana, 131
Combattimento di Tancredi e Clorinda, 55, 127, 132
madrigals, 130
Marian Vespers, 84, 108
L'Orfeo, 84, 108, 131
stile concitato, 132
Morley, Thomas, 55
Morzin, Wenceslaw, Count, 141
Mozart, Leopold, 34, 36, 41–42, 55, 84, 109, 126–127
Mozart, Wolfgang Amadeus, 12, 15, 16, 25, 26, 52, 57, 67, 68, 69, 80, 83, 93, 95, 123, 124, 196–199
Idomeneo, 135
The Magic Flute, 112
and Monteverdi, 134–135
music rich in contrasts, 136
orchestration, 91
"Paris" Symphony, 163, 196–198
performance practice, 127
placement of instruments, 85
Sinfonia Concertante, K. 364, 125
tempo indications, 56
Muffat, Georg, 151, 153–157, 163, 171–172
Muffat, Gottlieb, 33, 145

Neidthart, Johann Georg, 118
Niedt, Friedrich Erhard, 37
North, Roger, 109

Oistrach, David, 96
Ortiz, Diego, 104

Paganini, Niccolò, 26, 109
Palestrina, Giovanni Pierluigi, 181
Palladio, Andrea, 61
Pasquini, Bernardo, 154
Pergolesi, Giovanni Battista, 178, 192
Peri, Jacopo, 129
Pesenti, Martino, 175
Philip II, Emperor, 185
Piccinni, Niccolò, 193
Plato, 50, 132
Praetorius, Michael, 59, 67, 77, 115, 181
Purcell, Henry, 166–167, 185

Quantz, Joachim, 32, 57, 112, 118, 185
Quinault, Philippe, 191

Quintilian, Marcus Fabius, 133–134

Rameau, Jean-Philippe, 37, 38, 188–189, 190–195
Reincken, Johann Adam, 164
Rinck, Gottlieb Eucharius, 152
Rode, Pierre, 109
Rousseau, Jean-Jacques, 37, 192
Ruckers, Andreas, 74

Saint-Simon, Count, 185
Scheibe, Johann Adolf, 37
Scheidemann, Heinrich, 164
Scheidt, Samuel, 175
Schmelzer, Heinrich, 109, 150, 154, 156–157, 181
Schneider, Marius, 63
Schönberg, Arnold, 88
Schubert, Franz, 123
Schumann, Clara, 125
Shakespeare, William, 186
Simpson, Christopher, 55, 104
Speer, Daniel, 115
Stainer, Jacobus, 101, 103, 104, 113, 153, 157
Stein, Andreas, 74
Steinkopf, O., 115
Stokowski, Leopold, 14
Stradivari, Antonio, 71, 74
Strauss, Johann, 30, 33
Strauss, Richard, 15, 29, 77, 79, 95, 118, 122, 125
Stravinsky, Igor, 88, 122
Stockhausen, Karl Heinz, 124–125
Sweelinck, Jan Pieterszoon, 164

Tartini, Giuseppe, 109
Tasso, Torquato, 132
Tchaikovsky, Piotr Ilyich, 15, 122, 125
Telemann, Georg Philipp, 93, 105, 159–163, 176, 187
Tostalgo, Peter, 140
Tourte, François, 94–95, 102
Türk, Daniel Gottlieb, 36, 185

Uccellini, Marco, 108, 175

Vejvanowsky, Pavel, 153
Verdi, Giuseppe, 133
Vieuville, 145
Viotti, Giovanni Battista, 109
Vivaldi, Antonio, 46, 55, 83, 109, 139–143, 175

Wagner, Richard, 14, 23, 25, 67
Walter, Bruno, 49
Walther, Johann Jacob, 109, 184, 186, 187
Weber, Carl Maria von, 93
Werkmeister, Andreas, 65
Willaert, Adrian, 84
Wolf, Georg Friedrich, 37

Zarlino, Gioseffo, 62